Sports Illusion,
Sports Reality

To the memory of Bob Harron

Sports Illusion, Sports Reality

A REPORTER'S VIEW OF SPORTS,
JOURNALISM AND SOCIETY

Leonard Koppett

Houghton Mifflin Company Boston   1981

Library of Congress Cataloging in Publication Data

Koppett, Leonard.
    Sports illusion, sports reality.

    1.Sports—Social aspects—United States. 2.Sports
journalism—United States. 3.Mass media—Social
aspects—United States. 4.Sports—Social aspects—
Canada. 5.Sports journalism—Canada. 6.Mass media—
Social aspects—Canada. I.Title.
GV706.5.K67   302.2'3   81–6367
ISBN 0–395–31297–3   AACR2

Printed in the United States of America

A 10 9 8 7 6 5 4 3 2 1

Contents

Preface

THIS BOOK grew out of a lecture course I began giving at
Stanford University in the late 1970s. It was a very informal arrangement. I was a working sportswriter, recently
planted on the West Coast by the *New York Times* for logistical
convenience, with no academic credentials. My value, if any, lay
in the viewpoint I could give from thirty years or so of practical
experience on the major-league sports scene and a continuing
connection to the outside world. The once-a-week class would be
sandwiched in between traveling assignments. The fact that I
lived a few blocks from the Stanford campus was a factor. The
Department of Communications, which encompassed journalism,
was my administrative milieu.

The computerized departmental machinery dubbed the course
"Sports Culture," before I had given the matter of title any
thought at all. I didn't like it. It conjured up an image of mutated
microbes in some biology-lab test tube. I proceeded to ponder,
and settled upon "Sports, Journalism and Society" after a long
period of indecision about the appropriateness of the comma. But
the next year, there it was in the catalogue again as "Sports Culture." And the next year. And everyone at the Department of
Communications kept referring to it that way.

It didn't really matter, but it did help convince me I was on the
right track with my central theme — that *preconceptions* about
sports outlive explanations. Preconceptions have to originate
somewhere. In sports, they are formed by what newspapers,
radio, and television tell us, in such great quantity from an early
age, about the subject.

Explanations have to, or ought to, originate in reality: they should tell how things work. Well, I had learned a good deal about how the sports business works, and how sports journalism works. Maybe if I first explained these enterprises, it would be easier for us to see through (or confirm) preconceptions about how our interest in sports affects our society. At that point, it would become possible to examine more sensibly the cultural impact of sports (which is a more accurate way of putting the issue). After all, the assumption that sports do somehow affect society was what led to the preconception of calling the course "Sports Culture." Thus the format in which my course, and eventually this book, developed.

The phrase "tell it like it is" has come to symbolize the approved goal of "honest" journalism, even though some of the people who gave it widest circulation were consciously lying. In this book I make no such ambitious claim, but I do guarantee to "tell it like it seems from here."

For what it's worth.

Introduction

IN 1980, millions of Americans who cared nothing about spectator sports, along with the millions who did, suddenly found their attention claimed by four major "general news" stories displayed prominently on television screens, newsmagazine covers, and the front pages of newspapers.

The president of the United States led a movement to boycott the Summer Olympic Games in Moscow, relating his policy decision to issues of war and peace.

College administrations across the country were shaken by revelations that academic records had been forged, credit had been given for nonexistent and nonattended courses, funds had been misappropriated, and bribery had become endemic in the certification of athletes as eligible for college teams.

A threatened strike by the major-league baseball players, averted only at the last moment in a crisis atmosphere, stirred surprising anxiety throughout the population, and would have disrupted expensive television formats (as the Olympic boycott did).

And in the struggle for command of the latest commercial frontier — cable and pay television in all its forms — sports programming, especially that involving live games, emerged as a key battleground.

How could this be? Why would athletic games, designed entirely for entertainment and recreation, acquire the power to influence to such a degree international relations, domestic politics, important segments of the economy, the educational system, and the public psyche? To understand, we must begin by recognizing how unique this phenomenon is.

As mass entertainment, intensively commercialized spectator sports play a larger role in American culture than in any other society, past or present. In no other country today do the amounts of money spent, tickets bought, games played, livelihoods involved, words printed, hours televised, or spinoff industries concerning sports match American totals, either by absolute or proportional measure. And in no earlier time, of course, was there any possibility of following sports on such a scale, because no remotely comparable capacity for communication existed.

Other societies have at times organized vast physical-culture programs for their citizens. As far back as ancient Greece and Rome, the Olympic Games and gladiatorial combat absorbed the attention of spectators, although restrictions of geography and social class limited their scope. But the particular combination of huge investment, nearly universal awareness, and frequently passionate concern that characterizes today's sports world is unique to the America of the twentieth century. The sports establishment engages in day-in, day-out glamour-manufacture of "big league" teams and stars, drawing simultaneous nationwide attention through professionally developed marketing procedures used for avowed commercial purposes.

What does this peculiar role of the sports establishment reveal about American society? How does it affect national life and popular attitudes? Why does it have the form it does, how did it develop, and where is it headed? Who controls it, who benefits, who suffers, and who escapes its influence?

Such questions have become, in the last twenty years, popular topics for inquiry in the academic community. Countless theses have been written on one aspect or another of the sports scene. Psychologists, sociologists, and economists have carved out professional specialties as teachers and writers on this subject. Law school journals have been flooded with analyses, most of them about antitrust questions that have embroiled professional sports for decades. Degrees are being awarded in "sports administration." Mainstream philosophers and authors have published books examining the phenomenon. Serious treatment of commercial sports life in novels and films, unheard of a generation ago, has become common and has produced works of quality.

Within high schools and colleges, among students, teachers, and parents, the values and stereotypes of sports "as we know it" are being challenged and reconsidered as never before. Yet most of this discussion takes place in a factual vacuum. It confronts reality fragmentarily, if at all.

The two standard fact-gathering devices used in most studies are the questionnaire and the interview, and both are hopelessly inadequate. Questionnaires are too limited, in what can be asked and in the number of replies that can be analyzed, to generate significant information beyond what is already obvious in a mercilessly documented activity. (Any questionnaire an individual scholar or small group can handle is too limited, that is. It would be possible to design some that are comprehensive enough to produce new knowledge, if enough money were available, but this hasn't been done yet.)

Interviews are worse, because subjective factors loom so large. Among other things, people prominent in sports have long since become professional interviewees, accustomed automatically (and probably subconsciously) to manipulating their interviewers. In other types of academic investigation, the interview itself is usually a rare experience for the person being questioned, and if that person doesn't feel some motivation to share information, he or she refuses to cooperate. In sports, the obligation to cooperate is ingrained (since publicity is the industry's lifeblood), and the skills of grinding an ax or satisfying the questioner's expectations are fully developed. Courtroom lawyers know the difference between ordinary witnesses and expert witnesses for developing information — as distinct from convincing a jury — under examination. But in this sense, experienced sports figures are almost always adulterated commodities when questioned about themselves. (Again, sufficiently exhaustive cross-checking would solve the problem, but academic investigators don't get that opportunity.)

Most of all, however, these studies fail to focus on the crucial link in the chain: the role journalism plays in the interaction of sports and culture. It is the public's *perception* of sports — the general public's and the various specialized publics' — that counts. The business of staging games relies on the impressions of the customers, and those impressions are formed only through the connecting link of words and pictures. Only through newspapers, magazines, radio and television sets, and occasionally a book can the consumers — the spectators — get the information they need to make the entertainment entertaining.

This odd relationship does not apply to other forms of entertainment. We don't need "news" about the book business to enjoy reading a book. We can listen to music, look at paintings, watch a movie, attend the theater — or hike, fish, play Ping-Pong, go swimming, or play cards — perfectly well without a steady flow of current information about others engaged in that activity. We do need background information about the subject itself, which we can acquire through books or direct instruction as our interest grows. But we don't need constant, up-to-date journalistic input to enjoy those pleasures, while we do need exactly that to enjoy sports as spectators.

It's the awareness that the New York Yankees and Los Angeles Dodgers are playing in the World Series, with all the overtones of who they are, how they got there, what the World Series means, and so forth, that makes the occasion exciting. If the same eighteen individuals, in casual dress, played exactly the same game on some public-park diamond, the event would have no impact at all.

My approach, therefore, is this: In order to explore the many and profound effects that mass spectator sports have on American society, one must begin with the recognition that the producer — the promoter staging the event — and the consumer — the fan — can touch each other only through journalistic media. One must then determine how the sports business works, how journalism works, and how the two interact. Only after that, from a firm factual base, can one examine how sports affect society (and vice versa), which effects are desirable and which are undesirable, and what can be done about any of it.

The first two parts of the book, then, are unavoidably expository. The sexy social commentary can come only after we agree on what we're talking about. You don't put carts before horses, even though it's the cart you want to ride in. So Parts I and II can serve as a textbook for how sports and journalism work, and why.

Parts III and IV take on the issues the term *sports culture* suggests: What effect do these activities, and our perceptions of them, have on society as a whole? These chapters are far more personal and opinionated, intended to stimulate thought — and disagreement — as much as to explain. The ideas presented there are disputable, controversial, timely, irritating, or brilliant, according to your reaction; but they can't be addressed at all outside the context Parts I and II provide.

To begin with, we must define some terms. *Sports*, in our discussion, will have a narrow meaning. It will refer only to the commercialized segment of athletic games aimed at a large audience. By this definition, recreational activities (such as hunting, fishing, jogging, swimming, skating, camping, skiing) are excluded — not because they don't engage millions of people and dollars, or because they are less worthy, but because they are irrelevant to an understanding of our chosen theme.

Nor will we include even standard sports, such as baseball, when they are played on a noncommercial level in sandlot, school, Little League, pickup, semipro, low minors, or industrial leagues. These, too, are important in their own right, but not relevant. And we won't deal with the sports structures of other countries, except in passing or for the sake of comparison, because our concern is this society, at the present time. It is easy to be misled by apparently clear-cut similarities or contrasts when comparing another culture to our own, and superficial reference to the unfamiliar won't help us understand the more subtle forces at work here. Even in so closely related a culture as Britain's, the functions of both sports and journalism are distinctly different from ours.

But we will include Canada in our definition of "America," because Canada's professional sports practices are so closely tied to those in the United States. Canadian cities belong to major leagues in baseball, hockey, and soccer, once did in basketball, and may soon in football. The word *American* will be simply a convenient way of avoiding the more cumbersome *United States and Canada.*

Mexico, the Caribbean, and Central and South America, on the other hand, are entirely outside the scope of our discussion, even though American baseball has strong ties to those areas. The cultural differences are immense, and the impact on the American fan's perceptions is slight.

Journalism is the process of gathering and disseminating information and opinion about current events. It is distinct from history, instruction, entertainment, advocacy, investigation, activism, research, and philosophic analysis, although it uses and contains elements of all those things.

The term *news media* is often shortened to *media,* and this can lead to confusion. The *medium* is really a mechanical device — the printed word, the audible sound, the visible picture — and the *media* are really printing presses and broadcasting equipment and film and screens and tape, used for many purposes other than "news." For our purposes, journalism's most important function is that of delivering news, through whatever medium.

Finally, I must define myself. A first principle of journalism is to evaluate the source. A reader should have some guide to credibility, some indication of the basic viewpoint and possible prejudices of the writer. A newspaper's name is such a label: we are more likely to trust an account of an international crisis in the *New York Times* (no matter who actually wrote it) than in the *National Enquirer.* But if a racehorse's record appears one way in the *Racing Form* and another in the *Times,* we may have more confidence in the *Racing Form.*

As for me, my ideas are based on more than thirty years of daily sports coverage for New York newspapers and reflect whatever bias that experience implies. Those with firsthand knowledge of the television business, of a small-town paper, of running a ball club, of being an athlete, or of coaching in school or college would see some things from another angle.

Still, since no one can avoid speaking from some sort of vantage point, a reporter has some advantages. He is required, by training and job demands, to learn about and comprehend other people's activities. A player may learn what reporters do, but he doesn't have to. A reporter, on the other hand, must learn what players, as well as managers and coaches and politicians and fans, do. The reporter must also strive for objectivity, balance, accuracy, and thoroughness, a set of desirable qualities in the examination of any subject, whereas those who deal with other aspects of the sports world don't necessarily have to sharpen such skills. So if anyone in sports can produce a comprehensive overview, the reporter is the one who has the best chance.

I grew up in New York City — the Bronx, Manhattan, and Brooklyn in turn — during the 1930s. I entered Columbia in 1940, spent 1943, 1944, and 1945 in the army, and returned to finish school in 1946. Before the interruption and afterward, I worked in Columbia's publicity office and as a campus correspondent for the downtown papers and for out-of-towns.

In 1948, I went to work for the *Herald Tribune,* the morning-paper rival of the *Times.* In 1954, I moved to the *Post,* an afternoon tabloid. In 1963, I joined the staff of the *Times,* which sent me to California in 1973 to simplify the logistics of covering events of New York interest taking place in the western half of the country. I left the *Times* in 1978 and now work for the *Peninsula Times Tribune,* the local paper in Palo Alto, where I live. Meanwhile, I wrote half a dozen sports books dealing with explanation or history, and did some television commentary, a little teaching, and a lot of column-writing for the *Sporting News* — one column a week since 1968.

My newspaper assignments centered on the major-interest sports — baseball, football, basketball — with a heavy dose of the legal, labor-strife, and congressional-hearing news, which the *Times* treated more extensively than most papers. Consequently, my examples are drawn disproportionately from people and incidents connected with New York — not because New York is special (although it is, in some respects) but because that's where I happened to be most of the time.

Although I will not try to document every statement made on every subject, I will distinguish clearly between what is fact and what is opinion, and between what are generally accepted views and what are my own particular (and perhaps peculiar) ideas.

PART I

The Sports Business

1. The Product

"It isn't enough for a promotion to be entertaining, or even amusing: it must create conversation."

— Bill Veeck, 1965

JONATHAN SCHWARTZ is a sensitive man of forty, the author of a critically acclaimed novel and collection of short stories, a fine musician who became well known in New York as an exceptionally literate, low-key disc jockey and commentator of sparkling originality. Because his father, Arthur Schwartz, was one of America's most successful composers of popular songs for Broadway shows and Hollywood musicals, Jonathan grew up on terms of intimacy with show-business celebrities, seeing with sharp eyes their backstage actuality as well as their up-front glamour. Because of his own talent, inclination, and adult experience, he has exceptional insight into how the affluent society operates and what it feels, as well as a hard-headed appreciation of the mechanics of illusion.

Jonathan Schwartz is also a dedicated baseball fan who roots for the Boston Red Sox.

Why the Boston Red Sox? Because when he was eight years old, he was in Boston with his father (who was working on a show headed for Broadway) during October, while the Red Sox were playing (and losing) the 1946 World Series.

How hard does he root? Well, in September of 1978, the Red Sox, who had been leading the league by a wide margin in August, lost four straight games to the New York Yankees in

Boston, by scores of 15–3, 13–2, 7–0, and 7–4, and fell into a tie for first place with the Yankees.

Jonathan watched that series, with increasing agitation, on cable television in his apartment in upper Manhattan. In the seventh inning of the final game, unable to bear it any longer, he walked out of the house with nothing in his pockets but fifty dollars and a Visa card, went to the airport, flew to Los Angeles, rented a car, and started driving into the desert toward Palm Springs. Only when he was about halfway there, did he bring himself to stop at a phone booth and call back to New York (where it was past midnight) to apologize to his girl friend for his abrupt and unannounced departure.

That's how hard.

In his more than thirty years of passionate involvement with the Red Sox, Jonathan has had some soul-satisfying thrills. But he's had a larger number of soul-ravaging disappointments, most of the latter at the hands of the Yankees. Finally, in October 1978, the Yankees beat the Red Sox again in a single playoff game for first place, and Jonathan refers to the entire two-month period as "a nightmare."

Jonathan Schwartz's experience demonstrates, as a particularly vivid example, the essential nature of the commodity a sports promoter has to sell.

An illusion. Specifically, the illusion that the result of a game matters. To Jonathan Schwartz it matters deeply, in his most private feelings, how a game comes out. And millions of others, every day, feel the same way. These are the sports fans of America on whom the entire industry is based; but every now and then tens of millions of others also share this unique emotion.

When the American hockey team defeated the Russian team in the 1980 Winter Olympics at Lake Placid, and then went on to win the Gold Medal, there was nationwide rejoicing. People actually danced in the streets. A crowd at Radio City Music Hall in New York City, a large fraction of which consisted of children assembled for a Sunday-afternoon family-type show, went wild when the victory was announced.

This was, clearly enough, an extraordinary situation. The president of the United States had recently called for a boycott of the

Summer Games scheduled for Moscow, because of the Soviet invasion of Afghanistan. The Russian hockey team was acknowledged to be the best in the world, having beaten even the top professional teams, and it had dominated Olympic hockey for some twenty years. The American team, composed mostly of collegians in their early twenties, was thoroughly identified as an underdog in a sport long dominated by Canadian and European players.

As an unexpected victory in the David-versus-Goliath mold, it would have been exciting enough. But combined with patriotic overtones and national pride at a moment when it seemed the Cold War was being revived, the triumph took on overwhelming significance. The outcome of a few hockey games became profoundly important to an entire population, not just to rabid fans like Jonathan Schwartz.

But realistically speaking, why should it have made any difference at all? We can easily see why the result makes a difference to those playing, those running the business, those connected with some ancillary business, and their families. And it's easy to see why the outcome matters to anyone who makes a large bet. But the hockey games had absolutely no real-world influence on relations between the United States and the USSR, on the arms race, on what was happening in Afghanistan, or even on the question of participation in the Moscow Olympics.

Nor does the outcome of a Red Sox game — any Red Sox game — have any effect whatsoever on Jonathan Schwartz's job, earning power, writing talent, living conditions, health, or personal relationships, except to the extent that his voluntary emotional commitment allows it to have an indirect effect.

That commitment is to an illusion — an illusion so strong and so long ingrained that beyond a certain point the attachment is no longer entirely voluntary. And the sports business consists of finding ways to create and maintain this illusion.

Many promoters, probably most, don't realize that an illusion is what they're selling. They think their real business is building winning teams, or competing for the entertainment dollar, or providing the public with excellence to marvel at, stars to identify with, and excitement in a congenial setting. They think they're selling tickets, or victories, or "names." And of course all these factors are part of their business. But the fundamental thing is the illusion. Without the emotion that the illusion generates, all the rest would collapse. What's more, the illusion must be strong enough to capture even as sophisticated a mind as Jonathan Schwartz's. And when unusual circumstances give the illusion extra strength, it takes hold of the minds of many who are not normally sports enthusiasts. The fan, after all, has nurtured his interest by paying attention to his chosen sport for years. But the ordinary citizens — including children — who exulted over the United States hockey victory didn't care about hockey as a game, knew nothing about the players involved, had never heard of any of the opposing players, and couldn't even tell you how the championship was determined. (The winner was established by means of a complicated formula unlike the one used to decide ordinary league standings or elimination tournaments.) They were reacting, purely and simply, to the symbolism of "a United States victory," regardless of its nature.

But Olympics come up only once every four years, and international crises follow no regular schedule, so there is an important difference between a fan's reaction to the Red Sox and the general public's reaction to the Olympic hockey team. The latter, because it is so atypical, illustrates the power an illusion can generate. "Regular" events, on the other hand, dominate their followers' minds for years.

This, by the way, is as good a way as any to distinguish "mass spectator sports" from other athletic and recreational activities. Mass spectator sports are the ones that succeed in keeping the illusion of importance alive in large numbers of people over long periods of time.

To the participating athlete in any sport — an amateur running cross-country, a club tennis player, a weekend golfer struggling to break 100, or a quarterback in a Super Bowl game — the importance of the event is no illusion: it's real. He or she is there, doing it, personally experiencing victory or defeat and expended effort. Of course, the degree of intensity is different for the World Series pitcher than for the Tuesday night bowler. But whatever the personal significance may be, it is not illusory. One can elect not to participate in the first place, but one can't elect to ignore the result and its consequences if one does participate.

For the fan, however, the choice of caring or not caring is always available. Emotional involvement can be disconnected at any moment, for any reason — and just as easily reestablished — entirely as a matter of whim. (This degree of freedom has been heightened for sports in the age of television: it's much easier to switch channels in a moment of pique than to get up, walk out of the park, and make your long way home.)

Nor is the promoter, who must have something to sell, the only one who needs the illusion. The consumer needs it just as much, to have something to buy, to become a fan. The entertainment value of sports lies not in the physical actions observed but in the feelings aroused in those who interpret the meaning of those actions. The caring, in this important sense, *is* the entertainment.

That's why it can be so boring to those who don't care. How and why the illusion works will be explored in detail in Part III. For now we need only recognize that the business does rest on a particular illusion.

Aside from this indispensable foundation, other elements go into making sports marketable entertainment. There is built-in suspense: the outcome of any contest is undecided when it begins. There is identification: with stars as individuals, teams as entities, and outcome as victory or defeat. We can combine these elements into a formula:

> The illusion engages our emotions.
> The suspense engages our intellect.
> The identification engages our spirit.

In this scheme, "artistry," in the sense of grace and style, becomes quite secondary. How an athlete moves, as distinct from the result he achieves, may be enjoyed for its own sake, but only as a bonus, or side issue. A last-second basket, no matter how clumsily achieved, satisfies all sports values. A ballet dancer's leap, in contrast, acquires meaning only through its own perfection. The goal in the dance is not to transport one's body from one end of the stage to the other but to convey the meaning by the *way* the movement is made. The goal in sports is simply to achieve a tangible result — ball in basket, body over crossbar, puck past goalie — regardless of appearance. Even though, as a rule, athletic grace and effectiveness go together, only the effectiveness is of primary concern.

In some sports, style *is* primary and a part of the competitive scoring: diving, gymnastics, figure skating, and equestrianism. It is probably not a coincidence that such sports have never attained a mass-spectator commercial following in this country, despite the strength of their appeal to limited numbers here and to large numbers elsewhere in the world.

The American sports fan, conditioned to placing all emphasis on tangible results, is uncomfortable with scoring that depends on a judge's opinion of form. We accept the inescapable condition that every contest requires judging of some sort, but limit that acceptance to the determination, by umpire or referee, of physical facts — in-bounds or out, contact or no contact, ball or strike, fair or foul. We may dispute a particular decision, and enjoy doing so, but we don't question the idea that the fact was capable of being determined objectively. But we seem reluctant to accept the much more subjective judgment involved in awarding points for "correct" body alignment or other semiaesthetic factors.

In that connection, Clive Barnes, the distinguished dance and drama critic, went to the heart of the matter when he first came from England to work for the *New York Times* in the 1960s. Inevitably, an editor asked him to go to a sports event and write a piece about the similarity between an athlete's actions and ballet. (The reasoning goes, we have pictures in the paper every day of some baseball or basketball player in midair, and I've seen pictures of ballet dancers in midair, so there must be some profound connection between baseball and ballet. Honest. Editors think that way.) Barnes agreed to go to a New York Met baseball game at Shea Stadium on a Saturday afternoon and write a piece for the Sunday Sports Section, right from the scene.

Barnes watched, asked questions, reflected, and wrote a delightful story that included the line, "of course, to anyone accustomed to the mad, crazy pace of cricket, baseball seems a bit slow." He went on for several hundred words and finally came to the point, which went something like this:

As for the connection between baseball and ballet, there is none. But since I've been given this space, may I use it to call your attention to a correction. On page 39 of the Sunday Drama Section, which went to press earlier in the week, I have written that ... Please read that to be the correct information, which is ...

This anecdote says even more about the mechanics and psychology of the newspaper business than about sports, and we'll return to it in a later chapter. For now, it's enough to hold firmly in mind that we must recognize what sports are *not* in order to understand fully what they *are*.

All right, then. Exactly how do spectator sports differ from other forms of entertainment? They must have something peculiarly their own, or people wouldn't spend money to choose them over older and better-established diversions. What characteristics can we list that don't apply equally well to fiction, movies, theater, music, art, dance, circus, vaudeville, or television quiz shows? Here are seven:

1. Comprehensibility
2. Continuity
3. Readability
4. Coherence
5. Hazard
6. Low cost
7. Vicarious experience
   a. Violence
   b. Triumph
   c. Second-guessing
   d. Patriotism

Let's consider each in turn.

COMPREHENSIBILITY

The good guys and bad guys are always instantly identifiable: "my" team and the opposition. The score is always posted on the board, making clear who's ahead, regardless of how little the spectator may know about the mechanics or rules of play.

The game's basic idea — score a goal, advance toward the goal line, hit the ball safely or catch it, tap the ball into the cup — becomes self-evident after a minimum of observation.

And the rules of play, once learned, are self-consistent and relatively easy to follow (since they were devised with exactly that in mind).

Generally speaking, one can acquire a satisfactory level of knowledgeability about a sport with much less educational background and conscious effort than one needs to reach a comparable level of appreciation in the arts. This is one reason why children, whose receptivity to illusion is high anyhow, form a large portion of the sports audience.

CONTINUITY

Sports competition, when well organized and publicized, creates its own continuing history, and this in turn becomes a sustaining force for the illusion. Yesterday's result and tomorrow's possibility are very much a part of today's game, not only as points of comparison but as factors in determining a team's progress toward a championship.

Other entertainments lack this ingredient except in special circumstances. Serialized stories and soap operas seek continuity, but serials have relatively few installments and soap operas never reach definite endings. By and large we watch plays, listen to concerts, or read books without regard to the content of the last play, concert, or book we experienced. In sports, the relationship to earlier events is automatic, almost always present in the forefront of consciousness, and part of the melodrama that is unfolding.

READABILITY

By reading an account of a sports event, one can get considerable satisfaction and almost all relevant information for future satisfaction. This unique quality gives sports a dimension not present in other forms of entertainment. The experienced sports fan can see, in his mind's eye, the plays described in an account of the game, and can absorb all the incidental information encompassed under the "continuity" heading simply by reading or listening to the radio. The score, the league standings, individual records, the play that decided the game, the trade of a player to another team, the prospects for the coming season — all these are absorbed as fully by readers as by those actually present at the games.

In fact, this indirect experience of the sports event is not only possible but necessary. Very few people have the opportunity, let alone the inclination, to attend every single game played. But enjoyment of the game you do attend is influenced by your awareness of previous results (which give significance to the present contest), and such knowledge is obtained only by reading or hearing about the games you missed. Before long, the reading itself becomes an active pleasure. *Knowing* the outcome becomes a satisfaction apart from seeing it happen.

No comparable indirect experience is possible with the arts. We can't read, day after day, about how some musical comedy came out. We can read news and gossip about the activities of theater people, about their personalities, about their plans; and we can read critiques and evaluations of their performances. We cannot, however, match the content of "yesterday, Reggie Jackson hit three home runs and led the New York Yankees to a World Series victory over the Los Angeles Dodgers" with a statement like "last night, Montserrat Caballé sang *Tosca* beautifully." The second announcement is merely an assertion, containing none of the substance of the performance; and simply being told the performance took place isn't very exciting. But the report on what Jackson did *does* deliver much of the substance of the event, as well as all of the relevant historical background, so that it becomes just as much a part of the absent fan's total view of baseball as if he had seen it in person.

The United States hockey team's Olympic triumph demonstrated this point. Many people who were merely told the bare fact that the U.S. team won celebrated just as spontaneously and fervently as those who had watched the game on their television screens. A roomful of music lovers would not react in a comparable fashion to the announcement that "Zubin Mehta just finished a magnificent performance of Beethoven's Ninth!"

It is easy to underestimate the power of this special characteristic. The fact that it differs in intensity for different sports is also often overlooked. But baseball, football, and boxing, by their nature, are more easily written about in a journalistic format than games like basketball, hockey, tennis, and bowling; so it is no mere accident of history that the first three became bigger business than the others.

COHERENCE

All three of the above elements help make sports a tight, closed, reliable system that makes sense to the person who follows it. In the rest of life, especially during the last two generations, we have been surrounded by oppressive uncertainties. Traditional religious beliefs and social distinctions have been blurred. Problems of personal morality, political allegiance, economic choice, and acceptable behavior seem ever more fuzzy. Scientific discoveries, from relativity to genetics, have moved far beyond the ordinary person's grasp. Atomic bombs and atomic plants generate in us a sense of disquiet at the very least. The generation gap widens. National leaders tell us they have no answers to crises that are brought to our attention more relentlessly than ever. The motto of modern life could very well be "I don't really know."

The sports fan, on the other hand, feels he does know as much as he wants to about that comfortably restricted universe, or can know if he makes the effort. Everything is orderly and definite: A hit is a hit, a win is a win, a champion is a champion, an average is an average, and there's no need to argue about it or to prove it.

It is very soothing indeed to retreat periodically, for a couple of hours, into a simplified cosmos where rules can be relied upon and where the limit on knowledge lies only in one's willingness to pursue it.

James ("Scotty") Reston, one of America's most distinguished political columnists, called attention to this central source of pleasure on the eve of the 1979 World Series:

> The baseball battle between Baltimore and Pittsburgh will soon be over. The hits and errors will be clear, and the heroes and goats will be identified, and very soon everybody will know who won and who lost. Not so in politics, economics or foreign policy . . . In sports, if

not in politics, there are clear rules, boundaries, foul-lines, end-lines, goal lines, and referees or umpires to decide by instant decisions or instant replays what really happened. This gives a certain security to the scene. No wonder, then, that when everything else is uncertain and confused, it is easier and more popular to concentrate and choose up sides between the Pirates and Orioles.

Reston's insight is based on experience. Before moving into the higher echelons of the *New York Times,* the Washington establishment, and serious political analysis, he covered baseball and served as a road secretary for the Cincinnati Reds.

The air of certainty is, in itself, an illusion. Not one fan in a thousand really knows the intricacies of professional play, or the business procedures involved, and most fans acknowledge their limitations. But they believe wholeheartedly that all such details are *knowable,* that they *could* be known if the fan wanted to take the trouble to find out. Psychologically, sports offer an island of stability in a confusing, shifting cosmos.

Contemporary art, on the other hand, stresses ambiguity as much as contemporary science and politics do, and even the most classical art forms are subject to conflicting interpretations. Their very appeal lies in layers of meaning that can't be pinned down too specifically. No one can tell you how Beethoven's Fifth Symphony "comes out." On a less sophisticated level, even a murder mystery has the reader wondering who is on which side.

HAZARD

Modern, affluent, high-technology societies produce relatively few true-life hazardous experiences. There are plenty of dangers around — driving a car, flying, exposure to pollution or radiation, illness — but most of the time most of us don't feel threatened. We are assured that safety precautions surround us, from inoculations against disease to government-inspected elevators, and we take this security for granted. Most of us consider it a blessing. Yet the capacity to feel danger, to be at risk, has been part of the human race's survival machinery throughout its existence, and a certain pleasurable thrill is associated with that sensation. The

profits made from roller-coaster rides and horror movies are indications of the commercial rewards to be reaped by catering to
that instinct.

Sports titillate that response to danger in a way, or at least to an
extent, that other entertainments don't. Once we make an emotional investment by choosing to root for one of the contestants,
the nervous excitement that accompanies each step toward victory or defeat is an exhilaration quite different from our everyday
equilibrium. To increase or systematize this feeling, many people
bet — a lot or a little, according to their inclinations — "just to
make it interesting." Pure gambling addresses this need, but
sports provides the only means by which people can bet and at
the same time enjoy other "content." There's very little betting on
whether or not the soprano will hit the high C on a given night, or
on which suspect will be unmasked as the murderer at the end of
the play.*

In other times and places, there would be less appetite for this
aspect of entertainment. Life on the frontier, on a farm with crops
dependent on the weather, in wartime, in a depression, in a society that has primitive hygiene, or under an oppressive regime
carries its fill of realistic risks. In the America of the last century
or so, the craving for artificial (and vicarious) risks has grown.

Identifying with the sensation of danger, as distinct from actually being in danger, is as old as literature. A "willing suspension of disbelief" must be made by an audience before the events
on stage (or on the printed page) can become moving or amusing.
Sports, however, reach the same state more directly. The only
suspension of disbelief needed is the initial one, the acceptance of
the illusion that the outcome matters. After that, every game and
every play is truly dangerous, in the sense that it will either succeed or fail. We are one step closer to reality. To feel involved in a
hazardous situation in fiction, we must make a conscious

---

* When the television series "Dallas" captivated England and set off "Who
killed J.R.?" speculation on a massive scale, however, British bookmakers (who are
legal and respectable businessmen) promptly set odds and took millions of pounds
in bets on the identity of the assailant, who was to be revealed in subsequent installments. Whether this proves that art imitates life, or life imitates art, or neither,
isn't clear; but it certainly proves that bookies and publicity geniuses know how to
imitate a good gimmick when they see one — the gimmick being a type of gamble
usually associated with the outcome of a game.

effort to suspend disbelief with each new story. With respect to sports, we make it only once, early in life, and retain it. And the elements of continuity and readability constantly reinforce it.

LOW COST

Buttressing all these elaborate theoretical considerations is the highly practical matter of cost and accessibility. For the promoter, staging an event costs relatively little. For the consumer, ticket prices are relatively low and tickets are relatively abundant. What's more, the sports fan doesn't have to buy a ticket at all to derive substantial benefit from "following" the games — a by-product satisfaction he can't get from unattended concerts or un-read books.

In San Francisco, a box seat for a Giants' baseball game costs $6; for a 49er football game or a Warrior basketball game, the cost is $12. A box seat for the opera is $35, and a downtown movie ticket is about $4.

But suppose you go to one movie a week for six months. You spend 26 times $4, or $104, for 26 three-hour segments of enter-tainment — and *only* those segments. Between visits to the movie house, you get no significant movie-related entertainment for your money.

Now suppose you go to one Giant game every other week (since the team is on the road half the time). You spend 13 times $6, or $78, for only 13 three-hour segments; but you also get a total of 162 "entertainment units" of considerable interest and in-volvement from the 162 games the Giants play. If you care — and the basic premise is that you do — every Giant game played en-tertains you to some degree, even if you never buy a ticket at all. So even the cheapest entertainment ticket, to the movies, delivers less "value" over a period of time than the sports ticket.

As for television, which is free to the particular consumer (or seems to be free, because the viewer doesn't dwell on the indirect price of commercials and taxes), the advantage of watching sports is equally great. The only dimension a movie — let's say, *Gone with the Wind* — offers is the movie itself. It may be great, but when it's over, it's over. The televised sports event, however, includes its own "news-information" component and delivers all those continuity and coherence values that transcend any single isolated game.

As for the promoter — the club owner — producing the "show" requires very little in the way of equipment, nothing for expensive "creative" talent (such as writers or composers), and nothing for construction of sets and the like. The salaries of the performers, their transportation and housing, insurance, maintenance of an office staff, and rent are the main items of cost. But a movie or theater producer must pay for all these anyhow, plus creative talent, elaborate machinery, and renting the appropriate facility in the face of stiff competition.

The television industry, particularly through the networks, shows conclusively how cost-efficient sports presentations really are. It is dazzling to read that CBS pays the National Basketball Association $18 million a year for television rights to a program that gets less-than-average audience ratings. But when you realize that this package gives the network about ninety hours of air time at $200,000 an hour, and that it costs as much as $500,000 to produce one pilot of a half-hour situation comedy that may die at first exposure, it begins to make sense.

VICARIOUS EXPERIENCE

Violence. Just as response to danger has been bleached out of our daily lives, so has physical violence — not only in its most common sense of damage and hostility but also in the sense of great physical exertion encompassing intensity and passion. The urge remains; the opportunity to give it socially acceptable expression, even in such rudimentary forms of release as chopping wood or hunting small game, is practically gone. Sports offer an acceptable outlet. For athletes the experience is direct, and the widespread participation in contact sports despite substantial risk of injury demonstrates its attractiveness.

For spectators, the mechanism works on two levels — identification and vocal expression. When we watch two football lines clash, sadistic or other buried forces may or may not be involved, but a less subliminal message is certainly delivered: we see physical force attain an objective. No release from frustration can be more direct than the smashing of some tangible restraint, and contact sports give us a steady stream of restraint-smashing images with which to identify. It isn't a secret desire "to see blood" that's important here, whether or not this exists in any particular spectator; what's important is the open desire to see an obstacle destroyed, an opponent overcome, a restraint broken by simple, nonintellectual, physical strength.

This may explain, incidentally, why soccer has been slow to gain maximum mass-spectator appeal in America, despite the fact that it has such popularity in much of the rest of the world. In our traditional sports (including basketball as it is actually played, with considerable contact), the strength factor is close to the surface. Soccer's restrictions on physical interference — the very elements that make it such a good game to play and that heighten its artistry — convey a sense of limitation to the American spectator, a limit on the amount of aggression that can be discharged by identification with unbridled physical effort. Our taste for this sort of vicarious discharge is well established in the three main story lines in American movies — Westerns, crime, and war. And in spectator sports, we get a large dose of this catharsis.

We also get the opportunity to yell and scream in a setting where society accepts such behavior, and this is catharsis too. A shout is itself a physical act, and psychologically a violent one. Vocal expression of rooting interest, in the form of exhortation of your team or invective heaped on opponent, referee, or your own team (for a mistake), is a kind of release not allowed in theaters, concert halls, offices, or living rooms. Here again, the special appeal to children is obvious. Where but at a ball game are they allowed to holler and jump up and down without being told to stop?

Triumph. Closely related to vicarious violence, but distinct from it, is the satisfaction derived from "beating" someone. This goes beyond mere "winning," to the idea of defeating an opponent. In a competitive society such as ours, countless varieties of contests are going on all the time, but the enemy does not always have a personalized identity. One can "win" a lottery, or a place in a desirable college, or a good job, or the gamble of producing a Broadway hit. Succeeding where others necessarily failed is inherent in such a "victory," but the direct experience of overcoming a specific foe is not.

The complex emotions stirred by one-to-one triumph, like one armored knight unhorsing another, can find release in sports as in no other recreational context. The enemy is present, identifiable, and given, by definition, a fair chance. When the enemy is beaten, forced to yield, brought into submission, mastered, conquered, or proven inferior, deeper (and more primitive) layers of human experience are touched than when one experiences simple enjoyment of the prize won. That's the difference, in quality of feeling, between winning the Tchaikovsky piano competition and winning the Heavyweight Championship of the World. And it is a bigger difference for the spectator than for the participant.

One may wonder whether, on the average, males and females differ in this response. Have males been conditioned, during the centuries of personal combat and hunting before industrialization mechanized such things so recently, to invest greater ego values in the idea of "beating" someone? And is this why sports on average appeal more and in a different way to young boys than to young girls? Qualified psychologists can (and probably have and certainly will) probe such questions. For us, the significant point is to recognize that this distinction between winning and beating does exist, that it is an important element in the total set of illusions, and that it is allied with hazard and violence in affording the vicarious release of tension.

Second-guessing. A mental equivalent of this frustration relief is the second-guess, or Monday-morning quarterbacking. The "he shoulda" syndrome is omnipresent in our lives, from business to politics to cooking (although jokes about back-seat drivers have become obsolete now that everyone is in the front seat driving his or her own car). The ego boost one gains by being able to say "He [famous, rich, talented] was wrong and I [just plain me] was right" is tremendous.

For the sports fan, the chance to indulge is maximized by all the elements already cited: comprehensibility, continuity, coherence, and so forth. Every fan believes he knows enough about this neat and familiar "universe of discourse" to have an opinion about whether this manager should have bunted, that coach should have called a pass play, or this player shouldn't have taken a "bad-percentage" shot. Even those who in their rational moments know how limited their knowledge really is enjoy indulging in the game of second-guessing. Those who take themselves more seriously can get terribly worked up over such issues.

In the everyday world, second-guessing (about the economy, foreign affairs, political campaigns, murder trials, lawsuits, or the tempo chosen by a symphony conductor) is feasible but not widely practical. It takes a special interest and considerable intellectual effort to amass the raw material of information needed. In the arts, while second-guessing is possible it is generally fruitless, since the event doesn't lead to a "result" and the work is whatever it is only because the artist conceived it that way and not some other way. We can imagine an alternate work, but not really the same work altered.

In sports, however, the second-guessing mechanism is gloriously accessible. Not only do large numbers of "ordinary" people feel they have the requisite knowledge, but they also get a daily supply of fresh and adequate raw-material information through newspapers, radio, and television. Very few people get their kicks by telling themselves, while watching a movie, "the director should have made her wait two more beats before speaking the line, and then panned to the letter on the dresser." Almost anyone can say, "he shoulda got that pitcher out of there before he gave up that last homer." In general, sports promoters understand very well how valuable the desire to second-guess is to the fan's continuing interest, and they work to stimulate it.

Patriotism. Since World War II, conventional patriotism has been declining in America, in response to social fashion and polarized political views. Yet the impulse to be patriotic — feelings of pride, loyalty, unity, protectiveness, willingness to sacrifice with respect to your "in-group," and readiness to fight any "out-group" that appears hostile — runs deep in all societies. Since fans attach a feeling of loyalty to a particular team, spectator sports give them a legitimate outlet for the emotion that accompanies patriotism, without embroiling them in the more complex issues it raises.

Much of the rooting interest that constitutes the basic illusion centers on regional loyalty: in most cases, people root for a team that "represents" their city or area. Usually, that team's triumphs and defeats are taken as a reflection of the community as a whole, even by those who pay no attention at all to the sports scene as such. That's why city and county governments, civic leaders, and prominent businessmen get entangled in questions of team location and major-league affiliation.

On an even broader canvas, high school and college varsity teams serve as focal points for patriotic impulses toward their particular institutions. Such loyalty is an especially powerful force among teenagers, who are much concerned with peer-group reactions anyhow. A varsity team, because its success or failure is definite, measurable, and publicized, is the most visible image-maker for any school. Rooting for a team and sharing its ups and downs, therefore, serve as both training in and substitute for orthodox patriotism.

•

The seven qualities we have just isolated — from comprehensibility through vicarious experience — are somewhat arbitrary and overlapping. But by putting them in this form, we have demonstrated the one that I believe taps the deepest part of the psyche, the yearning for order that I have called coherence. Sports fans love to make lists, memorize statistics, collect trivia, follow schedules, arange lineups, keep score. They are willing to swallow the original illusion — that it matters — because they must, if they are to open the door to that cozy universe in which everything can make sense, and in which they can engage in the happy pursuit of definite answers.

Each sport exploits a different mix of the characteristic qualities, according to its nature. And that's not surprising. If each major type of game didn't have a distinct profile, it wouldn't be needed and couldn't make room for itself in the marketplace alongside a previously established sport.

Baseball stresses continuity, readability, cohesion, and second-guessing. Each play is clearly visible. The batter, pitcher, and fielder perform their roles solo. There is a game every day. There is no clock, and every action can be recorded. All this lends itself to the maintenance of valid and voluminous statistical tables, and gives maximum opportunity for legitimate second-guessing about well-identified tactics and strategy. It is lower than most games in comprehensibility, because the goals and procedures involved are not self-evident and take a long time to learn; but it is played so often, and broadcast and written about so much, that it offers abundant time to do the learning.

Football is also low on comprehensibility, which may explain why it has not taken root in any other country. It is very high in continuity, readability, coherence, hazard, violence, second-guessing, and patriotism. In structure, it is a model of warfare, making use of idealized battlefield tactics drawn from infantry, cavalry, and artillery actions. Its infrequency — it can only be played about once a week without crippling all the players — enhances its readability and makes every game an important social occasion, especially in high school and college. Every play starts from a set position, which makes anticipatory second-guessing possible, but what really happens on any given play is not very visible from the stands. (Coaches study films. Television viewers wallow in replays.) The time element and the odd-shaped ball, which bounces unpredictably, increase the sense of hazard.

Basketball is high on comprehensibility, since the main idea is taken in at a glance. The frequent rebounds and missed shots and the influence of the clock make it very high on hazard, and it is sufficiently violent because of the constant motion. Basketball is as good as football as far as patriotism and social importance in schools are concerned. Its cost is very low indeed. As a "seamless" game with ten men moving simultaneously, with few set-play starts and an indescribable eventfulness in each minute of play, it is low on readability and second-guessing, and less than ideal in coherence, although still very good. Its saving grace, in regard to coherence, is the frequency of scoring, each basket being a moment of definite result.

Hockey and soccer are seamless like basketball but are low-scoring because a goaltender is present. This heightens hazard but decreases the satisfaction derived from coherence. On the other hand, the low scoring makes writing and reading about these games easier. They are less easily comprehensible than basketball (because they contain "offsides" provisions about player location that are not self-evident) but more easily grasped than baseball and football. Hockey includes overt body contact while soccer does not, and that component of violence probably accounts for hockey's greater commercial success in America. In addition, hockey has the unique fascination that gliding on ice provides. It increases the speed of movement (of players and puck) to such a pace that it is billed "the world's fastest game."

Boxing is personal combat stripped bare, the ultimate in comprehensibility, violence, hazard, and low cost. It is eminently readable because the raw material consists of individual personalities without the complications of technique, and long periods between the bouts of any one fighter bring boxing some of the benefits of football's social arrangements. It is low on coherence, so-so on second-guessing, easy to bet on, hard to determine scoring, and very strong on primitive patriotism, in terms of the ethnic or national identity of the fighters.

Horse racing is based firmly on hazard: the chance to bet. Without legal wagering, it would be a narrow special interest. It is instantly comprehensible, high in continuity and coherence, and insignificant in violence and patriotism. And very, very expensive.

One could analyze every sport in this way. Flirting with danger — real danger — is obviously a basic appeal of automobile racing. Golf is easily comprehensible but uninteresting unless one digs into techniques, and it is almost impossible to see in its entirety as a spectator. Tennis rules are less obvious than golf rules but easily grasped, and tennis is the most visible of all sports. But it is devoid of violence and low on coherence (as presently organized) and continuity. Both sports are expensive, and both tend to depend for spectators on those who play the games themselves (however casually). Track and field ranks near the top of the scale in comprehensibility, continuity, readability, coherence, and low cost — and near zero in hazard, violence, and second-guessing.

So there's the product: an athletic contest suitable for marketing, to which can be attached the illusion that the result — a result implacably defined as winning or losing — matters intensely to the spectator.

The next question is: How is this product organized and marketed, and how did it get that way?

2. The Structure

"I am not in baseball for my health."
— Charles Ebbets, owner of the Brooklyn Dodgers, 1912

PACKAGING SPECTATOR SPORTS is, in itself, a triumph for the element of comprehensibility. But no Madison Avenue genius invented the formula. It was arrived at by trial and error. The basic unit of organization in team games is the league. This seems so natural to us that we forget (or never realized) that it is a relatively recent development, which was devised only in the 1870s by operators of professional baseball clubs and quickly became the model for other sports.

A league structure has two key characteristics. First of all, to determine a champion, a schedule is made in which each team plays every other league member, and a record is kept of victories and defeats. The team with the best record wins, so every victory has exactly the same value in the league standings, regardless of when it was scored or who the opponent was. The second characteristic is a strong central government that sets and administers rules about team composition and playing conditions.

Individual sports follow the tournament principle. Here, the basic rule is that the loser of a particular match is eliminated from further progress toward the championship. We are most familiar with this in tennis, but by stretching the theory, the tournament principle can be applied to races (involving humans, animals, or machines) and the informal free-lance arrangements common in prize fighting.

The tournament principle is so powerful that it appears in team games, at the end of a season in the form of playoffs. But as a means of day-to-day commercial success, it has some fatal drawbacks, most of all the possibility that the best gate attraction will be eliminated early in the competition. In tournament play, past victories count for nothing but the right to advance to the next round, so the identity of the opponent becomes paramount. That is, the significance of the match varies with the importance of the foe, so that not all victories are equal. The eventual champion may never have to face his highest-rated rival. In team sports, therefore, the ultimate measure of success is league standings — the won-lost record. In individual sports, it is the number of prizes, expressed in money or medals or trophies.

A good way to appreciate the importance and originality of the league idea is to contemplate how it began, with particular attention to the case of one Albert G. Spalding. The essential rule changes that created baseball out of older bat-and-ball games were worked out in the 1840s in the New York City area. American social life in those days followed established English patterns, and baseball "clubs" proliferated. A club chooses its own members, makes its own rules of procedure, and invariably draws its members from a particular social class or profession. The early baseball clubs reflected that orthodoxy. One club would be composed mostly of clerks, another of mechanics, another of wealthier "gentlemen," and so forth. All professed strict amateurism, in keeping with early Victorian ideals.

But America was not, of course, England. Even on the Eastern seaboard it was part of a frontier civilization, inundated by waves of immigration. The barriers of social position were not as rigid as in Europe. In a culture attuned to self-reliance, competition, wresting a continent away from wilderness and Indians, and making the most of individual opportunity, the idea of "recreational sport among social equals" paled alongside the satisfactions of victory in a competition. So clubs soon began to seek out good players to be members, instead of relying on "appropriate" members to become good ballplayers.

By 1858, there were enough clubs (twenty-two) to form the National Association of Base Ball Players. They needed common playing rules and some way to exchange information about the authenticity of a particular player's membership in a club. After the Civil War, which only served to spread the popularity of the game as men from every section of the nation were thrown together in armies and prison camps, the National Association blossomed. Regional and local conventions were held under its auspices, and by 1867 it had more than three hundred member clubs.

Enter Mr. Spalding.

Albert Spalding was sixteen years old and lived in Rockford, Illinois, about eighty miles northwest of Chicago, just south of the Wisconsin line. Rockford had two adult baseball clubs, the Forest Citys and the Mercantiles. Two years earlier, in 1865, Spalding and a schoolmate named Ross Barnes had organized another team, the Pioneers, composed of boys under sixteen, and had challenged and beaten the Mercantiles. Spalding was the pitcher, Barnes the best hitter. The Forest Citys promptly invited Spalding and Barnes to join them, despite their youth.

The Forest City team started to win fame throughout the area as Spalding, excused from school by an understanding principal, pitched several victories. The big shots, however, were the Excelsiors of Chicago, and the most celebrated team of all was the Washington Nationals, composed of "government workers" who were making a 3000-mile tour of the "West" by boat and train. On July 26, 1867, the Nationals were to play the Excelsiors in Chicago.

On July 25, the Nationals scheduled a "warm-up" game with the Forest Citys, who traveled to Chicago for the privilege. Spalding, holding a summer job as a grocery clerk for three dollars a week, had to give up a day's pay (fifty cents) to take his turn on the mound against the famous Easterners. He pitched and won 29–23, which was not an unreasonable score in those days of underhand pitching. The Nationals were stunned. And when, the next day, they walloped the Chicago Excelsiors, 49–4, the full dimension of the Forest City achievement was plain.

Within a few days, Spalding had an offer from a wholesale grocer in Chicago: forty dollars a week as a bill clerk. Spalding had no experience or qualifications for such a job, and the going rate for a newcomer would have been five dollars (which would still be 60 percent more than he was making in Rockford). Why this magnificent offer, then? Oh, yes. He would be expected to pitch for the Excelsiors.

Spalding agonized at the prospect of "violating at least the spirit" of Association rules prohibiting salaries for playing ball. His mother agonized at the thought that he wouldn't finish his senior year of high school. By the time he accepted, the 1867 season had ended, but off to Chicago he went.

As it happened, he never did pitch for the Excelsiors. The wholesale grocer went bankrupt during the winter. Spalding took a job selling insurance for an agency owned by his uncle, but a fire caused losses that wiped out that agency. He went home to Rockford, to a warm welcome, and was given two part-time jobs as a bookkeeper, "with the understanding" that he would pitch for the Forest Citys. This was, remember, 1868.

The star player of the Washington Nationals was George Wright, the shortstop. He had been a star in New York, with the Gothams, but had suddenly turned up on the Nationals' roster, where his occupation was listed as clerk at 238 Pennsylvania Avenue — an address that happened to be a public park. At the end of the 1867 season, George's older brother Harry, an English-born professional cricket player from Staten Island, was put in charge of the Cincinnati Red Stockings. He hired four players openly, for salary. The National Association now acknowledged that amateurism was being widely ignored, and accepted professionalism as "legal," though frowned upon.

In 1869, the Red Stockings became the first fully professional team, with each of its ten players — including George Wright, at shortstop — signed to a season-long contract. The Red Stockings toured the country (even California, just connected by railway to the rest of the continent), and didn't lose a game until June 1870, when a crowd of 9000 paid fifty cents apiece to watch them face the Atlantics in Brooklyn.

Then in 1871, ten clubs gathered in New York and formed the National Association of *Professional* Base Ball Players. One of the ten was Forest City of Rockford. Another was the White Stockings of Chicago. And a third was the Boston Red Stockings.

Boston? Yes. The Cincinnati Red Stockings had disbanded after the 1870 season, and Harry Wright had been hired by backers in Boston to start a team there. He took along the name, and his brother George. And he went scouting for other top players.

Wright knew all about Spalding and Barnes. He offered them about $1500 each to come to Boston. They accepted.

What emerged was almost an all-star team. Under the new Association rules, clubs still made up their own schedules and retained much autonomy in other ways. A whole generation of players like Spalding had grown up accepting the best offer wherever it arose. In Boston, they found fame, prosperity, and artistic success. For four straight years starting in 1872, the Boston Red Stockings won the championship. Spalding was recognized as the best pitcher in the land, Barnes as the best hitter for average, and George Wright as the best all-around player and home-run hitter. But the clubs were't making any money, and one after another folded. The few strong teams aroused little interest except when they played each other; yet the Association was obliged to accept for "championship" play any club that met its conditions and the ten-dollar entry fee. By 1875, the disparity was so great that Boston's record was 71–8 while the Brooklyn Atlantics, who placed thirteenth and last, were 2–42.

By hiring professional players and trying to sell tickets, the clubs had entered the business world, but they weren't being run as businesses. One club owner who had a better vision was William A. Hulbert, one of the backers of the Chicago White Stockings. Early in 1875 he approached Spalding about coming back to his "native" area. During that season, he signed Spalding, Barnes, and others to Chicago contracts for 1876, violating Association rules about making such deals in advance. But by then he and Spalding had already formulated their master plan: They would not wait for the Association to discipline them, but would start a new association of their own, inviting only the strongest teams to play only attractive games. They would call their group the National *League* of Professional Baseball *Clubs*.

It was the last word that changed everything. In the National Association, the clubs had been sovereign states, their policies determined by their citizens, the players. In the National League, the clubs became less sovereign, under the rule of a central government, and the players became employees rather than citizens.

As Spalding was to write later, this setup recognized the universal distinction between labor and capital. Management must have full control of operations; the workers must concentrate only on production, under management's supervision. Players (workers) came and went, and their policy judgments were inevitably influenced by short-term gains and character flaws. The "club," under professional management, would have a long-term existence, and its directors could make intelligent, farsighted business decisions no matter what individual players did. The problems of players jumping from team to team, gambling, fixing games, and engaging in rowdyism could hardly be controlled when the players, as a group, had control of the affairs of each club. The League, through tightly managed clubs, would be able to keep things in order.

It worked. The National League began in 1876 with eight teams, survived challenges by selfish clubs and expelled them, got itself on a firm footing by 1880, and is now more than a century old.

In 1876, Spalding not only took over as manager and pitched the White Stockings to the championship but also opened a sporting goods store in Chicago and, along with the Wright brothers and Al Reach, launched what would eventually become the largest monopoly in that field. He was twenty-five years old, turning twenty-six in September.

Why dwell on this at such length?

Because the Spalding-Wright-National League story contains all the elements still at work in commercial sports.

The league structure means all contracts go through a central clearing-house. A player who violates some regulation is disciplined by expulsion (however disguised) from the whole league, not just from the team he fought with.

It means a territorial monopoly can be established for each member of the league.

It means annual championships under similar conditions, a continuity of records, and a simple central identity that transcends the movement of any one player or group of players.

It provides a mechanism for limiting salaries, and for making one maverick club conform to the views of the group.

It supplies "impartial" schedule-making and assignment of game officials, instead of leaving such sensitive issues to negotiations between competing clubs.

It makes possible (through assessments and other cooperative ventures) aid to financially weaker clubs when necessary, to keep the league stable, and it increases public-relations potential.

And it gives the fan the simplest possible automatic daily focus of interest: the won-lost standings as the teams progress toward a "pennant" (so-called because the original National League constitution pledged the league to buy the champion a pennant "costing not less than $100").

Basketball wasn't even invented until 1891. Pro football grew in the 1920s, as did major-league hockey. They followed the baseball procedures without questioning them, because they could see how well baseball had succeeded.

And the lessons of Spalding's day — that club managements must have control, that player movement must be regulated, that a central office must exist, that one-sided competition kills spectator interest — have never been seriously questioned since.

The structural principles also work in college and amateur sports, under different designations. Colleges call their leagues "conferences," and their central offices aren't quite as strong as those in professional sports, but the same advantages are obtained.

We can now make some general statements and construct some charts that apply to all commercial sports. In commercial sports, the goal is always the same: to sell tickets. "Selling tickets" is our code word for generating income. It includes, naturally, the indirect income from television, radio, concessions, parking, programs and scorecards, advertising, and anything else management can translate into dollars.

Winning is *not* the goal of the *business*. It's a valuable means of attaining the goal of selling tickets — not only now but for future seasons. Winning *is* the goal of the individuals playing, and of that part of management responsible for choosing players. But the *club's* goal is to sell tickets. That's its reason for being.

In every club, there are three levels of personnel: the *owner,* whose goal is profit (which may be measured in prestige and effect on other business interests as well as in dollars); the *management,* whose goal is to produce a winning team while managing financial affairs in a way that won't dissipate profits; and the *player,* whose goal is to be part of a winning team and to excel individually, since these are the only ways to advance his own career. In practice, then, the owner thinks about end result: he wants his team in the championship game at whatever cost he considers to be reasonable. The management thinks about how to obtain the best players and train and lead them. And the player thinks about how to play effectively.

How similar these various functions are in different settings becomes apparent in the following table, which presents information from the standpoint of an individual club, college, or tournament.

CLUB ORGANIZATION

Function	Pro	Major College	Amateur
Owner	Club owner	College president	Various federations U.S. Olympic Committee
Management	Field manager & general manager	Head coach & athletic director	Local units of federations
Player	Career professional	Student	Nonprofessional
Player controlled by	Hire-fire	Eligibility	Certification
Reward to player	Salary	Scholarship	Glory
Discipline	Fine & suspension	Ineligibility	Ineligibility
Avowed goal of management	Profit	Prestige and fund-raising	Power and travel
Truer goal	Prestige	Job security	Maintain power
Unstated goal	Low pay	More scholarships	No pay
Means to goal	Sell tickets	Sell tickets & recruit	Stage events
Formula for reaching goal	Win, make stars	Win	Find stars
Financing	Investors	Donations or appropriations	Sponsors
Landlord	City or self	Self or city	One-shot sponsors

A similar table can be constructed for leagues, associations, and other groupings of individual teams or events:

LEAGUE ORGANIZATION

Function	Pro	Major College	Amateur
Head	Commissioner or league president	NCAA & conference commissioners	International associations, sport by sport
Scheduling	By league	By team	By promoters
Playing rules	By league	By NCAA	By international associations
Player control	By league	By NCAA & conferences	By international association, AAU/TAC, and IOC
TV control	League nationally, team locally	NCAA nationally, conference locally	Promoter of event
Labor representation	Player association in a league	None	None

In non-team sports outside the college or school ranks, a different table is necessary:

NON-LEAGUE ORGANIZATION

Function	Golf	Tennis	Boxing	Horse racing
Central authority	Professional Golfers Association (PGA)	International federation	None*	National associations
Legal status	Private	Private	Licensed by states	Licensed by states
Scheduling	By PGA	By promoters	By promoters	By tracks or "meetings"
Decision to participate	Player	Player	Fighter or manager	Owner of horse
Financing	Sponsors	Sponsors	Promoters	Track
Choice of site for major event	PGA	Promoter	Promoter	Track
Reward	Cash prize	Cash prize	Cash guarantee	Cash prize

* In practice in the United States, the World Boxing Council and the World Boxing Association have little practical influence.

The *promoter* arranges the staging of an event, signs up the participants, rents the facility, raises the money, and makes a profit, if there is any. He performs the functions that the league and club owner are responsible for in team sports. The *sponsor* puts up the money, underwriting expenses and prizes. This is usually a corporation or local booster group that becomes involved because of some public-relations value received. An analogy in team sports is the college that finances its football team.

Using tables such as those above, we can plug in any particular sport or team and identify how its decision-making processes work. All basic policy decisions, always, are made at the level of club owner or the equivalent. Simply by tacitly accepting a decision made at a lower level, the owner approves it; but it is impossible for a lower decision to stand against the active disapproval of the owner. All practical business decisions, within the policy set by the owner, are the province of the general manager or athletic director.

All playing-efficiency decisions are the business of the field manager or head coach.

All eligibility questions are handled by the league, the college conference, the amateur certification body, or some other group outside the control of a particular team.

The player has only one choice: accept the conditions or don't play. If the "player" is Muhammad Ali, of course, the rest of the structure will go to any lengths to win his acceptance. All stars have great bargaining power because their services are desired. But structurally they have no influence.

Where an effective labor union exists, such as the Major League Players Association in baseball and equivalent organizations in professional basketball and football, the players have some input into policy matters. They have exactly the same power unions have in any industry, no more, no less, and their only ultimate weapon is the strike.

This system has evolved (and is still evolving) for one reason only: to bring in money from the public, and to distribute that money in appropriate ways to the participants. It certainly brings in the money, to the tune of billions of dollars each year. And the money is certainly distributed to many people, all the way down to the hot-dog vendors in the ballpark.

But is it distributed "appropriately"?

That's a question open to bitter argument. So the next thing we will look at is how the pie gets sliced.

3. Cutting Up the Pie

"... to each according to his needs."

— Karl Marx

BEFORE YOU CAN cut up a pie, you must have the pie.

The traditional recipe for rabbit stew starts with "catch a rabbit." The formula for making money is just as simple: "draw a crowd." That's not the only moneymaking formula, but it's one of the few basic ones, and the one on which sports entertainment depends.

The true ancestors of the World Series and the high school football game are the carnival, the circus, and the religious festival. The youngest member of the lineage is the suburban shopping center. If you can gather a large number of people in a central place, you can sell them things; and if you can keep them there more than an hour or two, you can sell them food and drink along with anything else. That's the principle behind a central marketplace, from which cities originated.

But on a less-permanent basis, the best and easiest way to draw a crowd is to put on a show of some kind — a ceremony, a dramatic presentation, acrobats, bull fights, jugglers, singers, dancers, animal trainers, anything that differs from the routine of the lives of the people in the district but is easily comprehensible.

Generating commerce may be the furthest thing from the minds of those who actually perform, but there is always someone around who recognizes that their activity creates a context for trade. And it doesn't take long for the performers who didn't think of it originally to recognize that commerce is going on around them, and that they ought to get a piece of it.

There's a big step, however, between stating the generality — a show will draw a crowd of potential customers — and figuring out exactly how to wind up with a profit. To bake a pie you need some sort of kitchen and the appropriate ingredients, but you also have to know how to cook. The mere availability of the equipment isn't enough.

Paul Muni, a famous actor, liked to tell of an aunt who was renowned for her delicious apple pies. When asked for her recipe, she would say, "You put on an apron, you go in the kitchen, you wash your hands — and you make apple pie." Muni used the story to illustrate his belief that acting could not be broken down into a this-is-how-you-do-it program that an artist could pass along to anyone looking for the recipe.

The same thing is true of sports promotion. You do it however you do it, and equally successful geniuses in the field have used strikingly different methods. What they all have in common, however, is the usable ingredients, and these can be identified. There are only a few fundamental sources of income. There is a longer list of necessary expenses. What's left over is the profit. Only after that does the central question arise: Who gets to keep how much of the profit?

Let's start with income.

ADMISSIONS

Almost any kind of show will draw attention, but only past a certain stage of attractiveness will the show make people willing to pay to see it. Ball games and other sports have that kind of attractiveness (gained, as we've seen, by producing the illusion that the result matters).

One way to collect money from spectators is to beg — to pass the hat around or hope that coins will be tossed. Street musicians do this, and ball clubs did it in their earliest days. (The mechanism is exactly the same in church collections, although the purpose is quite different.) But this method depends on spectators with a strong sense of conscience or gratitude, and lets many others watch for free. It is better, if the attraction is good enough, to make anyone who wants to watch buy a ticket. That, in turn, requires an enclosure to keep non-ticket buyers out, and reasonable accommodations for those who do buy. The usual minimum is a place to sit and unobstructed sight lines.

When you have such a facility, and a show that arouses interest, ticket sales become the primary form of income.

FOOD AND DRINK

The enclosed facility creates an unexpected advantage. Not only must people pay to get in, but, once in, they have little inclination to go out. As they get hungry and thirsty, they accept whatever refreshments are made available on the premises.

Once the promoter enclosed the grounds for the sake of selling admissions, he automatically obtained physical control of the areas where food and drink could be sold. During a market-square performance, people can wander around different shops, but inside a ballpark they must buy from the licensed vendors inside, or go through a great deal of trouble (and miss part of the show) to go outside and come back. So the promoter, who may or may not have contacts in the food business, gives concession rights to someone who does. This outside party handles "the concessions," and the promoter shares in the profits.

Hot dogs, peanuts, popcorn, soda pop, and beer — especially beer — have been the staples of sports concessions from the beginning more than a century ago. Nowadays, menus have been expanded to include hamburgers, ice cream, candy, pizza, soup, and so forth, and in San Francisco's Candlestick Park you can even get little carafes of wine. Vendors circulating through the spectators, counter-stands in back aisles, and actual cafeterias and restaurants are now common.

Only older people remember that in the days of vaudeville and burlesque, theaters had "candy butchers" hawking their wares in the aisles (as they also did on railroad cars). But everyone is familiar with the popcorn-and-candy counter in movie houses today. The principle is the same in sports. A captive audience not only must buy "your" product instead of someone else's; it will also happily pay inflated prices for the available concessions. If someone rang your front doorbell and offered to let you have a half-cooked hot dog on a crumbly bun for $1.25, you'd laugh or curse, but you'd certainly refuse. Millions do it blissfully at ball games, though, and the cry "Getcher hot dog here" became part of our cultural language long ago.

OTHER CONCESSIONS

Once organized to sell food, you can sell other things as well — pennants, dolls, sweatshirts, any kind of souvenir properly labeled to play on the emotions aroused by the spectator's identification with the team. First and foremost, you can sell a scorecard, or program, that gives names, numbers, and other information about the players in the game. ("You can't tell the players without a scorecard" is a venerable American adage that many a manager, club owner, and newspaperman has amended ruefully to "you can't tell the players *anything.*") What used to be the nickel scorecard (with a free pencil) has grown into a $1.50 "souvenir program" with lineup insert.

Another recent development is parking fees. Until World War II, most of the ticket buyers arrived at the ballpark or arena by public transportation and walked in. There wasn't much a promoter could do to make money out of their mere arrival. But once the private automobile (and suburban stadiums) became dominant, a major source of revenue arose. A car must be parked in some degree of safety while left unattended, and within reasonable walking distance of the seat. That means parking lots on the grounds or adjacent to them, and the public can be made to pay for that. A fee of two dollars per car is not uncommon today. Multiply that by several thousand spaces a day, and it adds up to real money.

In some cases, all the parking money belongs to the promoter. The Los Angeles Dodgers, for instance, own their own stadium area. Sometimes the landlord (usually the city or county) controls the parking, and the promoter gets some share of the money. And in some cases, especially in pro football and indoor-arena sports, none of the parking money goes to the club.

But such differences are more technical than real. As long as parking generates significant income anywhere along the line, it shows up in what the other acceptable lease arrangements are. Income is income, and for general understanding it is well to keep one's eye on the ball — income minus outgo — without getting lost in details.

BROADCAST RIGHTS

Newspapers are invited to send their reporters to ball games without charge, for historical and other reasons (to be examined in the next chapter). So are broadcasters, if all they intend to do is prepare an account or an interview for a news program that is analogous to a newspaper.

But to carry a complete event play by play, on radio or television, a broadcaster must pay the promoter. In return, the broadcaster gets exclusivity — something the journalist doesn't have. Essentially, the promoter takes the position that a listener or television viewer is a potential ticket buyer who is satisfied in another way. On the one hand, he is a lost customer for that particular game; on the other, he is being bombarded with an elaborate ad for all future games. By balancing these two forces, the promoter can calculate how much he should be paid for the rights in order to avoid a net loss.

ADVERTISING

In the ballpark, the spectators look at the scoreboard every few moments for essential information. The space adjacent to the scoreboard is, therefore, a premium location for display advertising. Exactly the same principle is followed when newspaper or magazine ads are placed next to interesting reading material. At baseball and soccer games, the inside surface of the fence around the playing area is used for this purpose. When television enters the picture, the advertiser gets out-of-park exposure whenever the camera sweeps by.

The scoreboard or program is another natural habitat for advertising. So are various heavily trafficked ramp and access areas inside the arena. Total advertising revenues are small compared to ticket sales and broadcasting rights, but they require so little upkeep and initial cost that they become significant profit factors.

INVESTMENT

Until the last twenty years or so, promoters depended on actual ticket purchases for incoming cash and often had to borrow money for between-season and start-up operations. (One of the chief sources of such loans was the concessionaire, who wanted the club to stay in business so that he would have an outlet for his wares). But since season-ticket sales became a substantial factor, this has changed. In most cases, season tickets must be paid for in full before the season begins. This puts a whole year's cash into the promoter's hands before he starts paying salaries and other expenses. This cash can be deposited to draw interest, or invested in some other way, and it results in a double gain. The promoter doesn't have to pay interest on the money he no longer has to borrow, and he draws income from the money he can invest.

If a football team like the New York Giants can sell 60,000 season tickets at $80 each ($10 a game for eight home games), it can have $4.8 million on deposit before the first game. Some portion of the television income ($5.6 million in this case) may also be received before the season begins. If, let's say, $6 million can sit in a bank at 6 percent interest for even three months, that's $90,000 right there — and skillful money managers have still better ways to manipulate funds.

EXOTICS

A luxury box in pro football can cost up to $50,000 "rent," apart from the tickets and concessions involved. This money is divided, in some way, between the promoter and the landlord. A luxury restaurant, usually called a "Stadium Club," may be profitable. Such extra forms of income (which can be huge, as in the case of the luxury boxes, or modest) are limited only by the imagination of the promoter.

•

Out of the club's income, certain inescapable expenses must be paid. These include:

- Salaries to players
- Salaries to coaches and scouts
- Salaries to administrative executives and office staff
- Contributions to various pension and medical-benefit plans
- Game-day wages (ticket takers, ushers, cleanup crews, etc.)
- Travel
- Hotels and meals on the road
- Playing equipment and uniforms
- Office equipment
- Rent, or share of maintenance, or both
- Insurance
- Taxes (income and local)
- Advertising and publicity
- Player development (operating a minor-league team, or scouting players to be drafted, or both)

This list may not be all-inclusive, but it gives you an idea where the money is spent. Players rarely think about such expenses when they see themselves as the "source" of all profits.

Incidentally, the share of the gate that goes to the visiting team is not an "expense" in this sense, because it is simply exchanged for the visiting share your team gets when it goes on the road. For a particular club, this equation may get heavily out of balance in one direction or the other, but for the league as a whole it balances out.

And that brings us to profit.

From a strictly financial point of view, profit has three elements. There is the net surplus of income over expense. There are various kinds of tax advantages. And there is the effect the sports operation has on other business interests of the club owner.

The net surplus is self-evident from the income-costs list above. It can, of course, be a deficit, and often it is.

The tax advantages usually involve capital gains, depreciation of the value of player contracts over a period of a few years, and the writing off of business expenses that cover other activities. For example, a chauffeur-driven car is a legitimate business expense for a club owner attending his club's spring training in Miami. It certainly takes him to the ballpark and back. But it may also take him elsewhere at other times. For that matter, the whole stay in Miami is justified by the club's presence. This is a trivial example, but the art of making a business pay for the proprietor's varied activities is well developed in American commercial and political life. Club owners have not been backward in this respect.

One specific type of tax advantage shades into the third category of profit. A loss in one business may be matched against a gain in another to reduce tax liability, if the right corporate arrangements are made; and a gain may turn out to be less taxable if losses from elsewhere can be used to counterbalance it. Here, too, the creativity of accountants and lawyers hired by major-league sports organizations is not inferior to that found in other industries.

But taxes are not the only way an owner's other business can benefit. With rare exceptions, club owners are already prosperous before they become club owners, and that means they have other substantial business interests. If they didn't they couldn't buy or start up a major-league club.

Since a ball club is such a big attention-getter in the community — and we've pointed out that getting attention is one of a club's primary activities — the man who owns it is automatically a local celebrity. This means free advertising for his other business interests. If he sells insurance, practices law, runs a restaurant, brews beer, or deals in real estate, the fact that he is constantly identified with such activities to an enormous public helps those enterprises.

Beyond the value of just plain advertising, the owner's sports connection makes him an important community figure in the "booster" sense (since much of the public has accepted the illusions involved in rooting for a local team), and the resulting good will is a recognizable business asset.

Both the advertising and the good will tend to increase the

owner's ability to draw customers to his other business, whether it's a store or a bank or a tavern. In some cases (when the owner is a brewer, for instance) the demand for the other product is actually increased directly. And in general, if the sports franchise stimulates business activity in the community in any way, the owner's other business, as a part of that community, will gain in some way.

Any businessman can benefit from community activity on any level, by supporting the arts, or producing plays, or financing a playground, or sponsoring local sports tournaments or semipro teams. But the big-league franchise owner has two immense advantages — exclusivity and daily news potential. No other businessman in that town can own *the* ball club. And the club gets attention every day it plays (and most days in between), not just when it opens for business or when a gift is announced.

In addition to advertising advantages, the club owner's increase in personal prestige is an asset to his other business interests because "star quality" is of value. Business associates love it when the owner can get Mickey Mantle or Johnny Unitas to play a round of golf with them, and he himself becomes someone it's "fun to do business with," even when the athlete isn't present.

Technically speaking, those are the only elements in profit: surplus, tax breaks, and outside business gains. When we speak of cutting up the pie between employer and employees, those are the only factors that can be measured, even indirectly.

But the most important true "profit" to the franchise owner is an intangible: there are enormous ego rewards. All the vicarious thrills mentioned in the first chapter are available to the club owner in the most heightened form, with one important extra: the sense of power and command that goes along with thinking of "my" player and "my" ball club.

Being identified as a celebrity is a reward in itself to those who care about it. And those who don't care about it are less likely to buy or keep a ball club than those who do. Being a power in the community, a decision-maker whose advice and support are sought for countless projects, is heady stuff, apart from its tangible benefit to one's other business interests. Hobnobbing with other celebrities on an equal footing, and thereby arousing the envy of friends and rivals who may be equally "important" but far more anonymous to the public, is a satisfaction not purchasable by mere cash. It happens in restaurants, parties, country-club locker rooms, board meetings, and other daily rounds.

Most of all, however, there is the pure reward of supporting, and making it possible to experience, something one enjoys. Wealthy people who get their kicks from operas or symphony orchestras contribute large sums to keep those organizations functioning. If they love art, they endow museums. Ordinary people pay for the recreation by buying tickets. The wealthy movers and shakers, on the other hand, make sure their preferred form of entertainment is available by financing it.

The club owner, in most cases, is doing exactly the same thing with an entertainment he loves, and would be getting his money's worth even if the ball club, like the opera, had a deficit every year. Happily, most ball clubs don't.

In the profit structure, then, the formula can be put: Net surplus is number 1, tax advantage number 2, outside business benefits number 3, and ego rewards number 4.

Numbers 2 and 3 help create profit even if number 1 is a loss. And numbers 2, 3, and 4, lumped together, operate to make actual net loss worthwhile.

Oddly enough, exactly the same formula applies to players, although they are even less willing to acknowledge it than club owners. Players see their salaries (and side benefits such as pensions, medical care, and expenses) as their only "profit." But they too have tax-break possibilities, they too can enter other businesses in which their status as celebrities will give them an edge over the competition, and they too get fantastic ego rewards when they win a championship.

What they overlook is that the "championship" would not exist if someone (other than the proud player) didn't go through a great deal of trouble to arrange it. If it is true that the ego satisfaction of the promoter depends on the performance of "his" players, it is equally true that the ego satisfaction of the winning player depends on the "performance" of the promoter in creating the context for the contest.

Abstractions aside, however, the real-world struggle is for a slice of the tangible, dollar-measured profits. And that struggle dominated sports in the 1970s.

In 1869, the Cincinnati Red Stockings became the first fully professional baseball team with all its players signed to season-long contracts. There was no league, of course. They toured the country to the tune of 11,877 miles, never lost a game, and attracted some 200,000 spectators. Their gate receipts came to $29,726.26. The player payroll was $9500. Call it 32 percent of gross income. Since the "other expenses" ate up 68 percent, leaving a net surplus of $1.39, the Red Stockings folded after the 1870 season.

The professional players then formed an association, the forerunner of the National League. We've already met Mr. Spalding, who became the star pitcher of the Boston Red Stockings. In 1875, the Boston club took in $38,000, of which the players got $21,000. Call that 55 percent of gross income. That didn't work either. The National Association folded, and was succeeded by the still-thriving National League in 1876.

Major-league baseball told a congressional committee in 1951 that in 1939 its gross expenses had been $12,000,000 and its player payroll had been $3,600,000. Call that 32 percent of gross income.

So seventy years after the first baseball team, the share of the pie going to the players was the same. In the meantime, the owners had learned how to get a better handle on "other expenses."

After World War II, baseball income started to rise sharply. There were more night games, more radio, and, after a while, more television, and the attendance figures increased greatly.

But salaries did not rise much. By 1950, they were only 16 percent of gross income. By 1970, they were 11 percent.

That's why, in the late 1960s, the players decided to turn their fraternal Players Association, which had dealt with little but pensions since 1946, into a truer labor union. They hired Marvin Miller to negotiate for them. By 1976, Miller's negotiations had brought them back up to 15 percent.

This whole history was possible only because of a "reserve system" developed in the 1880s. This prevented a player from offering his services to any team other than the one that held his previous contract, even after that contract expired. In 1976, the reserve system was finally cracked. (We'll see how in a later chapter.) By 1979, the player share was up to 27 percent.

Other sports, using baseball contracts and league practices as their model, followed the same path but not the same arithmetic. Pro basketball players, benefiting from competition between two leagues in the late 1960s, soon achieved 65 percent of gross income as their share. In the National Football League, which has greater television receipts than any other league but also many more players to deal with, the player payroll has been running about 20 percent, but the players plan to ask for a flat 55 percent in 1982.

What, then, is the "right" percentage performers can expect in a "labor-intensive" industry that has no large-scale expense for raw materials or machinery? More than one-third, say the players. It doesn't work that way, say the owners. It's a matter of keeping other expenses in line, too.

Unfortunately, reliable hard-core figures on this subject are not available — not to me, not to scientific researchers, not to the players, and not to Congress. A few clubs here and there have public stockholders and issue profit-loss statements, but these don't reveal much because expenses are lumped together into general categories.

Public statements by league commissioners and individual club owners to the effect that "lots of our clubs are losing money" and that a league, to exist, must "help its weakest member survive" are plentiful. Player claims that all teams are rolling in wealth are also easy to come by. The most neutral thing that can be said is this: At the end of the 1970s, the gross income of major leagues in baseball, football, basketball, and hockey substantially exceeded the gross expenditures.

And two factors suggest that the true profit picture wasn't so terrible. The first is that in labor negotiations, the owner side has never claimed inability to pay as a reason for rejecting a player demand. That's because such a claim, under the labor laws, would give the union the right to look at the books.

The other indication is the choice made by the National Basketball Association in 1970, when it agreed to merge with the American Basketball Association (to end the bidding war between them for star players), and went before Congress to ask for a special exemption from the antitrust laws so that the merger could be carried out.

The Senate committee in question was headed by Sam Ervin of North Carolina, who subsequently became famous in the Watergate hearings and in American Express card commercials. Senator Ervin said, in effect: "If you want to be exempt from the law of the land to carry out a commercial arrangement you say you need, you'd better show me your tax returns and other data to prove you really need it." The NBA respectfully declined and accepted having its merger blocked for six more years rather than open its books.

For our purposes, however, the small details really don't matter. Learned volumes have been published on sports economics, with impractical ideas piled on top of invalid theories based on inadequate numbers, and these have been quoted eagerly by one side or the other in the struggle for the right piece of the pie. All we need to know at this point is that the struggle goes on, that there's room for movement (and doubt) on both sides, and that it will continue to go on as long as there are commercial sports. Unlike in the games themselves, there are no good guys and bad guys in the conflict, only separate interests, and there's little point in rooting for either side.

As for sports bookkeeping, a well-known joke comes closer to the truth than any column of figures. A businessman interviewed three candidates for the job of bookkeeper.

"How much is two and two?" he asked the first.

"Four," he answered.

"How much is two and two?" he asked the second.

"Four," he answered.

"How much is two and two?" he asked the third.

The third one got the job. His answer was: "How much do you want it to be?"

4. Natural Alliances

"I think you can hit Warfield on the down-and-in pattern against them."

— President Richard M. Nixon, 1972,
by telephone to the coach of the Miami Dolphins

FEW TRADITIONS are as peculiarly American as the ceremony of throwing out the first ball at the start of the baseball season. When major-league baseball had a team in Washington (until 1972), no less a personage than the president of the United States was invited to perform it — and felt obliged to.

That's the important part: he felt obliged to. The sports establishment doesn't have the strength it does by accident. It has grown, and thrives, through natural alliances seldom identified by commentators. Its influence on our imaginations and social behavior is far out of proportion to its true economic power. The total amount of money taken in by all major-league baseball, or the National Football League, in one year (call it $300,000,000) is less than the amount made by a single supermarket chain (Safeway, for instance) in ten days. Why, then, does sports have the impact it does?

The answer is alliances. The sports establishment's activities suit the purposes of other and larger forces, and that community of interests is what accounts for the development of commercial sports and also for its resistance to significant change. Newspaper publishers and politicians got on the sports bandwagon early, not because they loved the activity itself (which many did), but because it proved to be such an excellent vehicle for their own use.

Let's look again at the basic element of sports promotion: "draw a crowd" or, by extension, "get attention." In analyzing why the central illusion — that the outcome of a contest matters to you — is successful, we've seen that a sports event is a highly efficient attention-getter. And attention, once focused, can be turned to profitable use by people other than the ones who focused it. Those others will rarely bite the hand that feeds them.

We can identify at least nine of these "natural alliances," all of them still going strong — although their relative importance has fluctuated over the years. These alliances are with newspapers, broadcasting, politicians, local business, real estate, the school system, local government, potential employees, and the general populace. With friends like that, the sports establishment can withstand a lot of enmity.

NEWSPAPERS

A major sports team, once established, is a guaranteed daily newsmaker. The newspaper depends for its success on the expectation of its readers. It can't be sure that a spicy murder case, a major election issue, or a disaster will occur every day to supply an intriguing headline. It can depend on a sports result. If a large number of people are interested in knowing about that result, they will be impelled to buy the paper to find out about it. Baseball and horse racing, therefore, became the backbone of early sports sections. They produced results virtually every day, at least through the good-weather months.

Each result, of course, stimulates interest in the next event. The process feeds on itself. A game draws a crowd. Those interested enough to attend are interested enough to read about it and talk to people who didn't attend. This creates a nucleus of potential newspaper buyers. The paper tries to reach that audience by writing about the game, and that makes additional readers aware of the subject. The more people there are who care about the game, the larger the potential reading audience; and the larger the number of readers, the greater the number of potential ticket buyers.

This mutual-aid process has been going on for well over a century and is as strong as ever. The presence of a fully commercialized team in a community helps the local papers, and no team can exist without regular exposure in the local papers. (Elements of the same relationship apply to lower echelons of sports activity, of course, but it is the "major" event that is fuel for the engine.) In the largest metropolitan areas, professional teams are the kingpins. And where a college or university is a leading institution in a smaller city, this "amateur" team gets equally elaborate local newspaper treatment.

This doesn't mean, however, that the newspaper and the sports promoter have the same interests in every respect. The promoter is not in business to sell papers, and the newspaper is not in business to stimulate his ticket sales or indiscriminately boost his product. But each business gains from, and depends on, the existence of the other.

Newspapers frequently contain strong criticism of a team's management or performance, but never any opposition to its existence. And there are many bitter arguments between a team's management and the press, but never a situation where the management bars the press from attending (and therefore writing about) the events.

BROADCASTING

To some extent, what applies to newspapers applies to radio and television stations, but only incidentally. In broadcasting, the community of interest lies in another direction.

Above all, a broadcaster needs programming. Something must be put on the air that will hold the attention of an audience. That something must be created. It may be a drama, a variety show, an audience-participation quiz, a lecture, a debate, even a news program or a musical performance; but someone has to arrange it and execute it.

Sports provide countless hours of ready-made programming, already put together by the sports promoter. All the broadcaster has to do is buy the finished product. But sports have some unique advantages, as we have seen, over other forms of art and entertainment. The chief of these is an inexhaustible supply of new "plots" and built-in excitement. As a staple of programming, supplying a given number of hours of "noninvented" material, sports are essential to the broadcasting industry. In television, weekend shows like "Wide World of Sports" demonstrate how the medium must unearth or even create "sports" events when not enough "regular" material is available.

But as an attention-getter already in existence, sports had an additional and special importance to broadcasters in the early stages of that industry. Baseball scores may have increased the sales of nineteenth-century newspapers, but they weren't vital to the very existence of newspapers. But before television could develop an audience, it had to persuade millions of people to buy television sets. And they would do this only if they knew, ahead of time, that there was going to be something they wanted to watch.

Baseball was that something, in the late 1940s and early 1950s, and other sports soon followed. "We had to have the rights to carry baseball games," said General David Sarnoff, head of RCA, in a speech twenty years later, "in order to sell enough sets to go on to other programming." And exactly the same process is taking place in the 1980s with respect to various cable and pay-television systems.

Why sports? Not only because the plots are ready-made and because there is a large supply, but because the newspapers, by advertising ball games for their own purposes, simultaneously advertise the broadcast of those ball games. No other entertainment program can get the benefit of that much free "news" space. (The "Who killed J.R." coup by "Dallas" is, again, an exception to the rule.) So the alliance between the broadcasting industry and sports is intensified by the alliance between the newspaper industry and sports.

POLITICIANS

Regardless of issues, party affiliation, official position, or personal qualities, anyone running for public office (or holding it) needs to be noticed. Politicians, by their nature, are expert at latching on to whatever draws attention, and they make every effort to associate themselves with "favorable" causes, however they define them. Well, sports events get attention. If the mayor throws out the first ball, thousands of people will see him and — more important — the newspapers and broadcasters will record the event.

But it goes much deeper than that. When a sports team is successful, as we have seen, it stimulates all sorts of positive emotions: local pride, identification with victory, pleasurable excitement, and so forth. If a public figure is associated with such feelings, it is certainly to his advantage.

What's more, sports are the common language of superficial social intercourse. When the Pittsburgh Pirates or Steelers are headed for a championship, everyone in Pittsburgh talks about how they're doing, even the vast majority of people who don't really care and don't follow such events to any substantial degree. Mention of some currently hot sports topic is simply a tacit acknowledgment of membership in a community, like commenting on the weather. In other cultures, royal family members or opera stars may serve that function. In America, sports do.

This is precisely the point of contact a politician needs: a pleasant, instantaneous, harmless but recognizable sharing of interest. He immediately brands himself a "good" Pittsburgher by saying, "Isn't it great about the Pirates?" So you won't find politicians attacking the *existence* of, or the current practices of, sports establishments that have demonstrated their hold on public attention. Like newspaper publishers and broadcasters, politicians have a stake in the *functioning* of the major sports in their area, as distinct from the fortunes of the individuals involved in those sports.

LOCAL BUSINESS

Businessmen, like politicians, need means of making instant contact with strangers, albeit for different reasons. The "social intercourse" element of sports talk and sports news is just as useful to salesmen as to candidates.

But there are more tangible benefits, varying in importance according to the particular type of business but having an indirect effect on all. To the extent that well-publicized sports events stimulate business activity, their presence is welcomed by the business community. Hotels, restaurants, and transportation services can measure their gains directly, but since any "traffic" — the going and coming of people through commercial districts — improves the business climate, sports help everyone in the area. The original impulses responsible for market town and carnival still have their counterparts.

REAL ESTATE

One type of business takes special interest in what the local sports franchise provides. Real-estate agencies, for housing or commercial property, depend more than businesses on the reputation or fame of their city. It is an article of faith in all American cities that "spreading the name" is beneficial to economic health, not to mention morale. The real-estate sector feels this more directly than others.

Let's consider one example. Simply by having a team in the major leagues, Kansas City is brought to the attention of people elsewhere millions of times. That alone would be worth something, but this asset is also accompanied by the desirable aura associated with identification as "a major-league city." In time, the absence of this label becomes a stigma.

Real-estate interests also benefit specifically from the location of a ballpark or arena that houses a popular team. Transportation lines leading to the facility (or placement of the facility on a particular transportation line) can create whole networks of municipal development. As early as the 1880s, a baseball club owner tried to move his New York team from Manhattan to Staten Island because he owned a rapid-transit rail line there, a ferry line from Manhattan, and an entertainment complex at the end of the ferry line. He was also negotiating a deal to have the Baltimore and Ohio Railroad make Staten Island its New York terminus. The scheme and the team failed, but the name of the team — the Mets — lives on.

In half a dozen of America's largest cities, in recent years, there have been animated fights and lawsuits about whether new parks should be located downtown or in the suburbs. But neither realtor nor businessman nor politician nor broadcaster nor publisher has spoken out publicly against the *idea* of having a team in these cities.

SCHOOLS

Here we shift to a more subtle, but no less real, common interest. Each school, private as well as public, is concerned with solidifying a distinct image, arousing loyalty to itself as a particular institution, and attaching positive emotions to its activities. Athletics, in the form of organized teams that represent the whole school (varsity) or simply represent a part of it (class and intramural units), are effective instruments for the achievement of such goals. Since the population of the school consists of children, game-playing structures are especially suitable.

To schoolchildren, the commercial sports establishment provides appealing role models for the school teams. Interest in the "big" teams, stimulated by newspapers and broadcasts, is easily transmuted, through imitation, into enthusiasm for the school activity. It is not an infallible rule that school sports thrive where local major-league activity is high — too many other factors complicate the equation — but there is a tendency in that direction. In any case, many school administrators and parents do see such a connection, and they have favorable attitudes toward the big-league examples their children react to so strongly.

And for all their faults, major-league sports are perceived as more desirable role models for young people than are other common street activities. That's an important subject to be dealt with later, but for now we can note that the school community, in any city, forms a large constituency fundamentally supportive of the sports establishment.

LOCAL GOVERNMENT, POTENTIAL EMPLOYEES,
AND THE GENERAL POPULACE

The remaining three allies of sports require little comment. To
the extent that a major-league presence stimulates business, it is
welcomed by the working people of the immediate area. There
are part-time jobs for ushers, vendors, and ticket takers. There are
permanent jobs for other club employees, as well as for those who
work for businesses that benefit from the club's presence (waiters,
taxi drivers, local shopkeepers). The actual number of such people is small in any given city, but they are visible and have an influence on community thinking. (And where the stadium or arena
is municipally owned and managed, such jobs are awarded as
patronage.)

Local government benefits from the opportunity to collect
taxes of some sort, from the enhancement of its identity (consider
the dateline *Anaheim*), and from whatever uses it can make of the
increase in commerce.

The general population gets free entertainment. It's free to all
those who read or talk about it, listen to the radio, watch television, or are simply not bothered by those who do. The presence of
the big-league team doesn't matter much to those who don't care,
but the proportion of people who get at least an occasional charge
from it is very large. This is why attacks on the sports establishment, as it has evolved and as it exists today, get so little result.

Sociologists, moralists, and business rivals of the existing system assault it regularly, often with admirable logic and great perception. But they misread reality if they think their target is simply "sports," or if they believe that support for the system is
"unthinking." The support is very well thought out indeed. As is
the case in all alliances, it is subject to shifting needs and changing circumstances, but it also has a momentum all its own. And
the sports establishment won't become vulnerable until the alliance starts to unravel.

But alliances, by definition, must have foes. In the case of
sports, the enemy that these forces are allied against is the very
thing critics advocate: change. Alteration of the basic characteristics of spectator sports would weaken exactly those forces the

more powerful allies want for their own ends. And even if someone proposed a new system that, in theory, provided more valuable compensation than the present one, the resistance would remain strong because the traditional allies have acquired a large
stake in understanding, manipulating, and solidifying the present
system. They know their way around. They don't want to go ex-
ploring.

So American spectator sports are supported by a very stable base.
Does that mean that the lucky promoter has all friends and no
enemies? Not at all. As we are about to see, he lives in a rather
exposed position, subject to conflicting interests from all sides.
But there is one key difference. His "natural alliances" work to
protect and enhance the existence of his institution. The "natural
conflicts" put pressure only on his particular identity. The conflicts may make his life miserable and ultimately drive him out to
be replaced by another promoter; but the alliances still secure the
position of promoter, which someone else will then occupy. The
troubles, in short, weigh much less than the supports.

5. Natural Conflicts

"I'm sorry, but I don't talk to the press."
— Rod Carew, 1980

THE ALLIANCE of interests between sports promoters and other elements of the community, while seldom noted explicitly, is apparent enough when identified. The natural conflicts in the world of sports, in contrast, often make news without having their true nature understood.

Some of these conflicts are deliberately soft-pedalled or actually put aside for the sake of a more important interest. The most obvious of these is the competition between one player and another on the same team for a more prominent role (and therefore more money). Team play would be impossible if individual jealousies and career-building concerns were given free rein. On the other hand, battling a teammate to win a starting assignment or to avoid being cut or sent to the minor leagues is the ultimate reality of any professional athlete's life. It would be a mistake to think such rivalries aren't always present just because they seem to contradict the dictates of good sportsmanship and teamwork.

The player-versus-player conflict is always there. Team management uses it as a spur to better performance, as well as a weapon in the economic war over how to divide the pie; and in an activity that calls for decision by combat, with substantial risk of injury and painful exertion demanded of the participants, psychological spurs are needed. Some players make use of this conflict consciously. Some who can't respond correctly to this element of competition wind up failing despite outstanding physical skills. Yet competition within the team must also be subordinated to the cooperative effort team play requires. And that's what makes sports different. Competition for position is common in most aspects of human life: in business, in politics, in the arts, and even in finding a mate. Usually, however, one isn't so directly dependent on a teammate-rival's excellence for one's own success. The player who wants his team to win a championship has to hope his substitute scores, even if that upgrades the substitute's position and downgrades his. This situation is not unparalleled in other areas, but it is certainly more intense in sports.

Less obvious but even more important is the conflict of interest between the player and his employer, the promoter. This conflict concerns the player's welfare. The accepted idea is that what's good for the team is good for its individual members, but of course that's not true. The man who can "play injured" effectively is certainly helping the team, and therefore the promoter; but he is risking his own career. In less drastic fashion, when a player is asked to switch to a new position or style because of team needs, the goal of the promoter clashes with the best interests of the individual player.

In practice, the promoter applies enormous pressure to get the most out of each player *now*. Prolonging a career is not something the promoter cares about, except in the rare case of a superstar whose mere presence boosts the gate. For the player, on the other hand, prolonging his career is the prime goal. The promoter, if he's going to continue in business, knows he'll have to replace the player before long no matter what, and is looking for maximum output. The player, no matter how altruistic, cannot "replace" himself. When his career ends, his world (in terms of sports identity) ends. So in matters of scheduling, travel arrangements, playing surfaces, medical diagnosis, roster and playing rules, and similar concerns, the goals of the player and the promoter are quite different.

All this is entirely apart from the direct conflict about sharing the profits. That's there too.

And finally, there is built-in conflict of interest between the player and the media. Media members find it comforting to say,

"The publicity generated through us is what makes possible the money players earn, so they should accept our comments and intrusions as a necessary part of that publicity." But that's true only to a degree, and in most cases a small degree. Actual criticism, ridicule, or violation of privacy is extremely painful for the player involved, and any one of these affects him in a detrimental way far more than praise helps him.

The recurrent fusses about access to dressing rooms, how a play was scored, who was misquoted, and what is "legitimate" news and what isn't have their roots in this entirely realistic adversary relationship. It is, to a large degree, kept in bounds by the same considerations that give teamwork priority over career building, but it's always present.

The media people are also at war with the promoter much of the time. Here it is important to note a distinction, which will be amplified in Part II, between the *editorial* function (print or electronic) and the *publishing* function. The alliance we dealt with in the last chapter was between the promoter and the *publisher* — the one whose central interest is circulation or audience rating. The editorial people — reporters, columnists, commentators, editors — are involved with the manufacture of the product the publisher wants to sell, and with the excellence of that product by journalistic standards. Such standards call for skepticism, criticism, digging out information someone would like hidden, passing judgment at least implicitly and other facets of "honest reporting."

To the person being reported upon, what the journalist sees as highest objectivity often comes across as sheer persecution. The fact that promoters tend to act paranoid, while reporters often exhibit self-righteousness in inverse ratio to the completeness of their information, only makes things worse.

Yet the adversary relationship is even more necessary to the promoter than to the reporter, although few promoters recognize this. The reporter's "objectivity," certified by the inimical nature of the media, is what gives the sports promoter's event credibility. This is a key point. A sports event is presented to the public as something "unrehearsed." The producer of any other kind of show needs journalistic attention only for advertisement of its existence and, it is hoped, praise of its content. But the complex set of illusions on which the marketability of sports depends requires public assurance that the contest is on the level.

For all practical purposes, the press is the only entity that can certify that a contest isn't a prearranged drama. When the press ceases to do that, as in the case of professional wrestling or roller derby, the public abandons the presentation as a "sport" (but not as an entertainment of another sort, since wrestling and roller derby still sell lots of tickets).

It is the public's perception of the press as independent, not motivated to help create artificial melodrama, that makes sports news viable. Otherwise, it would be nothing but a collection of reviews and gossip, as we have in the theater and movie sections of the paper, and promoters would have to pay for space in the form of advertisements.

So the media, as certifiers of authenticity and eager watchdogs of competitive integrity, perform a service the promoter could not buy at any price. To do that, and to retain their reputation for objectivity, media representatives must display their ability to criticize, ferret out facts, and make general nuisances of themselves. By the same token, excessive praise and friendliness shown by a promoter to "his" media compromises the impression of objectivity. Nevertheless, neither side enjoys the consequences of feeling opposed to the other, and friction is the rule.

So far we have, then, five innate conflicts:

1. Player versus player, over personal advantage.
2. Player versus promoter, over physical welfare.
3. Player versus promoter, over share of the pie.
4. Player versus media, over "favorable" treatment.
5. Promoter versus media, over "favorable" treatment.

There are four others, each involving the promoter's relationship with the outside world. These adversaries are the local government, some local politicians, business rivals, and the team's own customers.

Every major-league team occupies a substantial structure — a stadium or arena — that must be maintained in an elaborate and expensive way. In most cases, that structure has been built with public funds and is operated by some arm or subsidiary of local government. But even if the building is privately owned (by the team or someone else), it is probably located on land some government entity supplied in a special deal to acquire or keep the franchise. And even if the land is privately owned, questions of tax assessments arise.

One way or another, then, the promoter is the tenant and the city is the landlord. This may not be the case technically, but the relationship is always equivalent to that. And it is certainly not necessary to elaborate the thesis that tenants and landlords often find themselves in adversary positions.

In sports specifically, the promoter tends to think of the facility he occupies as a minimum necessity supplied in return for the indirect benefits the community gets from his presence. On the other hand, the government, which stresses those benefits when floating a bond issue or seeking court injunctions to prevent a team from moving away, has a day-to-day need to minimize its expenses — especially since its expenditures are a matter of public record.

In 1976 when the San Francisco Giants were actually sold to a group that planned to move the team to Toronto, some nineteen years still remained on their lease of Candlestick Park. The purchasers were ready to negotiate a settlement for the unused portion of the lease. They were prepared to pay $8 million for the team itself and up to $5 million for a settlement. Mayor George Moscone, seeking an injunction to delay the sale long enough to find a buyer who would keep the team in San Francisco, argued that if the team moved away, the total loss to his city would amount to $175 million.

Since the team itself cost only $8 million, Moscone was asked why the city didn't buy it and save $167 million. That question was never answered, but local buyers did appear and the team stayed. Even so, conflicts continued. Candlestick Park had been built in 1959 as part of the package used to attract the Giants, who had decided to leave New York but had other offers in Minneapolis. Used strictly as a baseball stadium, Candlestick had about 42,000 seats and was a big commercial success. Then the city decided to enlarge its capacity to 60,000 so that the 49ers, the local National Football League entry, could use it too. This meant installing artificial turf, to simplify changing the configuration of the stands and to better equip the stadium to withstand the wear and tear that would result from more frequent use. (It also meant a fifty-cent tax surcharge on baseball tickets, to pay for an enlargement the baseball promoter didn't want.) After some years, the football team decided that the artificial surface was too hard, and pressed for a return to grass — a move that the baseball team now opposed. The grass went back in, reviving the problems of infield dust blown about by the strong prevailing winds. In 1981 a new campaign began, to build a dome for it.

Similar sequences of events have occurred in a dozen other cities. If the lease terms are too "favorable" to the club, the city soon comes under political pressure to tighten them. If the landlord does well, the tenant feels he's paying too much. No matter what happens, conflicting forces abound.

The political conflict arises as the opposite side of the political-alliance coin. The attention-getting capacity of sports promotion is what politicians in office try to utilize; and the politician out of office can use precisely the same means to draw attention to his cause. Attacking someone prominent is a time-honored publicity ploy. In politics, many tempting publicity-generating targets must be eschewed because of the danger of reprisal. One can certainly get the populace worked up over scandalous revelations about a labor union's misdeeds, but one then risks the loss of labor votes.

A sports promoter, on the other hand, makes an ideal patsy for an out-of-office politician. The promoter is marvelously visible and can be attacked without danger of retaliation because he has no constituency. The thousands who love his team feel no affection for him as promoter, since the illusion he has created has focused their loyalty on the "team" aspect of the sport rather than the business aspect. So the same politician who has only praise for the team's star can safely pit himself against the team's "greedy" owner, and, by extension, against the incumbent politicians who have established their association with the team and made unconscionably favorable deals with it.

Landlords and politicians, however, are minor burdens compared to the one ongoing imperative every promoter faces: competition for his piece of the entertainment dollar. Here the promoter is in his most exposed position in the economic jungle.

Fighting his players for a share of profits, the promoter has at least some common interest. Both sides know that they feed from the same trough, even if they don't like to admit it. Conflicts with various parts of the surrounding society — media, politicians, local businessmen with some particular grievance — are at least somewhat mollified by the simultaneous existence of alliances with those elements. But on the battlefield of commerce, there are no allies. Especially in entertainment.

Entertainment is a commodity no one *must* have. Even if recreation of some sort is one of life's necessities, paid-for recreation is replaceable, and paid-for recreation that consists of watching someone else perform is easy enough to skip if money must be spent on something else. So the competition is not only fierce, it's constant. Whatever it is that persuades someone to buy a ticket, it must do its work over and over again, every time afresh, in a crowded marketplace full of innovators.

A few statistics will give us perspective. According to the United States Commerce Department, Americans in 1975 spent $66 billion (that's $66,000,000,000) on recreation. Of this about $4.6 billion went for "admission to specified amusements." These were broken down as follows:

Motion-picture theaters	$2,274,000,000
Legitimate theaters and opera, and entertainment of nonprofit institutions	$804,000,000
Spectator sports	$1,512,000,000

This means that for every $100 spent on "recreation" (which includes reading, camping, buying toys, paying for radio and television sets, and so forth), only $2.27 is spent on spectator sports.

But we know, from attendance figures and ticket prices, that in 1975 the four primary professional commercial sports organizations — major-league baseball, the National Football League, the National Basketball Association, and the National Hockey League — took in something less than $500,000,000, or less than one-third of the "spectator sports" total. This means that an entity as powerfully promoted as the National Football League had ticket receipts of not more than $150,000,000 at that time and was getting $.23 of every $100 of personal expenditures on recreation; and that $97.77 was going for other voluntary, pleasure-providing, free-choice non-necessities. That's a pretty large jungle in which to forage.

The conflict between a sports promoter and his business rivals should be obvious enough, but it receives surprisingly little attention in the literature of sports. Much is made of the "monopoly" granted a baseball club owner by his "exclusive franchise" for a team in a particular city in a particular league. But his competitors are not, in reality, purveyors of other baseball games but rather purveyors of all other forms of commercial entertainment.

The ballpark and movies house are in competition. An attractive television show can reduce the attendance at a basketball game. People — the components of the market — do not restrict themselves to only one interest. When Joe Louis fought Billy Conn, a Pittsburgh resident, for the heavyweight championship of the world in New York in 1941, the baseball game in Pittsburgh (between the New York Giants and the Pirates) was interrupted so that the crowd could hear the radio report of the fight over the public-address system. What's good for one promoter, therefore, is not likely to be good for another. While it is true that a general climate of high interest in sports is healthy for all, and that most club owners pay lip service to such an idea, to prove their civic virtue, the fact is that competition hurts.

Ben Kerner, one of the pioneers of the National Basketball Association's development, owned a team in Moline, Illinois, that was clearly not "big league" (even though nearby Davenport, Iowa, and Rock Island, Illinois, were also part of the market and the team was called the Tri-City Blackhawks). The team was in a league that also had clubs in New York, Boston, and Philadelphia. So Kerner moved his team to Milwaukee and prospered. But not for long. He moved in the summer of 1951. In the spring of 1953, the baseball Boston Braves became the Milwaukee Braves, and that region went baseball crazy (since, in those days, basketball prestige was zero compared to baseball's long-established big-league image.) No longer the biggest frog in a small pond, Kerner found another place to go. In St. Louis there had been two base-

ball teams for half a century, but the Browns had just moved
away (to Baltimore in 1954). The Cardinals were left, but there
was no big-league football team. And there was no professional
basketball team or hockey team. So he took his Hawks to St.
Louis in the summer of 1955 and made a fortune.

But twelve years later, partly because Kerner had shown that
St. Louis could be a good market, the city had built a huge modern stadium downtown, a National Football League team had
moved into the city to go along with the baseball Cardinals, and a
new National Hockey League team was moving into the only
large indoor arena that was available. Trapped in a small building (which had been a fine moneymaker a decade earlier, when
salaries and other expenses were lower), Kerner sold his team to
an organization to be moved to Atlanta, and got out of the business. Subsequent attempts to have a professional basketball team
in St. Louis, as the fourth-ranking big-league entity instead of the
second, have failed.

Even more striking cases can be cited, such as the problems
that arose when the baseball A's moved into Oakland, splitting a
market then held by the San Francisco Giants. The point is, any
one team's promoter is fighting for his share of the entertainment
dollar. Good weather in an area where people like to hike or fish
or go to the beach can wipe him out. So can bad weather and the
vagaries of the television schedule.

On the practical level, this business warfare takes place in the
battle for "dates." Choosing the most desirable dates for your
home games requires not only some degree of clout with the
landlord (who may have other tenants, such as traveling rock
shows or industrial exhibits, seeking the same time slot) but also
alertness to other events that will be going on around you, and
when.

Finally, there is the continuing guerrilla war between the ticket
seller and his customers. This sounds insane. Why would a seller
have conflicts with buyers of his product? Does a storekeeper argue
with his customers? Well, there are some authentic conflicts of interest involved. The fan would like maximum comfort: wide
seats, wide aisles, uncrowded concession stands, protection from
the weather, and an excellent view. The promoter would like

maximum income: as many seats as possible per square foot, an endless flow of concession purchases, and bodies occupying all the least desirable seats as well as the good ones.

The fan wants victory "at any cost." The promoter puts cost control first. Victory is desirable, of course, but only if it's possible in that context. Some fans want rowdies summarily removed, and expect intensive policing of the crowd. The promoter doesn't want to stop selling beer, nor does he wish to pay for an army. And so on.

As with every other decision, the promoter must try to balance whatever he does. Too much emphasis on advance sales can hurt gate sale and total attendance (unless you can sell *all* your tickets in advance, as some football teams do). Ticket prices have to be low enough to keep people coming, but not so low as to lose the necessary income. Creature comforts must be provided to a degree, but no concrete structure in which 50,000 people congregate will ever match the amenities of a luxury restaurant, or a living room.

A college football coach, commenting on the need to win often enough, once said, "You have to keep the alumni sullen but not mutinous." Substitute "customers" for "alumni" and that might well be the sports promoter's creed.

6. Legal Issues

"Courts are not the forum in which this tangled web ought to be unsnarled."

— Chief Justice Warren Burger, 1972,
in his decision on the Flood case

ALL THE PRINCIPLES of sports promotion discussed so far, from the nature of the illusion through the various alliances and conflicts, have remained more or less constant throughout the twentieth century. Circumstances and manifestations have varied greatly, of course, but the basic mechanisms have been recognizably similar. In the last twenty years, however, one aspect of the business that had been private and rather peripheral has become publicized and central: the relationship of sports to the law. It is impossible to get even a sketchy appreciation of how the sports business works today without examining its interaction with antitrust laws, labor laws, federal broadcasting regulations, and civil-rights legislation.

Every ball club (and every school) has always used legal advisers when needed. What has changed is the extent of the reliance. Lawyers have moved into primary decision-making capacities, because the legal consequences of an action must be weighed before anything is done. At the same time, players have learned to find legal representatives as a matter of course, to look after their personal interests. The trend to litigation in American life since World War II is not limited to sports, but it has brought about especially noticeable changes on the sports scene.

It is impractical and, fortunately, totally unnecessary, to spell out all the legal entanglements and their history. For our purposes, it is enough to pinpoint the kinds of legal questions that have dominated the sports business in the last two decades, and to note their effect on the business. The four areas we will examine are antitrust law, labor relations, television, and internal autonomy.

ANTITRUST

When the National League was formed in 1876 and became the prototype for all other commercialized sports, there were no federal antitrust laws. In the prevailing view of the business community at that time, monopoly was a natural and benign development of enlightened capitalism, and such devices as blacklisting, group boycott, and price fixing were considered legitimate.

By the time the Sherman Act was passed in 1890, the National League had already worked out the two basic mechanisms that would come under attack. With respect to players, a "reserve system" had been created that effectively bound a player to the team he first signed with, even after his contract had expired, forever or until the club unilaterally decided to let him go. With respect to other clubs, the idea of exclusive right to operate in a particular territory was inherent in the franchise. To enforce both concepts, and other regulations, the clubs acted jointly through the league, even though they were separate business firms, in a manner later lawyers would call "conspiracy."

In 1922, in a case involving one league conspiring to drive another out of business, the United States Supreme Court decided that baseball was not subject to antitrust laws because it was not "interstate commerce" in the sense of the Sherman Act as then interpreted.

In 1949, the reserve system was challenged by Danny Gardella, a player. At the district-court level, his case was rejected on the grounds that baseball was exempt from antitrust law. But at the appeals-court level, by a 2–1 vote, it was ruled that the issue he raised — about the legality of the reserve system and its limitation on a player's right to seek employment — was different enough from the previous ruling to be tried on its merits. Rather than risk having the by now highly questionable 1922 decision overturned, the baseball people made an out-of-court settlement.

But in 1952, the Supreme Court, in another player case, reaffirmed the 1922 finding, on the narrow legal ground of *stare decisis* — the concept that a previous decision is not to be lightly overturned. For thirty years, the Court's argument went, baseball had been allowed to operate and investors had placed money in it on the assumption that antitrust law did not apply to it. The Court wasn't going to upset their good-faith understanding, even though conditions (and legal interpretations) were clearly different from what they had been in 1922. If baseball did belong under the antitrust law, the Court said, it was up to Congress to pass a law saying so.

In the next few years, however, the same Supreme Court ruled again and again that other sports were definitely subject to the Sherman Act and all other laws. Only baseball had its unique exemption, and that was solely because of the historical accident of the 1922 decision. The Court made clear again and again that if baseball were considered strictly on its merits, at the present time, it too would be found subject to antitrust law.

Using antitrust laws as a threat and a weapon, new teams and new leagues were created in many sports. Using the same weapon, player unions in basketball, hockey, and football cracked their reserve systems. But in 1972, in the Curt Flood case, the Supreme Court again refused to overturn the 1922 baseball ruling, even while admitting that such a ruling was an "anomaly." It was up to Congress to straighten it out, the Court insisted, even though Congress had never said anything about exempting baseball in the first place.

So the situation today is this: baseball remains exempt, but only baseball. All other sports are subject to the antitrust laws and vulnerable to antitrust suits. When two leagues want to merge, they need special legislation to get permission (as the National and American football leagues did in 1966).

In one specific area, however, professional sports have been granted antitrust immunity on an ongoing basis: teams can act together, as leagues, to make national network television agreements.

Since 1951, dozens of bills have been introduced in Congress to clarify the relationship of various sports (including baseball) to the antitrust laws. Many full-scale congressional hearings have been held. But no such bill has become law, although some have passed in the House and some have passed in the Senate.

Because violation of the antitrust laws may entail triple damages as punishment, fear of losing such a suit has become a constant factor in business calculations in all sports. Antitrust questions remain vague and potentially dangerous in the still-uncharted continents of pay-television agreements, and the baseball players' union once found itself embroiled in an antitrust action about giving a single company exclusive rights for bubble-gum cards.

In the non-team sports, especially tennis, the antitrust laws have impeded various plans to unify the worldwide (or even national) tournament schedule. Any group that tries to make rules about which tournament may or may not operate on a given date, with specified star players, runs into antitrust threats by the local promoter involved.

LABOR RELATIONS

Rebellion by players against restrictions on their pay scales and on their freedom to negotiate with other employers is nothing new. In the late 1880s, before the Sherman Act, National League players formed a rudimentary union and, in 1890, actually pulled out and formed their own league (which failed within a year). Further attempts at unionization were beaten back before World War I and again in 1946, right after World War II.

In the middle 1960s, formal unions were developing in all the major team sports. The National Labor Relations Act confers many benefits (including antitrust exemption) to workers in a certified union bargaining with a defined set of employers, and not until players formed recognized unions under effective professional leadership could they achieve agreements on worthwhile minimum salaries, expenses, pension benefits, working conditions, and grievance procedures.

Today, even baseball umpires and basketball referees have

union organization. The essential point here is that in recent years sports promoters have become subject to the complex provisions of the labor laws in dealing with their players when negotiating industry-wide agreements (as distinct from individual player contracts). This increases the burden, and necessity, of obtaining legal advice at every step.

Historically, the relationship between employer and player was paternalistic: condescending on the owner's side and helpless on the player's side (even if a particular player happened to be well treated). Since unionization, the relationship is decidedly cooler and more distant, more difficult from the owner's viewpoint and more complex from the player's. Therefore, anyone who wants to follow the play-by-play of various contract squabbles, strike threats, and player-control regulations must become familiar with the requirements of the labor laws of this country. Most sports reporters and fans have found themselves woefully unequipped for such analysis, and deeply resentful of its necessity.

TELEVISION

The legal issues involved here stem from the difference in status between broadcast and print media. Under the First Amendment, newspapers and magazines are free of government regulation (although, of course, their business practices must conform to the law). But the content of radio and television programs is subject to supervision by a licensing body, the Federal Communications Commission; and the nature of the medium (in this country, at least) makes it difficult to draw a line between program-content practices and business practices.

In addition, the customary sports-broadcast relationship involves the buying and selling of rights to carry the program, a relationship that doesn't arise with respect to print coverage. What proprietary rights does a player have in the selling (for a fee) of his television-recorded actions? What rights does the visiting team have? What rights does the station carrying the game have when a cable system picks it off the air and rebroadcasts it? What sorts of combined arrangements are monopolistic, and what sorts aren't?

Questions of this type have been multiplying since 1960, and they have yet to reach full virulence. Again, what is relevant to us at this point is the existence of these bureaucratic and legalistic complexities, not the pros and cons of any specific regulation.

INTERNAL AUTONOMY

The player unions, through antitrust suits and implementation of the labor laws, have ended the era of arbitrary control of players by club owners. But what about league control of the club owners — the very concept that distinguished the formation of the National League and all that grew from it?

When Kenesaw Mountain Landis became the first commissioner of baseball in 1921, it became fashionable to refer to him as "the Czar." He was given, and in fact wielded, considerable autocratic power in an industry then desperate to establish an image of integrity, in the wake of a fixed World Series, other gambling scandals, interleague wars for star players, and suspicious financial dealings within the family.

The "czar" concept proved so vivid, and was so endlessly publicized, that it was soon institutionalized. After Landis's death, presidents of football and basketball leagues styled themselves "commissioners," simply to capitalize on the aura of authority Landis had given that term — while baseball itself stripped much of that authority from his successors.

To this day, most fans and the general public perceive a league commissioner as the "ruler" and ultimate arbitrator of that particular sport. Nothing could be further from the truth. A commissioner is an employee of the club owners who hire him. He is their most important employee, of course. He may have enormous influence behind the scenes, in direct proportion to his skill as a politician within a closed group of powerful men who usually distrust each other. He is their front man to the public, and holds public opinion as a card in his hand — a card Landis played well. But he doesn't have a penny invested in the business, and he has no vote in substantive matters (except, in baseball, to break a tie when the two major leagues disagree on an issue). He is much more a constitutional monarch than a prime minister. Rather than setting policies of his own, he carries out and legitimizes policies the club owners set.

The commissioner can make decisions only when the majority of his employers are willing to have him make them. But often, in fact usually, he is allowed to act in public as if he were "forcing" the owners to do something for greater, more noble, nonselfish interests. This is one of those key illusions that make the sports business palatable to fans, under our aforementioned categories of coherence and comprehensibility. Believing that a vigorous leader is really in charge is more satisfying than knowing that policies are established by the interplay of conflicting interests, as is the case in real life outside of sports.

So it is impossible to understand or interpret how a league works without realizing that club owners, and only club owners, make decisions about things that matter. Commissioners are allowed independence only on issues that matter less, or along lines tacitly agreed upon. This arrangement calls to mind an old joke. The husband says, "I make all the major decisions in my family: which party to support in the election, foreign policy, what to do about unemployment, military questions, supporting scientific research, and so forth. My wife makes all the minor decisions: what we eat, where we live, what kind of car we have, what we spend, how the kids dress and where they go to school, and stuff like that."

Only the club owners "own" anything, and leagues are merely the agencies through which their collective assets are managed. They hire and fire commissioners at will, and since the players have formed strong unions of their own, the ability of the owners to use the commissioner to discipline players or control their movement has been eroded.

What really rules every league, therefore, is a consensus among the more powerful (or more respected) club owners in the group. Leadership does not coincide with maximum financial power, but rarely does a financial weakling (relatively speaking) exert much influence on the other owners. Personality and a record of success determine which owners become leaders.

But there are differences from sport to sport, and these must be noted. Baseball took its present two-league form in 1903. Each league had a president who was truly powerful within league councils. Interleague matters (such as the World Series, and common rules about contracts) were handled by a three-man commission. After the Black Sox scandal of 1919, the idea of a strong one-man commission arose, and that's how Judge Landis got the title of commissioner. Each league still has a president, but he is primarily an administrator and an advocate of his league's position in joint councils rather than a "local ruler."

The National Football League was, from its beginning in 1920, a single entity. Its "commissioner" is actually the league president, and was known by that title until the public-relations experts got wise. He too is primarily an administrator, but because Bert Bell and Pete Rozelle turned out to be skillful leaders worth listening to, the public has seen them as stronger than the four baseball commissioners who followed Landis. The rival leagues that started up and were eventually absorbed by the NFL had their own "commissioners," but these disappeared in the mergers.

The same thing happened in basketball and hockey. In both sports, the "presidents" imperceptibly changed their titles to "commissioner," but no two-league setup ever arose: rival leagues always wound up being absorbed under the older league's commissioner.

Professional golf has a commissioner and no club owners as such, but the commissioner is frankly an administrator, and basic policy is set by an oligarchy of top players and the most important tournament directors. In tennis, there has been even less central control, and the top dozen stars and the top few tournaments (such as Wimbledon and the U.S. Open) have done as they please.

In boxing and racing, a "commissioner" is a state official, since those activities require state licensing. In college sports, conferences (leagues) have commissioners who make no bones about their status as super-housekeepers; they look after game officials, schedules, eligibility complaints, and so forth, and the member institutions set policy through college heads or faculty representatives.

In another respect, however, commissioners have come to play crucial roles as the lawsuits have multiplied. The legal activity has to be centralized, whether it be litigation or legislative lobbying, and it is the commissioner who has day-to-day contact with the lawyers representing the collective league interest. If a league loses a lawsuit, whatever has to be paid must come out of the pockets of the individual clubs, since the league itself has no appreciable assets. So the club owners are more dependent on the commissioner as a liaison with league attorneys than they used to be.

It isn't surprising, then, that Bowie Kuhn, commissioner of baseball since 1969, was chosen for that post after years of service as one of the lawyers representing the National League; that Lawrence O'Brien, commissioner of the National Basketball Association, is a lawyer who came to sports after a career in politics under presidents Kennedy and Johnson; and that John Ziegler, the commissioner of the National Hockey League, is a lawyer. And although Pete Rozelle is not a lawyer but a public-relations man by profession, he has spent so much of his time with high-powered Washington and New York law firms that he could probably pass a bar exam if necessary.

Kenesaw Mountain Landis was a federal judge (and a colorful, controversial one) when he was made commissioner of baseball, and he made the avoidance of lawsuits the cornerstone of his policies for a quarter of a century. His successor, Albert B. ("Happy") Chandler, was a United States senator from Kentucky. Next came Ford Frick, a journalist turned baseball executive, and then General William Eckert, a retired Air Force general with a background in procurement contracts. By this time, baseball's affairs were so snarled that the club owners fired Eckert summarily, spent months disagreeing on a successor from within their own ranks, and turned to Bowie Kuhn.

When Kuhn was hired, the owners restored to the office of commissioner some of the arbitrary powers they had regained after Landis's death. Unable to exert any direct influence over players once they unionized, Kuhn used his reinstated powers against individual club owners when necessary to carry out policies he favored (always with powerful support from *some* club owners). In 1976, he overruled an attempt by Charles Finley, owner of the Oakland A's, to sell three players to the Yankees and Red Sox for $3.5 million. Finley sued on the grounds that Kuhn had exceeded his authority, but the courts held that the commissioner had been granted wide latitude and could make any "good faith" ruling he chose, even if the ruling seemed unwise or unfair, so long as it wasn't conclusively vindictive or capricious.

A similar issue about the extent of a commissioner's power over his employers is involved in basketball cases concerning "excessive" compensation awards made by Lawrence O'Brien to teams whose star players signed elsewhere, as well as in the struggle to move the Oakland Raiders of the NFL to Los Angeles over Pete Rozelle's opposition.

So a 180-degree irony has been created: the institution of commissioner, set up by club owners as an effective weapon to keep players in line and to allow them to run their business as they pleased, has become totally powerless with respect to players and quite powerful against some owners. (The owners could, of course, fire a runaway commissioner, but such an action would have bad public-relations consequences.)

This has happened because of the club owners' vulnerability to lawsuits. Business rivals can hit them with antitrust litigation. Individual players (or their unions) can use labor-law and civil-rights violations as a basis. Television privileges concerning league-wide network arrangements can be maintained only by paying the price politicians demand (for example, lifting local blackouts for sold-out games). Avoiding lawsuits, or defending against them, requires far more centralization of decision-making than individual club owners ever expected to give anyone, and the commissioners, along with their staffs and attorneys, have become the Politburos of their sports.

Nevertheless, ultimate sovereignty still rests in the hands of the owners, acting collectively, since they can discard or overrule any particular commissioner if they are displeased enough. But because the commissioner listens to his lawyers, and each club owner listens to his lawyers, and the players (individually and collectively) listen to their lawyers, the practical result is that all the fundamental decisions are made by lawyers. That's how the sports business in America works, behind closed doors, in the 1980s.

But how do we know whatever we think we know about it? Only from what we read, hear, and see in the journalistic media known as newspapers, radio, television, magazines, and books. And to understand how we get the impressions we do, we now must look at how the journalism business works.

PART II

Journalism

7. Functions

"All the news that's fit to print"
— Motto of the *New York Times*

COMPARED TO SPORTS, journalism is a simple and straightforward business — at least in theory. The function of journalism is to deliver the news. *News* can be defined as "an occurrence of general interest happening now or recently." The key time element is "today." The key characteristic of a news occurrence is "out of the ordinary."

We can expand a bit on the function of journalism. What journalism is supposed to do is gather information and deliver it to a medium (printing press or loudspeaker or television screen or film) that can, in turn, deliver some fraction of the collected material to the public. Quickly.

The goal of those involved is the universal goal of business in this culture: to make a profit. The means of making a profit is to satisfy the reader/listener/viewer enough to make him come back to the product day after day. This is done by making the material sufficiently informative and entertaining, and in this respect advertisements are no less important than "editorial" matter. (An ad, after all, brings the reader news about something currently available.) The materials used to carry out the means are "straight news" (as defined above), features, analyses, opinions, pictures, and live voices. Sports pages and sports programs obviously cut across the entire spectrum of journalistic activity. But they have hybrid aspects, to which we'll return.

In size, the journalism business dwarfs sports. The gross income of all professional baseball, football, basketball, and hockey teams lumped together does not reach $2 billion. Daily newspapers in the United States collect more than $13 billion a year from advertising alone — and that's just newspapers. But sports has a disproportionate importance because it commands such continuing loyalty among its followers, as is exemplified by the "alliances" we referred to in Part I.

Meaningful statements about "journalism" reach a dead end very quickly if we don't allow for the different emphasis each medium demands. Daily newspapers stress news in the most orthodox sense, and surround it with amusing features. Radio and television stations stress entertainment, journalism being only one part (and a minor part) of their activities. Of course, both groups expend enormous effort in both directions — informing and entertaining. But a newspaper can succeed without entertainment sections, as long as it delivers news (for example, the *Wall Street Journal*). And a radio/television station can exist on entertainment programming with virtually no news content (beyond the minimum required by FCC regulations).

To put it another way, people don't continue to buy a newspaper devoid of news, no matter how good its features; and people don't tune in a radio or television station regularly unless it provides entertainment (comedy, drama, music, adventure), no matter how good its news segments. Yes, there are exceptions. There are all-news radio and (just beginning) television stations. But these form such a small fraction of the total, and are such special cases, that they don't invalidate the generality. The generality is: newspapers depend on news, and electronic media live off entertainment.

Books and magazines, by the nature of their production processes, cannot be "timely." Therefore they hold their audiences by stressing opinion, analysis, and special interests not thoroughly covered in the daily mass news market.

Since sports events are, by design, timely events, they are relatively less important to books and magazines than to newspapers and broadcasters. Sports contests are time-bound because everything is geared to arousing desire for the *next* event. A promoter can't make money out of people remembering last year's World Series, whereas a book publisher or movie producer can continue to make money by reissuing a Shakespeare play over and over.

Therefore, the indispensable people in newspaper journalism are the news gatherers: reporters and those who assign, edit, and supervise them. In the broadcast world, the indispensable people are the "creative" talent — writers, actors, directors, and producers who can put together a show, whether it has news content or not.

Despite the differences, however, there are even more fundamental similarities between the print media and the electronic media. They can be charted this way:

		Responsibilities	
Activity	*Main goal*	*Newspapers & Magazines*	*Radio & Television*
Set policy	Profit	Publisher	Network or station
Set strategy	Produce what satisfies policy	Editor	Editor/director/producer
Carry out strategy	Produce what satisfies editor	Reporters & staff	Performers & technicians
Measure of success	Set rates for advertising	Circulation	Ratings

This table suggests an analogy to the structure of sports organizations, which we examined in chapter 2. The publisher is equivalent to the club owner. The editor is equivalent to the manager or coach. And the reporter is equivalent to the player.

Just as no player, however skilled, can function in isolation, but must be part of a team and league in order for his play to have meaning, so no reporter *in journalism* can function out of context. An author can write a book, play, or poem on his own and become involved in the mechanics of disseminating his product only after it is finished to his satisfaction; but a reporter is inseparable from the mechanics of news production. His product exists only to the extent that he can get it into print or on the air at the designated time, in the designated way.

All too often, neither sports people nor reporters themselves pay attention to this basic condition. But it permeates both activities and accounts for the sort of impressions formed by the public. To the public, it is not Leonard Koppett who covers a particular baseball game, it is the *New York Times*. Individual reporters come and go, as individual players come and go. Some are better, some worse. But the identities that last are those of the team and the newspaper, and it is the relationship between those two business entities that determines our view of sports, not the relationship between, for example, a manager named Billy Martin and a reporter named Dick Young.

This is even more true of television, although the force of the broadcaster's personality tends to obscure the relationship still further. The connection, and therefore the impression conveyed, is between the National Football League and a network, not between, say, Chuck Noll (coach of the Pittsburgh Steelers) and Howard Cosell (sports broadcasting personality without peer). Noll and Cosell carry out their particular duties in their own inimitable ways, which are uniquely effective and for which they are well paid, but they don't *determine* what their duties will be. Art Rooney (owner of the Steelers), Pete Rozelle (on Rooney's behalf), and executives of the American Broadcasting Company (or even its parent corporation) do the determining.

The lines of command are of transcendent importance, and widely misunderstood. Readers usually assume that a writer is expressing a personal view, or that his newspaper has some explicit policy guideline that he has been told to express. Listeners react the same way to broadcasters. In reality, there are few "views" and fewer "instructions." The policy decision that counted was the one to cover or carry the event. What follows is more or less automatic, and the results are remarkably similar, in the end, no matter who the individual reporter is.

This should not be surprising. In non-sports areas of journalism, the decision about the newsworthiness of an event is made *after* something has happened. (An election is an exception, but the generality holds.) In sports, most of the time, the newspaper is dealing with a *scheduled* event whose newsworthiness is the outcome, not the taking place. Its readers (those who will turn to the sports page) know ahead of time that it is taking place, and they expect an account of it. So the paper, by deciding to send a reporter to cover it, and by committing itself to print the story no matter how the game comes out, has already gone on record with its news judgment. How much more true must this be in play-by-play radio or television, where the station actually pays for the right to carry the game?

We must not expect, therefore, to find consistent criticism of the *existence* or *nature* of sports events in journalistic media already convinced that these events will help sell papers and get an audience. Criticism of particular people or situations is a different matter, and is often avidly pursued for selfish as well as altruistic ends. But the only people involved who could seriously question the *value* of attention paid to sports are publishers and network executives who have the power, if they so choose, to make their organizations not pay attention. They haven't done so yet, and it is unlikely that they will in the foreseeable future. The business of journalism is news. Sports events make news, automatically, for the large segment of the population that takes an interest. Thus journalism is married to spectator sports.

Before we look in greater detail at the mechanics of journalism and some related issues, one point needs reinforcement. We defined *news* as something timely and out-of-the-ordinary. The classic example, which became so hackneyed that it is hardly ever heard any more, is "Dog bites man, not news; man bites dog, news."

Omitted from that formulation is the "who." By news standards, the "who" is all-important. While there is nothing intrinsically newsworthy about any dog biting any person, a dog nipping the ankle of the queen of England would make news worldwide. So would a story about Lassie biting anyone at all. By the same token, the fact that some unidentified shepherd in Central Asia bit his dog, playfully or malevolently, would not cause a stir on the press-association wires of the world.

This element of identity is particularly relevant in sports. The news is welded to the idea of who did it, and in what context. A sandlot player driving a baseball 500 feet does not make "news," although this is certainly an exceptional event that takes place in the present, and a cause for comment in his community and, possibly, activity by baseball scouts. But Reggie Jackson driving a baseball 350 feet over a fence in Yankee Stadium during a World Series game is sports news of the first order. The "what" is inseparable from the "who."

News, then, is the core of journalistic activity. There can be no opinion or comment until an event has been reported and has become widely enough known for the commentary to make sense. *Getting* the news must, of necessity, precede *presenting* the news. How is this done in the realm of mass spectator sports, where the promoter has a direct financial stake in making the news easy and practical, and the journalistic media are aware that they must be thorough and prompt to satisfy their highly knowledgeable audience? Let's find out.

8. Methods

"Get first names."
— I. A. L. Diamond, 1940, as editor of the *Columbia Spectator*

THE SOURCE of almost all information is someone else's
words. A little bit — a *very* little bit — comes from eyewitness observation, but even then it usually takes someone's explanation to make the observation completely clear.

To find out anything, you have to ask someone who already
knows. Your original intellectual equipment — language, arithmetic, names of objects — came from the words of adults around
you (parents, teachers, and others). Once able to read, you can
learn more by looking something up — that is, through the written words of someone who has already found out. When you play
tennis for the first time and serve a fault, for example, someone
must tell you (through spoken or written words) what it means
when the ball doesn't land in the service court. Eventually, you
can tell for yourself whether a serve is good or not, but that's only
because you've already had it explained to you at some point in
the past.

So the first law of journalism, which is information gathering,
should be: ask. Right? Not exactly. The First Law is: listen. The
Second Law is: ask. The Third Law is: pay attention to what you
see, so you'll know *what* to ask.

Why the distinction between "listening" and "asking"? Because the important part is what you hear — the information
coming in. The question is merely an implement to start the flow
of material that will enter your brain through your ears.

Much can be learned without asking direct questions, because people around you talk anyhow, and many things will be made understandable by what they say. Naturally, the more you already know about a subject, the more you can fill in the parts you don't know from brief remarks made about it.

Also, in a social context where your identity as a journalist is known to all concerned, and where an elaborate mixture of preconceptions, prejudices, attitudes, and images already exists in the person you're talking to, direct questions should be husbanded. If you go up to Hank Aaron's locker after he has hit his 715th home run, surpassing Babe Ruth's record, and you want to probe his psyche about that historic moment, and your first question is, How old are you? it is not likely that the information you really want will emerge, nor is it likely that he'll regard you as very bright. If it matters, he'll expect you to know the answer, and he'll know it's easy to look up, so to him you'll simply be identifying yourself as unqualified. His subsequent answers, or more important things, will probably be guarded and impatient.

Since you are unlikely to be alone on such an occasion, you may learn more if you simply listen to the subject's answers (and volunteered statements) in response to other questions, and don't ask anything yourself until a particularly relevant point arises. (Am I advocating a free ride on the questions of others? Of course. Let *them* ask the dumb ones.)

However, if you are alone, or if Aaron is being uncommunicative or simply waiting to be asked, it is best to start a conversation going with an innocuous remark like "That was some blast," or "It must feel good to have that over with," or "It was cold out there, wasn't it?" — anything at all that will elicit a perfunctory and common-courtesy reply. Then, by listening, you can learn what line to follow to work the conversation around to the things you really are interested in, giving him the impression in the process that you are an intelligent, sensible, responsible, aware, reliable, and good-natured person to whom he can speak with only normal reservations.

On the other hand, if you're waiting at the finish line of a marathon run that has "seniors" entered, and you talk to the first of these to finish, someone you've never seen before, the question "How old are you?" is a perfectly appropriate beginning.

That technique is suitable for print journalists, but not for the electronic kind. They have microphones in hand and need the actual statement, in the subject's own voice.

But that's a show business necessity, not an information-gathering necessity. In journalistic terms, it's the content of the answer to information-seeking questions that matters most, and the attractiveness of "in his own words" is secondary.

These distinctions between media will get individual attention in the next few chapters. For now, the main point is that all information comes from someone else; and the reader or listener will lose sight of the true situation if he or she does not cling stubbornly to that awareness. The reporter is *passing along* what someone else told him, no matter how pompously, arrogantly, or authoritatively he presents it. To judge the validity of information, therefore, the consumer must be willing to judge both the reliability of the source (which is never the reporter) and the reliability of the reporter (who must convey accurately what the source said, without being able to vouch for the absolute truth of the source's information).

One would think that eyewitness evidence is primary in sports coverage. Most sportswriters like to think this. After all, we know all about how the game is supposed to be played, our attention is eagerly focused on each play, and we are given good sightlines. If I can see that Kareem Abdul-Jabbar was goaltending on a shot, even though the referee didn't call it, and if the slow-motion replay confirms my opinion, why should I have to ask anyone about what I saw?

As a fan, I don't. As a player or coach, I don't. As a play-by-play broadcaster, I don't. But as a journalist I do, because one of the principles of reporting is to avoid jumping to conclusions. The evidence I saw through my eyes must be checked against other possibilities before I can pass on the best estimate of reality. What I saw may be utterly convincing, but I must at least ask those involved if something else, of which I was unaware, intervened. Chances are, nothing did; but I still must ask, to confirm the fact. That's one difference between reporting and spectating.

So no matter how we twist or turn, we're stuck with the fact that a reporter is a conduit between the source and the reader/listener. In practice, the process is cumulative: After I have seen a hundred football games, I can recognize when pass protection breaks down — but only because I have already asked, many times, in comparable situations. And even at that, I have to check *this* time (if the incident is important enough to deal with), to make sure there was no hidden, exceptional factor that I didn't recognize.

Managers and players, usually with hostility or self-pity, often say to reporters, "You saw it, write it. Write what you saw." They are wrong. A reporter is supposed to tell what happened, not merely what he saw. To fill out what he saw he must listen, ask, and — above all — comprehend.

O.K. How do reporters do it? Let me list the ways:

1. By informal conversation. This is unquestionably the best and most productive method in sports, where people live in a benevolent environment dedicated to providing entertainment. After all, everyone involved is aware of the goal of providing enjoyment, generating publicity, and prolonging a comfortable existence. Getting adept at such conversation is an ongoing process summed up by the word *experience*.

2. By reference to printed material, which is abundant.

3. By direct question-and-answer sessions, often under deadline pressure.

4. By formal press conferences, at which the answers generated are available to all and the subject is very careful to follow his prepared line.

5. By in-depth one-on-one interviews, which require the active cooperation of the subject.

6. By off-the-record, private exchanges of information — the only means, in the long run, by which a reporter can become experienced enough to comprehend significant developments when they arise.

7. By learning enough about the field being covered — baseball, politics, physics, law, police courts, or whatever — to feel at home in it as an informed layman.

All seven of these methods are used continually by all journalists, print and electronic, in overlapping fashion. But in the case of sports, methods 1, 3, 4, and 6 raise a special issue, or at least a special form of a more common issue: the problem of access.

The natural habitat of athletes is the locker room. That's where they can be found in relaxed circumstances before and after games, and in dramatically tense circumstances immediately after a tough game. It is the best place for reporters and athletes to mingle.

Method 1, the informal conversation gambit, used to be accomplished more naturally on trips, when teams traveled by train. There were club cars and dining cars on trains, and card games in the sleeping cars, and many of the journeys were overnight. Hotel lobbies were also automatic meeting places when baseball teams played mostly day games — and when hotels had lobbies. But since 1960 or so, even casual contact has depended on the locker-room setting. The familiar discomforts and fragmented social contacts of today's air travel, motel-like hostelries, and night games destroy the kind of camaraderie "the road" used to produce.

Direct question-and-answer interviews (method 3), given right after a game, can't be done anywhere else in proper fashion. Time is an element, for morning papers and radio reporters, and the alternative of a staged press conference is a journalistic disaster. The press conference (method 4) is suitable for planned announcements, but not for spontaneous information gathering. And off-the-record relationships (method 6) are virtually impossible to maintain outside the locker room, when a "closed" clubhouse policy poisons the climate. Reporters, therefore, want an "open" clubhouse policy.

Traditionally, promoters have recognized that access to players is good for their business. The sports business depends on the free advertising afforded by "news coverage," and the promoter doesn't want to put obstacles in the way of those who supply it. But traditionally, players and coaches have wanted privacy just as much, and have fought for "cooling-off" periods, other time restrictions, and off-limits areas (such as the trainer's room).

Until the last fifteen years or so, the balance of power lay with the promoters, and by and large they supported open clubhouse policies. Nowadays this is the exception rather than the rule, because many things have changed. Among these new developments the proliferation of recording devices; the presence of women reporters; the increased power of professional players over their own affairs; a general animosity toward the press that has spread through society as a whole; the recent ascendancy of television over newspapers as the promoter's most powerful ally; a less militant group of sportswriters (more abrasive, perhaps, but definitely less militant); and the general development of the public-relations bureaucracy. But while conditions have changed, the need has not. There is no way to get information except by talking to the people involved, and the locker room is the place to do it, as much as the club will let you.

Another of the important changes in the old equation has taken place in journalism. We have been living through a quote-happy age. There was a time (say, up to about 1950) when newspaper writers were very selective and sparing in the use of quotes. Then editors began to realize that radio audiences were hearing their heroes speak at length, in their own words, and that this gave a much greater impression of immediacy than did an occasional sentence with quotation marks around it attributed to Joe DiMaggio. Soon after, the television audience was seeing facial expressions as well as hearing the words, and the editors caved in. "Get quotes," they told their writers. "Lots of quotes."

This was good thinking, because it was true that the challenge had to be met, and it was also true that many good quotes had gone unrecorded (or even unheard) in the old days. But it didn't take long for this sensible response to turn into a fetish, and by the early 1970s it was standard newspaper practice to replace information with quotes. Mickey Mantle saying "Today is Tuesday" became a more valued story, in the eyes of many editors, than a writer pointing out that Mickey Mantle could no longer throw from the outfield. "Get somebody to say he can't throw — his manager, an opponent, Mantle himself — and you've got a story," an editor would tell his writer. "But nobody wants to read your conclusions and statistics."

Whether or not this was a correct estimate of what people wanted to read, it raised other problems. Quotes in a newspaper can never be completely accurate, because of space considerations alone, and they certainly have to be edited for grammar and decency as well as conciseness. At the same time the demand for quotes was growing, the wordage of newspaper stories was shrinking. It soon became possible (and common) to have stories full of quotes and empty of information.

Those being quoted want to be quoted "accurately" — that is, complete with all the qualifications, weasel words, special meanings, and backtracking they try to include in an answer once they realize their words may make some kind of trouble for them. When speaking into a microphone, they feel confident that what will come out is exactly what they say. Since this assurance is impossible with print media, their already present feelings of distrust and resentment toward reporters become magnified. The reporters, in response, try to quote them more thoroughly, partly out of a sense of fairness and partly to soothe the feelings of those they must deal with the next day. The result is even more quotation and less story.

For example, let's suppose Reggie Jackson hits a ninth-inning homer off Gaylord Perry, winning the game for the Yankees. A reader might be interested in knowing what kind of pitch Jackson hit, especially since the reader may know that Perry has a reputation for throwing illegal spitballs. I can go to Jackson, find out that he hit a fast ball, and include that information in my story in a total of four one-syllable words: Jackson's homer was "off a fast ball." I can, if I want to uphold the quote mystique, make a short paragraph: "I hit a fast ball," Jackson said.

But if I get involved in "accurate" quoting, by transcribing from a tape recorder, I'm going to wind up with something like this: "Uh, yeah, he threw me a fast ball . . . he was trying to get it down and in, but got it just out over the plate a bit too much . . . yeah, I could tell it was going out when I hit it . . . No, you can't say it was a bad pitch, he's got me out on pitches like that lots of times, he's a great pitcher and I just got him this time . . . Did the wind help it? I don't know, maybe it did and maybe it didn't . . . Yes, it feels good when you get a game-winning hit, but they pay me to do that . . . and they pay him to not let me . . . That's right, today is Tuesday and tomorrow is Wednesday." And so forth.

Quotes, like anything else, are only as good as their content. As a rule, a *description* of an action in quote form is marvelous for radio and television, and a waste of space in print. A printed quote acquires value when it is an intrinsically colorful expression, a startling statement, or a formal issue where wording is important.

And since time never stands still, quotes have bred their own unnoticed antibodies. Everyone learns by imitation. Kids mimic the actions of their heroes. In the 1960s, as I wended my way through clubhouses and dugouts and basketball arenas, I gradually became aware that things were starting to sound familiar. After a close game, winners would be appropriately humble and losers appropriately calm but determined, in terms I had heard before. It didn't take long to pin down what was happening: These athletes had grown up reading the quotes (and hearing the voices) of their predecessors, and were reproducing — quite unconsciously, I'm sure — the statements that seemed to be expected in those circumstances.

My own stories of a decade before were being fed back to me by a new generation of athletes. In 1971, Ron Swoboda, determined to make the right big-league responses, was telling me what he had heard Duke Snider say in 1961, not because Swoboda was insincere or unoriginal but because he had formed his ideas of what was appropriate through the medium of my profession. Swoboda later became a sports broadcaster. It's easy to see how inbred this kind of thing can become.

Meanwhile, another by-product results. Players grow up expecting to be quoted whenever there are reporters around. At the very least, they can never be sure when a comment will be quoted and when it won't. This exacerbates the tension and increases the demand for clubhouse privacy. It undermines the relaxed informality that could lead to amusing and revealing quotes, and creates a heightened hostility that promotes stuffy, self-conscious quotes. And most reporters, influenced by the demands of their editors and their own upbringing, perpetuate the process by stalking quotes as if with a butterfly net.

Where this all leads, however, is full circle: Whether you quote them or not, you have to talk to the people involved to find out anything, and the reporter's job is to find out. Find out what?

Who did something: "The Yankees ..."

What they did: "The Yankees defeated the Red Sox, 4–3 ..."

How: "The Yankees defeated the Red Sox, 4–3, on Reggie Jackson's ninth-inning homer . . .

When: . . . last night . . .

Where: . . . at Yankee Stadium . . .

Why: . . . to take over first place in the American League East."

Those are the six elements of a "lead," drummed into the head of every journalism student in this century, and probably before that. In the orthodox, old-fashioned news story, these elements are supposed to be included in the opening sentence. In features, or in the "new journalism" (which sometimes bears a striking resemblance to the "old baloney"), structural demands are much looser, but the six questions are supposed to be dealt with sooner or later in the story.

If you can answer these six questions about any subject, you have the rudiments of an informative report. You can elaborate it to book length or keep it in one paragraph, but you have addressed the news content of that incident. If you can't, you are journalistically incomplete.

So before a reporter can worry about putting his information into usable form and transmitting it, he must obtain it. And that's what reporters do, whether they assume the trappings of literary figures or choose to act like characters in a road-show production of *The Front Page.* They find out who, what, how, when, where, and why, and everything else flows from that.

9. Obligations

"Nevertheless, it moves."
— Galileo Galilei, 1633

THE JOURNALISTIC FUNCTION, to gather information for dissemination, is well defined. What about journalistic obligations? These are not as easy to state. Where ethical questions are involved, views differ widely these days. If there is a consensus, which I doubt, it has been shifting rapidly. Journalistic ethics is a subject that will have a chapter all its own at the end of this section. There are, however, many practical obligations, on what can be called the operational level, that ought to be spelled out because they, too, affect the sports–journalism relationship in profound ways.

We will keep our focus on the reporter, since he is the direct contact between the sports establishment on the one hand and the public (his listeners and readers) on the other. The internal journalistic forces to which the reporter is subjected will show up clearly enough in the background, but the reporter is the individual at the vortex. (In this discussion, the term *reporter* includes columnist, feature writer, and news-program broadcaster.)

There is one, and only one, standard for reporting: get it right. Whatever it is, you have to report it correctly — the score, the date, the spelling, first names, details, explanations, quotes, sequences of events, anything and everything. Get it right. You cannot, and need not, deal with every conceivable aspect and every available detail of the event you cover. But whatever you do use, get it right.

No virtue justifies being wrong — not your brilliance of expression, the delight of your audience, the boost of your circulation or ratings, the depth of your insight, or the speed of your delivery. If it's not correct, it's lousy journalism. And no deficiency — lack of grace or the absence of some other attractive quality — can negate the journalistic value of a report that's correct. A poor account may be unsatisfactory on many levels (and should be avoided, it goes without saying), but it has journalistic validity if it delivers correct information.

The First Law, we said, was "listen." The Prime Directive is, "Get it right." So the journalist's first obligation to his craft (which is to say, to himself) is accuracy. Not accuracy to the extent required of engineers, surgeons, or courtroom witnesses, because the hurly-burly of daily news transmission doesn't permit that. But within the limits of the rough-draft, first-approximation, calling-your-attention-to-what's-going-on-in-the-world   activity called journalism, the reporter must strive for all reasonably attainable accuracy.

The conscientious pursuit of accuracy is known as objectivity. Objectivity does not mean having no viewpoint. That is impossible for a conscious being. Everyone has preferences, prejudices, accumulated impressions, and already-drawn conclusions, along with less identifiable likes and dislikes. Being objective means not letting your preferences distort the accuracy of your account, to whatever extent you can be aware of distortion. (To the extent that you're not aware, you can't control it).

Objectivity, in this sense, is the exact equivalent of the scientific method, a centerpiece of Western civilization. It is the idea that experiment and observation will be recorded however they occur, rather than accordance with some prior theory or hoped-for result. The journalist's obligation is to do his best to tell what actually happened, as distinct from what might have, should have, or would have been nice if. Only if he does this, accurately, can the "ought-to" elements of society begin to deal with whatever is going on.

So to the First Law and the Prime Directive, we can add the First Principle: be objective. *Objectivity* leads to a fallout of definitions.

Opinion is the expression of a viewpoint based on objective evidence (that is, evidence gathered by conscientious pursuit of accuracy) and on reasonable conclusions. In journalism, all the evidence need not be stated or explicitly presented in each story, but the writer must have it available and be able to justify the opinion if challenged.

Integrity means limiting yourself to *honest* opinions, not viewpoints taken for effect or based on knowingly insubstantial grounds. It includes a strong dose of qualified experience.

Reliability means a high average, over time, of performing with Objectivity and Integrity.

These purposely pompous capitalized words have general applicability to all corners of journalism. For sports journalism, they are even more applicable.

The distinction between objectivity, which is attainable, and some artificial ideal of absolute disinterest totally free of value judgments, which is not, is crucial in sports. Every event and personality has a built-in point of view, and both writer and reader know it. In every game, there is a loser as well as a winner; but there is also a home team as well as a visiting team, and a favorite as well as an underdog. And in every nongame topic dealt with on the sports pages, some degree of prior familiarity with the images or circumstances under consideration is assumed.

A writer traveling with the Dallas Cowboys to a game in St. Louis will be sending a story back to the area where the overwhelming majority of readers care about the Cowboys (and those who don't care are not likely to be readers). The essence of his story must be, "Dallas wins" or "Dallas loses." At the same time, at the same event, the writer for a St. Louis paper must approach the story from the point of view "St. Louis loses" or "St. Louis wins."

It is futile to pretend that this is not a point of view, that this doesn't indicate, at least subliminally, an affiliation for the writer. It does. Nor would it make sense, in an area of life devoted to entertainment, for the writer to pretend "neutrality" as to the result. The writer must be aware of the direction of the emotional involvement of most of his readers, and must address it. Failure to do that results not in praiseworthy evenhandedness but in bland pointlessness. The "thrill of victory and agony of defeat," in the phrase made famous by television (for its own purposes), is part of the entertainment value of the event to the followers as well as to the participants, and the reporter must encompass that feeling. True objectivity, then, doesn't duck the issue of affiliation. It simply resists every impulse to *distort* what happened in accordance with emotional preference.

Suppose Dallas scores what appears to be the winning touchdown on the final play of the game, only to have it nullified by an offside penalty. The game then ends as a Dallas defeat. A story that reflects the frustration of Dallas partisans is perfectly objective; but a story that expresses outrage at officials who "robbed" Dallas is not. The fan is free to feel "his" team was "robbed." The reporter is not, but it is ludicrous to maintain that it is not "his" team. His assignment, in this case, is to cover the fortunes of the Dallas Cowboys, not, in some abstract fashion, the phenomenon of a football game taking place somewhere in the vast universe.

If the reporter can keep his judgment from being warped by his hopes or expectations, he has achieved objectivity. If he gets too involved in rooting for victory (or rooting for defeat, if he happens to dislike the coach or players), his capacity for getting the story straight will be compromised, and that's when loss of objectivity occurs. But feeling happy or sad at the result has nothing to do with the issue; the only thing that counts is what is actually said in the story.

Suppose, though, that the example is a little different. Suppose (as actually happened in a famous college game in 1940) the officials mistakenly give Dallas a fifth down on the final play, and Dallas scores the winning touchdown. The St. Louis reporter would be perfectly justified in using the term *robbed* to describe his team's defeat. And the Dallas reporter, to be objective, would have to call attention to the undeserved nature of the victory. This would then be only the starting point of a continuing story — what to do about the mistake. And at all times, the journalistic issue would be correctness: Were there five downs or weren't there? What will be done now? How did this happen? (In the Cornell-Dartmouth game of 1940, Cornell authorities "gave back" the 7–3 victory after seeing the films, and it's in the books today as Dartmouth 3, Cornell 0.)

In addition to rooting interest, a phenomenon that doesn't occur often in non-sports journalism, opinion and integrity carry extra weight on the sports page. In sports, opinion is inseparable from reporting. The phrase "an outstanding catch" is an opinion as well as a description. If a music critic says an orchestra played well, that is only an opinion (qualified or not, as the case may be). But if a reporter says Bjorn Borg played well in defeating John McEnroe, it is more than mere opinion, since the objective score also indicates that Borg played well enough to beat another good player. It is almost impossible to say anything about sports without making some sort of implicit value judgment.

But in sports, the reader has opinions too, ready-made and often highly qualified. He continually compares his knowledgeable opinions with those of the reporter. If a reporter (assuming he has the credentials for a qualified expert opinion) writes, "Approval of the SALT treaty does not seem likely," he may turn out to be right or wrong, but few readers will be in a position to challenge his judgment at that moment. But if a reporter writes "Borg was serving well," and a box score shows that 60 percent of his first serves were out, any tennis fan can tell the reporter is wrong.

Thus the knowledgeability of the fan puts a burden on the sports reporter, a demand for accuracy, thoroughness, and understanding that is greater than the burden placed on non-sports reporters.

The same applies to integrity. The fan of a particular team or sport reads the same writers and hears the same broadcasters day after day. Their credibility will quickly disappear if they are consistently inaccurate, intemperate in their opinions, or insufficiently objective in their approach. The integrity and reliability of sports reporters is subject to constant crosschecking that other reporters escape. Misspell the name of the president of an African nation, and the chances are no one will call it to your attention. But get one digit wrong in the right fielder's batting average, and the letters will come pouring in. It's that old illusion-of-importance at work.

So the obligation is: be right. But it is not the only obligation. To his employer, the reporter owes loyalty. To his audience, the reporter owes good taste, along with accuracy, thoroughness, and objectivity. To the participants in what he covers, the reporter owes all these things plus the test of relevance in what he chooses to report and the observance of confidentiality when that is invoked.

Loyalty to an employer means not challenging policies set at a higher level, and not supplying ammunition (through your status as an employee) to someone who has a conflict with your employer. It's not a question of blind loyalty, or "my paper right or wrong." You are not obliged to think your employer does everything right. But as long as you accept the employer's money, you are obliged to do your job the way the employer wants it done.

Examples? They're pretty simple. "That was a lousy, dull football game" is properly within the province of the sports writer. But "Football is a vicious, silly activity that should not be permitted" is not a proper approach to a game your paper sent you to cover. It may be a perfectly good theme for a story at some other time, if your editor (and publisher) decide they want to run it. But it is not right for you to decide, on an assignment, that that assignment is unworthy. You have every right to refuse to do what you don't believe in; you don't have the right to accept money for doing it, and then not do it, or oppose it.

Nor do you have the right to agree with, or give material to, outsiders who happen to be having a fight with your employer. "Why is your paper out to get me?" a much-criticized coach may ask. No matter what you think about the prejudices of your editor, you do not pursue this subject with the coach. Defend your editor if you want to, but don't curry favor (or excuse yourself) by confirming the coach's feeling of persecution.

Back in the 1950s, when I was working for the *New York Post,* I was in Chicago on a Yankee trip. The *Post* and Yankees were enemies at the time, since the *Post* had accused them of racial prejudice in not hiring black players. But Casey Stengel (the Yankee manager) and I were good friends, going back ten years to the time when he had first joined the Yankees and I had been on the *Herald Tribune.* While I was waiting around in a railroad station for the club train to leave, I spotted Stengel and Del Webb, one of the club's owners, near a newsstand, deep in conversation. I was wandering by the newsstand, looking at magazines, not thinking about them, but they thought I was eavesdropping. Webb asked sharply what I thought I was doing. I was startled. Stengel, realizing Webb had made a mistake, tried to repair things. "That's all right," he said to Webb. "His paper's no good but he's all right."

Stengel thought he was saying something favorable to me and about me. But he wasn't. He was implying that he could trust me, as an individual, to act differently from what my evil employer would like. I had to tell him, "I'm not here for me, I'm here for my paper; I *am* my paper as far as you're concerned. Think what you want about it, but don't think I'm separate from it." In my mind, I was avoiding disloyalty. And as it turned out, I got along better than ever with Stengel and Webb for years after that, because they understood my reaction for what it was.

To his audience, the reporter owes his best shot, just as the performer or athlete does. Fans pay to see athletes play and they pay to read the sportswriter's story. A reporter's best shot is objective accuracy, to aid the reader in forming his own conclusions. If the information can't be relied on, what good is it?

In sports journalism, however, the reporter should not lose sight of the fact that children make up a substantial portion of the audience. Some levels of sophisticated adult cynicism can be seen in proper proportion by adults but come out wrong when younger readers encounter them in newspaper write-ups. For example, it is no secret that athletes use a steady stream of barracks language. But reproducing this for effect, or for a laugh, or in the name of realism is not justifiable in regard to an audience not equipped to handle it. This doesn't mean that one should never deal with topics that are in bad taste; it simply means that one should do it only when there's an important reason to, and then in a way that makes the reason clear.

And that shades over into what the reporter owes the subject. Above all, he owes sincerity and awareness. The reporter must be conscious of the *effect* his words have on the people he describes. He can't shy away from hurting or criticizing, but he mustn't hurt *unintentionally*. He has to mean it. Ridiculing someone because it enlivens the story is not justifiable journalism, although it may be good writing and enjoyable reading; the ridicule must be substantiated by circumstances, according to the guidelines of objective opinion. The people being reported upon have families, friends, and acquaintances, and what appears in print about them affects all these people. Tough-minded, even merciless, criticism is a risk every public figure (including athletes) must be prepared to accept. But a cheap-shot insult, for the sake of calling attention to the cleverness of the reporter, is simply bad journalism. When stated in a misleading or distorted way, something that is "true" fails the test of objectivity.

The reporter clearly owes it to his subjects to make a reasonable distinction between private and public activity, between what's relevant and what isn't. An offensive tackle's speech impediment is not likely to be relevant; but a quarterback's is. Drinking and carousing, by athletes or reporters, is really nobody's business — until and unless it can be shown that their work is being affected. What makes such information fair game is not whether or not it happened but whether or not its occurrence relates to the public responsibility of the person involved.

Finally, and in the most practical terms, confidentiality must be observed, implicitly as well as explicitly. Otherwise, all sources of information — information can always be traced to someone's words — will dry up.

A player who says, to a group of reporters around his locker, "The coach stinks," can expect to pay the consequences of seeing that statement in print. The same player, saying the same thing to another player on the practice field, has the right not to see it in print, even though there may be a reporter nearby who has a perfect right to be there. The reporter can, and should, make a mental note that the player feels that way (at least at that moment); that's why reporters want "access." But it is background information fed into the reporter's memory banks and mental computer, valuable but confidential under the circumstances. It may enable him to understand more easily difficulties that arise later, but it is not legitimate quote material right then.

We can sum it up this way: "honest" journalism requires the ability to tell the difference between authentic honesty and lip service paid to it while actually practicing aggression, self-aggrandizement, revenge, exploitation, common snooping, or half-understood conclusion jumping.

And the reporter must accept the fact that he moves through a collection of people who feel hostile, or at the very least wary, in his presence.

"Is it raining out?" I once asked a third-base coach who had just come into the hotel from the street.

"Yes," he said, "but don't quote me."

10. Newspapers

"Extra, extra, read all about it, historical news is being made."

— Stephen Sondheim, 1959, from a song in *Gypsy*

FORM FOLLOWS FUNCTION, someone once said (or maybe it's function that follows form). Terrain dictates the plan of battle. And technological parameters determine, often in subtle ways, the content and style of different types of journalism.

Consider newspapers.

Most people, if told to put out a paper, would begin to think, "What will I say in it? How will I fill it with stories?" But that's starting at the wrong end of the process. A newspaper is a physical object that weighs up to seven pounds (a Sunday New York or Los Angeles *Times*) and has no value until it can be put in the hands of a reader.

So the first problem is *distribution*. How, and by whom, will the paper be delivered to people's doorsteps, newsstands, vending machines, candy-store counters, and other places that make it available? A fleet of trucks has to be loaded and leave the printing plant at the right times to make connections with trains, planes, and drop-off points, so that the army of local deliverers can do its work. This necessitates the establishment of a particular hour by which the physical object — the completely printed paper — must come off the press.

Getting it off the press is known as *production*. The mechanical steps that go into the printing of millions of sheets of paper in every twenty-four-hour period are incredibly complex, and their accomplishment is a daily miracle. Whatever the steps, they take a certain amount of time. Calculating back from the time the production and distribution processes must begin, we arrive at the *deadlines* by which editorial workers (writers and copyreaders) have to live. The deadline is inflexible. The most brilliant piece of writing in the history of mankind is worthless, to the newspaper, if it misses the deadline. And the most rudimentary information — "Red Sox win," for instance — is of considerable value if it beats the deadline and gets into print.

If a story is being written inside the newspaper office, its relation to the deadline can be dealt with directly. But if the story is being written at the scene of an event, as most sports stories are, there must be a way to transmit the written story to the office, so the production process can begin. This takes a given amount of time that also must be calculated backward again from the deadlines.

Finally, the size of the newspaper itself is finite. Each page can contain only so many words and pictures. The number of pages any day's newspaper contains is determined by the cost of newsprint (that's what the raw paper is called), the speed of the presses, the amount of advertising sold, and the exigencies of distribution. So all decisions about content must be made in light of the space available.

The requirements imposed by distribution, production, deadlines, and space have far more to do with determining what you read than do "creative concepts" in the minds of editors and writers. Editors and writers hate facing up to that fact, and it hurts their egos, but they can't escape it even if they refuse to admit it. (That's why Clive Barnes seized the rare opportunity, in his story about the Mets game, as described back in Part I, to alter a thought earlier congealed into type by the tyranny of deadlines, and why his gleeful act was cheered and envied by his colleagues.)

In sports reporting, the deadline problem is a constant factor. In general news, an important story breaks at deadline time every once in a while, but such occurrences are rare and irregular. The working day and the various time zones of the world can be plugged into a relatively comfortable routine. Writers and editors must work quickly, but they usually know what they have to deal with at least a couple of hours before actual deadline time. But ball games, by their nature, are undecided until they end — and most take place at night and on weekends. For morning papers, therefore, results crowd the deadlines every single day.

If the *New York Times* goes to press at 12:30 A.M. New York time, and the Yankee game in Los Angeles doesn't end until 1 A.M. New York time, the result will not be in the next morning's paper, and all the resources of the world's proudest news organization can't change that. The reader winds up mad at the *New York Times,* instead of at transportation systems or the earth's rotation; but that can't change anything either.

So all thinking about what will be in the paper begins with the question, What can we get into the paper? And each type of paper has its own restrictions and capabilities, around which have grown traditional functions. There are AMs and PMs, or morning papers and afternoon papers. A morning paper is prepared during the night and is intended to be read at breakfast time. It sums up the events of the day before. An afternoon paper is supposed to be on the street at midday or late afternoon, with a smattering of "today's" (early) news and more depth and sidelights on "yesterday's."

These traditions are especially strong in sports, although they've become blurred in recent years. The AM tells how yesterday's game came out, and the PM tells more about why, the consequences, and people's reactions. Theoretically, the AM assumes you don't yet know the result, and the PM assumes you do but want to know more about it.

Radio and television have forced changes in these assumptions, but they are still true to a certain extent. For the "big" events, such as major-league games and top tennis and golf tournaments, even the AM editor assumes the reader knows who won long before he gets the paper, and therefore demands more "afternoon-angle" content in the morning story. But this isn't as universally true as it seems. A large proportion of sports events of local interest (high school scores, new college coaches) aren't mentioned at all on the eleven o'clock news; a lot of readers, for one reason or another, miss something that is on the eleven o'clock news; and the electronic report is necessarily sketchy. So there are plenty of reasons to include traditional morning material in the sports section, including an important one that is seldom acknowledged: the file of past newspapers constitutes the only available historical record of sports results and is often referred to subsequently for a variety of reasons.

Of central importance to both AMs and PMs are the wire services. The Associated Press (AP) is a cooperative to which hundreds of newspapers belong. Its members are entitled to what it transmits, and it can pick up material from member papers (with credit). The United Press International (UPI) has a direct buy-sell relationship with its clients. These are live-coverage news services, and most of the sports news you see from outside your own immediate area originates with an AP or UPI reporter, who phones his material to a central office where the story is written and put on the wires. The wire services have some full-time reporters who cover major stories, but routine ball games are usually covered by "stringers" — local reporters hired to do piecework in their area.

Other wire services are more specialized. Large papers (such as the *New York Times,* the *Washington Post,* the *Chicago Tribune*) and various chains (Knight-Ridder, Gannett) sell their own material to other papers. Feature syndicates distribute comic strips, political commentary, and regular columns, concentrating on material for which the time factor is less important.

Within the paper, various editorial functions are relatively well defined. The *reporter* is the one at the event. He (or she) is usually called the "writer," but he may only phone information in to the office, where a rewrite man writes the story (or transcribes a dictated story, if the reporter can do that). In sports reporting, the reporter usually does write the story, and his name appears on it. But his primary responsibility is to collect information — score, quotes, description, whatever — since he is the only representative of the paper actually on the scene. In major sports, writers tend to have "beats" — ongoing assignments covering one team or one sport. That's how they acquire the status of experts.

The *copyreader* processes the writer's story. He reads it for corrections (which are often necessary, because the writer is working in a hurry), for clarity, and for grammar. He trims it to the exact size called for in the make-up (something the writer can't do if he's filing live from outside the office). And the copyreader also writes the headline. No single fact about newspapers is less understood by outsiders. Readers automatically assume that the writer, whose name is on the story, is responsible for the headline — which often gives a different impression than the full story. Ideally, the head and story agree. But in practice, the headline writer may misinterpret a point, the writer may fail to say clearly what he intends, or condensation may simply alter the flavor of a statement.

But it can't be otherwise. A headline has to fit, an exact number of units of type in a given amount of space, and a certain amount of skill is required to write it quickly. The reporter out of the office can't know ahead of time what count will be required, nor can he afford to spend time playing with such word puzzles.

The *editor* and his assistants (who are called "head of desk" or "slot man" when in charge of the copy desk) read all stories for content, decide on their size and placement, and make up the pages. The editor is also the administrative head of his department, assigning people to stories, deciding what should be covered, and so forth.

A big-city daily also has agate clerks (agate is the small type used for box scores, league standings, and other tables), editorial assistants (who used to be called copy boys), a secretary, and reporters or deskmen assigned to rewriting.

The *columnist* is the editorial voice of the sports section. He writes clearly labeled opinion rather than reports. A column is identifiable by some typographic device, a title or perhaps a picture of the writer. Most papers have one daily columnist, and their other writers do columns occasionally on topics connected with their beats.

Every large paper has different *editions,* which go to press at different times during the twenty-four-hour period, and each edition is somewhat different in content. In sports news, the different editions are of great importance because events end in time for some editions and not for others.

Suppose you are covering the New York Yankees for the *New*

York Times, and they make a trip to California that starts with a Tuesday night game in Oakland. The first edition of Wednesday's paper will require a story that "clears the desk" (is edited with headline) by 8:00 P.M. New York time Tuesday — two and a half hours before the game begins. So you write an "early story," essentially a feature with a "false lead": "Manager Dick Howser was encouraged by the recent play of Bobby Brown, the rookie outfielder, as the Yankees began their western trip in Oakland tonight . . ."

The next edition goes in at 11:30, when the game is in the third or fourth inning. You ignore it. Once the game starts, however, you send a "bunk lead" and a "running." A bunk lead is noncommittal: "The Yankees faced the A's here tonight." It can be followed by an "insert" the instant the game ends: "The Yankees won, 4–3." Meanwhile, your running story describes each inning (or summarizes only scoring innings) as it occurs, so the story is growing piece by piece back at the office. When the game ends, the whole story is ready for the printing process as soon as the brief insert comes through. That saves however many minutes it would take to write a story starting from scratch at the end of the game.

The running story may prove to be unnecessary, depending on when the game actually ends. There's another edition going to press at 12:45 A.M., and you just might make it with the final result. But if the game lasts longer, readers may be told, in the insert, "The teams were tied 2–2 after ten innings." In any case, when the game ends you start all over and write a new, coherent, readable story (which the running story can't be) as quickly as possible, aiming for the last edition (which might be at 2:00 A.M. or earlier, but can be held back a bit to make sure that at least some copies of the paper have the final story).

Then you go down to the clubhouse (if anyone is still there) or back to the hotel, and that night or the next morning get material for Wednesday's early story for the Thursday first edition. This report, whatever its angle, will try to sum up what happened in Tuesday night's game — because those who get the first edition never saw the result, which appeared only in the last edition. In effect, then, you are writing an afternoon-type story a day late.

That's what time zones and night games have done to traditional newspapering.

If you're covering the same trip for the *New York Post,* a PM, you don't get caught up in that kind of treadmill. You watch the game, make your clubhouse call, then sit down to compose your story, sending only one version of whatever you decide to write. (Usually, it's two stories, a "main" story and a "sidebar" or "notes," and on some nights you may also have a column to do — although the chances are you got that out of the way during the daytime.)

A PM writer does less typewriter labor but more thinking than an AM writer. Whereas he must choose his angle, the AM writer already has one: the game in front of him. But if the late game in California is very late and very eventful, the *Post* reporter will wind up writing a morning-type descriptive story, knowing the morning papers didn't get the result into any edition. And even in a routine contest, he'll put more details of the game into his story than he would for an eastern-time-zone game that ended in time for the morning papers to treat thoroughly.

These mechanical details control the contents of sports stories more than do the prejudices or viewpoints of writers. As consumer, the reader gets what they *can* give him rather than what they would like to give him.

Nothing illustrates the controlling force of technology more vividly than does the baseball box score. This method of summarizing a game was worked out before 1900, and it was designed to include information about fielding (putouts and assists) as well as hitting (at bats, runs, hits), in tabular form. Additional detailed information appeared in paragraph form under the table. An experienced baseball fan, studying a complete box score, could come close to reconstructing the progress of the game even when no play-by-play description was given.

When major-league baseball stabilized, the box-score form that was settled upon was determined by what fit conveniently in the width of a newspaper column printed in agate type. The headings (for each team) became AB, R, H, PO, A, E — at bats, runs, hits, putouts, assists, errors. Since errors are relatively few, it was easy enough to save space if necessary by eliminating the sixth column and including the errors (by name of player) in the paragraph portion.

For half a century, the box score in that form was as familiar as a law of nature. In the 1950s, however, the use of computers for transmission of information (and eventually for typesetting) began. Major-league box scores were already being sent only by the AP and UPI, since it would be a needless duplication of effort and expense to have each paper's writer draw up and transmit the same box. But when the wire services computerized their operations, the technological format they settled upon demanded only four columns per team. These became AB, R, H and RBI; and the box score no longer contains any record whatever of putouts and assists. This makes it impossible to "reconstruct" a game, and provides less (and less complete) information — not only to the reader of today's paper, but to anyone who wants to look up an earlier game.

Now this is not absolutely crucial information. After all, considerable thought went into making the value judgments that determined the new form of the box score, so that what was left out was deemed least important. The point is, these judgments had to be made in light of a *technical* necessity (four columns was an efficient size for the computer to handle) and not a *conceptual* desirability (a more complete summary of the game).

Of course the original six-column form was also technologically determined; it was simply suited to a different technology, fitting the convenient column width of linotype. It's not that evil computers have robbed baseball fans of information they used to get. It's just a fact of life that mechanical capability controls what the journalistic consumer receives.

Nonetheless, conceptual considerations are important in determining what goes into a newspaper. The idea is to sell the paper. It comes out every day. Reading it must become a habit. Therefore, the key need is credibility. Readers won't stick with a paper unless they find its information trustworthy and thorough. That's why objectivity pays off, and why newspapers make it their religion. And whether objectivity pays off or not can be measured by circulation statistics: the number of papers sold can be determined accurately.

But no one (except editors) reads every word of every issue. Readers turn first to the section or story in which they have a prior interest — a fact that makes sports results and stock-market tables so fundamentally important — and only after that do they turn to some startling item. There is no such thing as an "average" reader or "mass appeal." A newspaper is a collection of many constituencies, and its success rests on satisfying each sufficiently. Even within the sports section this is true. There are baseball fans who never look at a tennis story, and vice versa, but baseball must be covered well enough to suit the baseball fan and tennis well enough to suit the tennis fan. Space limitations force editors to make choices, but in the long run each of the many relatively small constituencies must be fed.

That's why hype and hysteria are counterproductive in the newspaper business. You can't aggressively sell sensation every single day. Even if you could find it, you would quickly immunize the reader to its shock value, just as a virus can acquire immunity to an antibiotic. In broadcasting, it's the other way around: hype pays off, and credibility doesn't count for much.

11. Radio and Television

"And now, a word from our sponsor."
— Traditional, circa 1940

BROADCASTERS, both radio and television, have no delivery problems at all. Their customers receive programs by a flick of a switch. And they have no mechanical production problems, beyond the placement of cameras or microphones, once their basic equipment has been installed. Whatever their performers do or say is instantly transmitted to the audience. But they have one tremendous problem print media do not: getting and holding the simultaneous attention of a huge audience.

A reader chooses what to read, when, and where, at the reader's convenience. The reader can skip, go back, reread, skim, change his mind, or get a back issue. A listener or viewer, on the other hand, is prisoner of the sequential presentation. In a news broadcast, for instance, the Yankee score is up there for two seconds. If you miss it, it's gone. Therefore, broadcast media necessarily depend on show-business techniques, which have evolved over centuries precisely because they are effective in holding audience attention.

Holding attention is the key economic need. A newspaper depends on income from ads in order to stay alive, but the value of the ads is related to circulation, a factual figure. The advertiser assumes that people who read news stories will also look at some of the ads — not all people at all ads, but in a conglomerate of constituencies. So the ads and the editorial matter don't have to be directly connected (although advertisers do specify which section of the paper they want).

In radio and television, however, the only hope the advertiser has is that the audience will remain tuned in long enough for the commercials to come on, embedded in the subject matter of the program. A reader's eye can skip effortlessly over the ad alongside his baseball story; but a viewer is much less likely to turn off the television set between innings while the game is on.

So broadcasters have to convince their audience to stay tuned in *now,* for the duration of the show. Hyperbole and artificial excitement help do this. A newspaper that is cool, critical, and detached about yesterday's ball game is building up its credibility without damaging the reader's enjoyment. But if a broadcast lets the audience think *this* game and *this* instant isn't so terrific that it can't be missed, it is not building a future following and is cutting off the present one. What's more, the broadcaster has no *countable* circulation figures to offer the advertiser. He has only ratings, which are statistical projections of large numbers taken from small samples. Whatever their validity, they put a premium on getting the largest possible audience for every program.

If a sports page devotes half a column to a yacht race that is of interest to only a few people, the thousands who read the adjacent football story aren't disturbed. But if a television station interrupts two programs watched by tens of millions to show something esoteric watched by only 900,000 viewers, it is courting disaster. And this is the key difference in journalistic approach: newspapers aim at a large collection of distinct constituencies; broadcasts aim at a large single audience during any given hour.

There's another significant difference. A print journalism reporter summarizes something that has already taken place, and even when he does a running story, it reaches the reader long after the fact. A broadcaster, on the other hand, can operate in real time, reporting results as they happen. For this reason, radio and television gear their sports operations to play-by-play broadcasts.

But play-by-play, strictly speaking, isn't journalism at all. It's better. It's a window to the real thing as it happens. In television play-by-play, the real reporter is the camera rather than the commentator. In radio, it's the announcer, who is skilled at description (far more skilled than most newspapermen) but is denied the essence of journalistic judgment, which is to collect, sift, rearrange, and make coherent *only the essential elements* of what went on, after the outcome is known.

Nor is the on-the-air interview journalism in the true sense, because the editing function is usually absent (at least in sports). This point can be argued, and I'm expressing a personal view; but the crux of the matter is that within the time limitations of a live interview, the person being interviewed has much greater control of what he says, and how, than he does when he faces a reporter who can go back and forth over the relevant ground and come away with the information he seeks.

For a play-by-play broadcast to exist at all, the station must buy exclusive rights from the promoter. This makes the station a co-promoter of the event to a far greater degree than a newspaper is, even when the alliances described in Part I are taken into account. And while co-promotion can be a thoroughly honorable, laudable, socially valuable activity, it cannot be called objective journalism.

Almost all the air time devoted to sports in America is play-by-play or the replay of past play-by-play. The amount of sports news on television in the 1970s was proportionately less than the amount of time devoted to newsreels in movie theaters in the 1940s. On radio there is much more sports reporting than on television, but still very little compared to newspapers, and it is heavily weighted toward "big" events. In general, news is only a minor part of the broadcast industry, which has more direct ties to advertising than print media do, and still closer ties to theater and music. On the other hand, news is the most important part of the newspaper business.

What consequences do these differences between print and electronic media have for sports and the perception of sports by the public? Broadcasts give people the chance to be absentee spectators, visually through television and in the mind's eye through radio. They enhance the same attitudes, impressions, and emotions developed in fans attending games. Newspapers provide sports fans with opinions, information, and ideas about what they *can't* see, outside the vicarious ballpark environment.

The main kick for the broadcast audience, then, is shared excitement. The main kick for readers is to pass judgment. A live event, seen or heard, is drama. A newspaper account is a review.

The play-by-play announcer is a representative of the club or league, and is accepted as such by athletes being covered and by the bulk of the audience. That's his proper role, and his appeal. This doesn't mean he doesn't call an error an error, or lies about who won; it just means he loses his effectiveness if he is persistently critical of the event in progress.

The newspaper reporter, on the other hand, is supposed to be neutral, and his effectiveness is lost if his audience loses faith in his objectivity. Erring in the direction of being hypercritical does him less harm than being a Pollyanna.

All the newspapers in the world, lumped together, can't match the effectiveness of one well-handled telecast of a live event. And all the television and radio stations in existence can't supply the fan with the special delight gained from studying league standings and batting averages at leisure. Neither group has a monopoly on virtue, wisdom, or venality. But each displays its qualities and drawbacks in its own way.

These days, athletes and promoters are highly conscious of the way broadcasting adds to their earning power, and they consider it a "friendly" medium. They view print journalists primarily as antagonists seeking ways to distort or discredit their precious images, and see no financial benefit to be gained from cooperating with them. But some promoters know better, because they recognize that the old symbiosis between press and sports promotion, and the new symbiosis between promotion and broacasting, are inseparable from a third symbiotic relationship between press and electronics.

Broadcasters have a crucial dependence on newspapers. The daily coverage of sports events, in print, is what builds up the climactic interest that induces people to tune in. In fact, viewers look in the paper to find out when to tune in. And almost all the factual material that goes on the air is originally unearthed, developed, and disseminated by newspaper reporters. The newspaper report of yesterday's game not only sells tickets for tomorrow's but also sells the broadcast.

Newspapers, in turn, depend on the television techniques used for major events to aid their coverage and stimulate reader interest. A national telecast guarantees newsworthiness. Network broadcasting makes available to newspaper reporters replays, slow motion, interviews, and insights that wouldn't be available otherwise.

In the movie *Oh, Men! Oh, Women!* David Niven, playing the part of a psychoanalyst, says at one point: "Of course men and women want different things. Men want women, and women want men." I'm not sure exactly how the analogy works, but it seems to me that the newspaper-television relationship is touched upon in that remark.

12. Books and Magazines

BOOKS, magazines, and weekly newspapers play only a
peripheral role in the sports-through-journalism interaction with society. They have their own values, but journalistically they are insignificant. The reason for this is the usual one:
technology. It takes longer to produce (that is, deliver to the customer) a book or a magazine than it does to produce a newspaper
or broadcast. And sports can't be separated from its immediacy.
The moment a contest is decided, its fascination begins to wane,
as interest in the next event (related to the one just completed,
and affected by the result) starts to build up.

The whole spectator-sport business is, as we have seen, dependent on the peculiar attractions of "today's" event. And there is
nothing a book or magazine publisher can do about that. So in
the sports field, these publications are relegated to a "secondary"
role. They can deal effectively only with topics *already* made
newsworthy by press and broadcast exposure. This is not true of
books and magazines in general. They often bring attention to
something that has *not* been big news recently, and they frequently reveal for the first time large areas of detail and knowledge not generally recognized until the book or article presents
them. This applies to everything from Charles Darwin's *On the*

Origin of Species to a letter by a Soviet dissident, smuggled out of Russia and printed in the *New York Times Magazine.* But on sports topics, books have no commercial viability unless they deal with the already famous.

Books and magazines can, and do, go far beyond what's in the daily sports diet, but only when they deal with topics daily newspapers have made familiar.

Here we must devise categories again.

Weeklies are only semijournalistic. They have avid readers to whom they serve as supplements rather than primary sources. They are a specialty interest, supplying information more specific (and more comprehensive) than the daily papers can. But while it is conceivable that a person reads *Time* or *Newsweek* once a week without paying too much attention to the same world-news topics in daily newspapers, it is inconceivable that someone interested enough in baseball to read the *Sporting News* won't keep up with the daily baseball scores.

So the *Sporting News, Pro Football Weekly,* and even *Sports Illustrated* (which is aimed at affluent leisure-time audiences even more than at fans) don't add to the *number* of those who take an interest in sports. They add to the *quantity of information* available to those already interested.

If weekly magazines develop something that's "news" on their own, the daily media immediately appropriate it (with encouragement from the weekly, which wants to advertise its existence and excellence even more than it wants the ephemeral glory of an "exclusive"). If weeklies report on live events, their deadlines prevent them from matching the timeliness of the other media.

Monthly magazines aren't even semijournalistic. The time element restricts them to dealing with features, exposés, pictures, tables, and analyses that can be prepared far in advance and are of value only after daily coverage has called attention to their subjects.

Sports books fall into several categories:

1. How-to. An enormous field that doesn't concern us, according to our definition of mass-entertainment spectator sports.

2. Records and statistics. These are absolutely essential to those who work in sports and to dedicated fans. Owing to the nature of sports, they require annual updates.

3. Biographies, revelations, and similar hot-property items. These are obviously "secondary," in that they capitalize on, rather than create, interest in the subject.

4. Histories. These books lean heavily on the nostalgia value inherent in the original process of accepting the basic illusion (that the result matters to the reader).

5. Coffee-table picture books. Essentially, these are pictorial histories of a vivid sort.

6. Analytic books. These have relatively little circulation or public impact (although they can influence those who influence). This book is an example.

What all these kinds of books have in common is the amount of time it takes to produce them. Generally speaking, about one year elapses between the time the author finishes writing and the reader starts reading. If the subject is World War I (for example, *The Guns of August*) or a presidential election (*The Making of the President,* for instance), the interval doesn't matter much to those who want to read about it. But a book about last year's pennant race, however glorious, comes into conflict with daily news about *this* year's pennant race. And the whole complex machine of sports promotion, newspaper marketing, and broadcasting is devoted to getting fans to focus attention on the *current* pennant race. A Barbara Tuchman book about World War I is not competing with high-powered organizations trying to sell tickets to World War III; but Steve Jacobson's book about the hectic New York Yankee season of 1978 is competing, in 1979, with all the elaborate attempts to sell tickets to 1979 games.

So books and magazines don't have much to do with the kinds of impressions people get about the sports world, at least not in a *primary* way. But they do have an enormous effect in another way. They solidify, reinforce, and perpetuate the impressions first produced by daily journalists. The stories that get retold, the cumulative nostalgia, the reputations that become frozen forever, the perceptions of "conventional wisdom" about sports — all of this is found in books. Babe Ruth is remembered today not as he was, or as he was written about in the newspapers of his day, but as he has been written about in books. The authors of those books used the newspapers of Ruth's day as source material, but they didn't limit themselves to it.

The Brooklyn Dodgers of the 1950s, depicted by Roger Kahn in *The Boys of Summer,* are *Kahn's* perceptions, not objective reality or even journalistic distortion. They resonate with the perceptions of those who remember the Dodgers of those days. Kahn's book (an excellent one) embeds that time in public consciousness more vividly, and more completely, than anything that actually happened, or was written about by anyone at the time (including Kahn, who was there).

The same is true of Jerry Kramer's *Instant Replay,* written by Dick Schaap, which describes the Green Bay Packers of Vince Lombardi's era; George Plimpton's various "I-tried-it" books; and for that matter, Ring Lardner's all-too-true fiction. In fact, the higher the literary quality of the work, the more firm the impressions that are perpetuated. But the origin of those impressions — even when the author contradicts some existing impression — can always be found in the daily journalistic impressions already created.

So in the book and magazine business, as in broadcasting, hype becomes far more important than credibility. The book is going to be sold *once.* It must call attention to its existence. It is relatively expensive, and the reader must make an active decision to buy and read it (which is not the case with habitual newspaper reading or the effortless turn-on of a broadcast). Something has to *convince* the consumer than it's worth the effort. That something is hype.

Magazines must do this every month, subscriptions notwithstanding. Inaccuracies will be forgotten long before the next exciting cover tries to seduce the readers. And a record of accuracy won't help sell a dull issue. As a consequence, magazine editors and book editors *start* with the idea — the headline, title, or cover — and then seek a writer who can substantiate it. (The writer may, of course, originate the idea, but the decision to proceed is the editor's.)

This is the exact opposite of the true journalistic approach, which starts with the information and then seeks a headline for it. The daily editor says, "Go find out what happened and we'll print it." The magazine editor says, "We know this happened, now go out and get me some good stuff about it." It is a fundamental, very important, and too-seldom-acknowledged difference.

Yet each approach is entirely appropriate to the needs of the institution that employs it. The function of news is to make known what's going on. The function of books and periodicals is to amplify and interpret what is already known.

In sports, therefore, periodicals lean heavily on pictures. The visual impact of sports action is enormously appealing in itself, on the souvenir and nostalgia level as well as aesthetically, and this is something daily journalism can't provide (because of the limitations of time, space, and the quality of newsprint for reproducing photographs, in the case of newspapers, and because of the evanescence of the image, in television). The daily press provides millions of words, saturating the intellectual interest of the fan, and few books and magazines can add to that. So it makes sense to emphasize art when putting out a sports magazine or book.

The basic trade-off is more detail in exchange for less timeliness. The basic difficulty is saturation by the daily media. Everything has its limitations.

13. Limitations

"Keep it short."
— Standard instruction to reporters

LIMITATIONS understandably are not characteristics people like to advertise about themselves. But it is foolish, and can be fatal, to deny them. A $10,000 automobile is a marvelous machine, but you wouldn't try to drive one through a six-foot-deep stream. Nor would you rely on a spiffy speedboat to carry you along a freeway. And if you expect a newspaper, television program, or book to supply something it can't provide, you will be at best disappointed and at worst misled.

Sports consumers, because they devote so much of their time to their chosen subject, develop a useful sense of some of the limitations of sports journalism. They don't expect a newspaper story to describe every shot in a basketball game, and they don't count on television to broadcast local high school batting averages. But in many important ways that are less extreme and less obvious, the American public holds great misconceptions about what's possible and suitable and what isn't, in the delivery of news.

By the same token, journalists themselves often lose sight of their proper functions. Because of ego, or sloppy thinking, or ambition, or ignorance, or imitation, or indifference, they often promise what they can't deliver, assert authority they don't have, and pretend to power that isn't really theirs. In the process, they fail to do as well as they could what they can and should do.

Accepting limitations doesn't mean giving up or copping out. It doesn't excuse the failure to make every effort to overcome escapable limitations, and to minimize the rest. But it does mean assessing reality correctly, and acting accordingly. There are some things journalists, print or electronic, cannot do, and some things they shouldn't do. These are worth enumerating for the consumer (who can then tell when his or her informant is going off the track) and for the journalist (who doesn't always give the matter enough thought).

A journalist *cannot:*

1. Predict what will happen.
2. Prove "beyond reasonable doubt" most of the propositions presented in his report.
3. Produce a "complete" account of anything.
4. Probe a complex subject, situation, or personality "in depth."
5. Investigate a crime (or anything else).

A journalist *should not:*

1. Advocate a cause (with one exception, to be noted).
2. Participate in the event being covered.
3. Manipulate people or events.

Sports reporting provides exceptional opportunities for believing that the first list is possible and the second list is permissible, so we should spell out these limitations more clearly.

The first question that occurs to people about any game is, Who's going to win? The sportswriter or broadcaster is identified as someone close to the situation, and is therefore considered an expert. So the question a reporter hears most often from people around him (including friends who should know better) is, Who's going to win? My answer always is, If we knew that, we wouldn't have to go through with the game, would we?

At the same time, trying to *guess* who will win is one of the chief joys of the whole entertainment. To explain who *ought* to win, for what reason, and under what conditions is not only the right of every fan but the pleasure. A reporter on the beat, or a columnist, has almost an obligation to give his analysis of what can be expected to happen. But when the recipient of that forecast loses sight of the fact that it is part of the "fun," and takes too seriously what is predicted, he is setting himself up for self-deception.

What sort of person would take a prediction so seriously?

• A player, official, or other club loyalist who considers a prediction of defeat a treasonous act. (The idea that a reporter isn't supposed to be "for" anyone seldom penetrates the competitive mentality.)

• A very young (or otherwise inexperienced) fan, who overestimates the consistency of fate and the wisdom of authority.

• A bettor.

It's the last case that makes trouble most of the time. No one who loses a bet likes the feeling. Most bets are made on the favorite (which is why it has become the favorite). The favorite was established by "expert opinion," and news of its identity reaches the public only through reporters of one sort or another. So when the game doesn't turn out the way it was supposed to, it's those incompetent reporters who are accused of misleading the losing bettor. And in the minds of some bettors, there's a worse possibility. There is no way Notre Dame can lose this week, N-o W-a-y! But it does lose. Could it have lost on purpose? Was "business" being done to rig the outcome for betting purposes?

Games, we know, have been rigged and will be rigged again. Larceny has not yet been eradicated from human activity. But suspecting larceny because a sports-page prediction proved wrong is a case of insufficient evidence. A conscientious journalist, therefore, calls his reader's attention to the difference between his analysis of the expected (which is an informational service) and his prediction of the outcome, which is pure game-playing for the fun of it. (If a prediction is made in all seriousness, as a guide to action, the one who makes it is a tout, not a journalist.)

Just as you should not depend on news media for dependable forecasts (even of the weather), you should not demand "conclusive" evidence of anything in such a context. A report of something is not a proof of anything. Its whole value lies in telling you that something is happening, so that you can, if you want, pursue "harder" information in an appropriate fashion.

The same applies to "completeness." Anyone who believes that the entire story of any event can be obtained from news accounts (or columnists) is probably beyond help. News is an indicator, a surface-skimming contact with the rest of the world. It tells the reader what further questions to ask; it doesn't supply answers.

In sports, however, news comes closer to being complete, for all practical purposes, than it does for most other subjects, for all the reasons we've already mentioned. Proportionately, the media give more attention to the mass-spectator-sports system than to, for instance, all congressional activity. And by its nature, sports material is essentially simple, straightforward, and heavily factual, having been arranged that way to make it marketable.

Even so, the limitations should be borne in mind. Yesterday's scores and the league standings are complete, final proof of how games came out. Stories about why and how are far from complete or conclusive, being necessarily selective and limited in space. Therefore, the popular idea of "probing in depth," so much in journalistic fashion during the 1970s, is for the most part a fraud. While it is true that a report which penetrates two millimeters below the surface is twice as deep as a report that plumbs only one millimeter, the fact remains that the whole field of journalism is inescapably superficial. Stories that psychoanalyze athletes, reveal interior motivations, or purport to elucidate the complexities of a football play or a basketball contract negotiation show much more about the arrogance of the reporter and the gullibility of readers than about the topics examined.

Watergate and all that went with it stimulated a romantic view of "investigative" reporting, instantly creating a generation of would-be heroes of the press. But aside from the once-in-a-lifetime circumstances of Watergate, it's important to recognize what actually happened to the *Washington Post* and its reporters on the road to glory: after months of exhaustive effort, they had *nothing they could use publicly* until a nonjournalistic action — McCord's letter to Judge Sirica — set things in motion. Once things began happening in the "real" world of courts and politics, the press could utilize what it had collected, but not until then.

The real achievement of the press in that case (and the true value of a free press) was its ability to keep the story alive, to keep pointing out the *need* for investigation, rather than carrying out the investigation itself.

These limitations on what journalism *can* do are not very controversial, once you pin them down. Ideas about what journalists *shouldn't* do are far more subjective, and here the argument is my own (and, these days, a minority position).

Reporters should not be advocates, marshaling arguments for or against a particular position, even if the position is unquestionably evil (war, pollution, oppression) or undeniably benign. This is not because a journalist should be divorced from social struggle, absolved of making moral judgments, or entitled to be above the battle. It is because he can't perform his truly useful function — to deliver information — if he adulterates it with partisanship. He simply won't be believed after a while, and the very thing he was after — to win adherents to a cause — will become unattainable. Whatever his goals, the best thing he can do is to present *factual* raw material that advocates can then put to use.

In sports, this issue arises most often when a journalist offers "support" to a coach under fire, or to a particular team or player — or attacks the same. Journalistically, either action is self-defeating. The meanest thing you can ever do to someone you disapprove of is to report *accurately,* without comment, what he or she says and does.

Reporters should not participate in the events they cover, should not try to affect outcomes, and should not project themselves and their problems into controversies. Sometimes (but not often) that's unavoidable, and there's nothing wrong with a reporter in effect disqualifying himself from a particular story, just as judges and others disqualify themselves from clear-cut conflict-of-interest situations.

Specifically, it's not a reporter's task to provoke a fight between a player and a manager by running back and forth between them asking and repeating inflammatory questions and quotes (accurate or not) until they explode. It's not up to a reporter to reveal a team's game plan ahead of time, or second-guess a referee's decision (as distinct from recording the second-guessing reactions of others to the call). The cliché, too often ignored, is: We *report* the news, we don't *make* it.

Nor should a reporter, as a member of a powerful institution, use his leverage to maneuver people or events into "making a good story." One common tactic is to print a rumor, with little basis, in order to elicit an interesting denial. Another is to use a partial or out-of-context statement, reinforced by headline condensation, to stimulate reader or listener interest. A third ploy is the "when did you stop beating your wife" type of question, which guarantees attention no matter how it's answered and makes follow-ups by the rest of the media likely, whether or not there was reason to pose the question in the first place.

These "shouldn'ts" are violated more directly, and more frequently, in sports than in other areas of journalism. They are widely tolerated and often praised. But they undermine the most precious asset a journalist can have: credibility. For a newspaper, as we've seen, credibility is more important than it is on the airwaves. For that matter, very little *sports* material on the airwaves has anything at all to do with journalism, so perhaps newspaper standards are the proper measuring rods and not simply a reflection of my own prejudices.

Beyond these generalities, the limitations of particular media can't be ignored by the consumer who wants to interpret correctly what is beamed at him. Newspapers cannot begin to match the *immediacy* of radio and television reports. And radio and television can't approach the *scope* of the subjects covered by newspapers, or the *tangibility* of box scores and reading matter that can be referred to at the user's convenience, repeatedly and consistently. And magazines and books can't be timely.

In a little volume entitled *Murphy's Law, Book Two**, there is a section called "Langsam's Laws" that should be kept in the forefront of consciousness by all those engaged in journalism; and it is even more important for those who read, hear, or watch it:

1. Everything depends.
2. Nothing is always.
3. Everything is sometimes.

Equally pertinent is "Green's Law of Debate," from the same

---

* Arthur Bloch, *Murphy's Law, Book Two: More Reasons Why Things Go Wrong* (Los Angeles: Price/Stern/Sloan, 1980).

volume: Anything is possible if you don't know what you're talking about.

Journalism, properly practiced, ought to help people identify
the impossible.

14. Statistics

"There are lies, damn lies and statistics."
— Benjamin Disraeli, or maybe Mark Twain, or both

A FEW WORDS about statistics, the care and feeding thereof, the way they can mislead, and their proper use. Numerical statements of all kinds, often presented in graph or tabular form, are staples of journalistic fare. Nothing else gives such a strong flavor of impartial, indisputable, factual information. Statistics also heighten the impression of exactness, are admirably concise, and seem unambiguous. Since all these qualities are deemed desirable for journalists, they use statistical material whenever they can.

This is especially true in sports, where numbers are built into the action and where most participants and followers have a lively interest in easily obtainable statistics. And since the sports journalist, more often than other journalists, is allowed to (and expected to) indulge in expressing value judgments, he or she uses numerical "evidence" to take a bit of the curse off this suspect subjectivity.

But the famous saying, "Figures can't lie but liars can figure," is not true. Figures can lie too. Using statistics correctly requires training and skill. Mathematics is needed, but it is not as important as logic and scientific method. Few journalists acquire, or even admit they need, background in such fields. Worse still, most readers are sitting ducks for half-baked statistical proof of some point or other. Even when the statistical information presented in a story is accompanied by all the appropriate ifs, ands, and buts, readers frequently ignore the qualifying statements and zero in on the kernel of distortion.

Only two aspects of sports statistics concern us at this point, however: how the statistics are actually used, and why. Since every game happens one play at a time, any aspect of it can be counted, and the accumulation can be turned into a statistic. At least one thing *must* be counted in order to have a result: the points scored. And at least the number of victories and defeats must be counted in order to have standings and a championship. These necessities precondition us for the acceptance and enjoyment of other numbers derived from recording the action.

What numbers? That depends, first of all, on what is convenient to count. Another determining factor is tradition — what has been counted in the early stages of a sport's development. (The whole idea of statistics is to compare, and there must be a body of past data to compare to.) Then (and definitely third in importance) comes the intrinsic significance of certain types of information. And finally, there is the search for originality and fresh insight, which, through counting more things or combining in new ways things already counted, leads to the creation of new statistics. This last factor is obviously an open-ended process that creates ever more numbers.

Who needs them? Newspaper reporters need them, to a degree, as an outgrowth of box scores and as a way to buttress general statements. Saying someone is hitting .385 seems a lot more convincing and objective than saying he is hitting exceptionally well. Fans need them as fodder for conversation and rumination, mental activities that go to the heart of fan enjoyment. Players and coaches need them to analyze their play and, more important, to make convincing arguments about points grasped simply by intuition, memory, or observation. But radio play-by-play announcers need statistics to fill time — and that's the real reason for the statistical explosion that swept through sports in the years following World War II.

A newspaper account of a major-league game rarely runs longer than 1000 words. A broadcaster, in the course of describing the same game during a period of two to three hours, has to use more than 25,000. (To give you an idea of how much this is, 25,000 words fill about 60 pages of this book.) What can the broadcaster say? Describing the batter's stance and how he fidgets with his cap, commenting on the weather, repeating the count and the score, setting the scene, telling an anecdote, giving a player's personal history, plugging tickets, leading into a commercial — all these things aren't enough. Statistics offer the ideal answer.

The writer, trying to condense and summarize, can say simply, "Dave Parker doubled." But the broadcaster has to talk for perhaps three minutes while Parker is still at bat, before he has done anything, so it is natural and easy to say, "Parker is hitting .285 as of now, with 86 hits, 12 of them homers, 4 triples, and 14 doubles." Then, when Parker hits a double, it would be pointless (and seem incomplete) to fail to say, "That was his fifteenth double of the season."

Before radio, the selection of which statistic to publicize depended on its quality: someone's opinion, right or wrong, that the statistic was important or interesting in itself. For example, Babe Ruth's fifty-fifth home run. With the advent of radio, the criterion became volume, so the broadcaster would have something to talk about. This led to less discrimination between a "worthwhile" statistic and any old statistic. But it also conditioned listeners to accept more statistics, and to get involved with numbers (because the numbers are fun and enhance the fan's illusion of being informed). Writers, in turn, picked up the habit, partly because they grew up with the same sort of conditioning, and partly in response to their newly conditioned audience.

Today, excessive use of statistics is endemic to the American sports scene. But excess, in itself, is not as bad as the widespread basic misunderstanding of what statistics are, and what they are not. Statistics, in sports, provide an indisputable record of *what has already happened.* They are not "probabilities," in the mathematical sense, of what might happen next. They can be used as one factor in deciding what to expect next, but only as a factor and only if used correctly, with considerable skill.

Computer users have coined the term "GIGO" — garbage in, garbage out. That's the most important principle of sports statis-

tics, and the most overlooked by fans, journalists, and participants. No mathematical manipulation of figures is worth more
than the validity of the original figures plugged into the equation.
What's more, all the sophisticated developments in mathematics
assume random, inanimate, unchanging-during-the-course-of-
the-example events. How a tossed coin or die falls, the distribution of ages in a population, the proportion of defective ball
bearings found in a sample taken from a machine trying to stamp
out identical pieces of metal — these investigations are the true
province of statistical analysis.

But in sports, most situations involve the conscious decision-
making, and reaction, of living human beings. Their actions may
or may not distort the statistical formula, but it can't be assumed
that they won't. When I throw a pair of dice, they don't "know"
that they came up seven last time, or what the odds are against
another seven. They roll however they will, and the mathematical
law that says there is one chance in six that they will add up to
seven is rigidly valid. But a man at bat is aware that he struck out
last time against the pitcher he's facing (or hit a home run, or
whatever), and he knows what the score is, how important the
game is, how the crowd is reacting, how he feels physically, and
what the consequence of his next act is likely to be; and he has an
idea about what the pitcher may try to do, knowing that the
pitcher knows about the situation.

Thus a statistic that says "This batter has 17 hits in 51 times at
bat against this pitcher over the last five years" does not mean
"He has one chance in three of getting a hit" in the same sense
that there is one chance in six the dice will come up seven. Each
roll of the dice is one of a series of *identical* tries (for all practical
purposes); but each time at bat is a *distinct conglomeration* of unprecedented factors, which include the consciousness of the participants. The two ivory cubes are the same cubes on each suc-
cessive toss, whereas the pitcher and the batter are different
human beings than they were yesterday, or even two innings ago,
when this time at bat comes up. The observation that "No one
can bathe twice in the same river" (because the water is flowing by)
goes back to antiquity. It represents the underlying truth about
the difference between sports statistics and mathematical statis-

tics. Yet the tendency of journalists, both print and broadcast, is to ignore this fundamental distinction, and the fans follow.

All sports statistics are valid *if* the way they are generated is kept in mind. The things to keep in mind are:

1. Exactly what has been counted and what hasn't? (A won-lost record includes all games played, and is valid; the number of touchdowns a team has scored, without consideration of how many chances it had to score and how many touchdowns its opponents scored, may or may not be informative.)

2. Does one set of numbers *automatically* cause, or imply parallel changes in another set of related numbers? (A player who seldom gets on base can't steal many bases; a football team with a weak defense against the run, and usually trailing in a game, will have "good" pass-defense statistics because its opponent won't bother to pass; a basketball player who seldom drives to the basket will have few free-throw attempts.)

3. Are there enough instances to make an average meaningful? (A .667 winning percentage with a 4–2 record does not mean the same as a .667 percentage with a 102–51 record.)

4. Is the traditional form of a particular sports statistic the relevant one? (From the beginning, baseball fielding averages have counted the number plays handled cleanly and the number of errors, but what really matters is the player's ability to cover a certain area. Thus a poor fielder who doesn't reach balls that go by for hits may wind up with a perfect fielding average.)

5. Is an *average* relevant in a particular area, or are totals more informative? (For example, one basketball player averages 20 points a game, playing an average of 40 minutes; a teammate averages only 5 minutes of playing time and 6 points. Isn't 1.2 points per minute better than 0.5? No, because there's a reason the substitute is playing only 5 minutes: he's not as good. And to suppose he would average 48 points a game if he played 40 minutes is a good way to flunk Elementary Common Sense 101–102.)

6. Are the quantities or identities involved really comparable? (The Giants of mid-1980 have a different collection of players than they had in mid-1978, so comparing their statistics is of limited value, although it may be of great interest to the passionate Giant fan. And the Willie McCovey who hit more than five hun-

dred home runs over a span of twenty seasons has little to do with
the Willie McCovey playing his twenty-first at the age of forty-
one.)

And yet, having said all this, we must recognize that statistics,
however imperfect, are the backbone of continuing fan interest
in American commercial sports. The historical pattern was set by
baseball, which lends itself to statistics, but all later sports have
tried mightily to develop their own sets of numbers, because
numbers are incomparable and inexhaustible conversation fodder. They stimulate the comprehensibility and continuity aspects
so vital to the sports promoter's product, and they are the ideal
raw material for the run-of-the-mill journalist. Journalistic judgment, or self-restraint, breaks down for a ridiculously simple reason. Statistics are overused because they are there.

In order to keep track of anything that will become truly significant — like the 44-game hitting streak with which Pete Rose
electrified sports in 1978, or Joe DiMaggio's 56-game streak of
1941 that remains the standard — one must keep track of *everything.* The statistician can't pick and choose, beforehand, which
numbers to record: he must do them all, every day, and add them
up every day, and start again the next day. When a writer does
this himself (as most writers used to, in the old days), he develops
a vested interest in the homework he has done. Keeping each
player's batting record leads him to share the fruit of his effort,
and he honestly becomes more interested than a less-involved
critic might.

But statistics-keeping long ago became the province of the professional publicity machinery attached to league, club, or player,
and all journalists are now inundated with mimeographed tables
and notes. This is fine and proper. I may want only one number
for my story: the number of times this season that Omar Moreno
was thrown out trying to steal. But to have it when I want it, I
must be given the full sheet with hundreds of current statistics
about the Pittsburgh Pirates. The statistician can't anticipate what
I may need, he can only give me everything available. But then it
is up to me to be selective enough, and disciplined enough, to *use*
only what I need.

Unlike a child at the dinner table, a reporter is not supposed to clean his plate of all items put before him. But nowadays, what is put on his plate is quite different from what used to be, and the difference leads us to more profound issues concerning the relationship of journalism to the subjects it covers.

15. Relationships

"The interaction leads to a charade. Reporters try to lead players to statements which will confirm the reporters' own preconceptions, and players try to avoid saying anything that will make them look bad ... The players and the reporters are bound together inextricably, like partners in a dance."

— Bill Bradley, 1976

THE RELATIONSHIP between journalists and public-relations people is central to the work of both, and determines more than anything else what information the public receives. But the journalist has other important ongoing relationships that influence the finished product: relationships to confidential news sources, to employers, to colleagues, to the public, and to the sources of profit.

Let's examine each in turn.

PUBLIC RELATIONS

Public-relations people used to be called publicity men, before sexism in language became an issue. The derisive term for them is *flack*. And the designation favored currently is "director of information." Whatever you call it, the task remains the same: to give a business (or government agency, or individual celebrity, or anything else) some measure of control over its contact with the public.

Public relations differs from advertising. In an ad, the space or air time is paid for by the advertiser, and he or she has total control of what the ad says. The price paid for such control is loss of credibility. And public relations also differs from promotion and marketing. These are concerned with direct actions to stimulate sales. But public relations clearly overlaps all of those areas and must be coordinated with them.

In general, the goals of a public-relations program are:

1. To circulate information about the client's activities.
2. To put those activities in a favorable light.
3. To suppress unfavorable information, or deflect criticism.
4. To do whatever is necessary to generate a favorable feeling toward the client in potential customers and in the public as a whole.
5. To attract as much or as little attention as the client desires.

All these goals are easier to attain if the public-relations (PR) person develops a friendly and trustworthy relationship with journalists. By and large, news of the client will originate at irregular intervals with some kind of announcement. Access by journalists to "principals" — company presidents, elected officials, movie stars — is severely limited and is usually available only through PR channels. Written releases, if important enough to be followed up, are the starting point of the reporter's work. Wherever a PR office exists, journalists are almost totally dependent on it unless circumstances warrant a serious and determined effort to bypass it.

In sports, however, the situation is quite different. Sports reporters have firsthand contact with the players and games they cover. News flows according to a schedule known long in advance, and results declare themselves. The event, simply by existing, generates its own publicity and has space allotted to it. Journalists could cover a sport effectively if it had no PR office at all — and they did so for decades while the present system evolved, with only the most primitive "publicity-man" functions being performed by various team officials.

The main function of modern PR in sports, then, is to provide efficient service and keep from losing, by default, the favored journalistic position presently enjoyed by sports. Competing for space isn't a major problem: that's already been determined by the newspaper's or station's policy. Getting favorable impressions isn't really controllable (or important): winning and losing, and star performance, determine that. Defeats can't be suppressed, and victories can't be manufactured (as the "who killed J.R.?" master stroke was manufactured).

This makes for a comfortable relationship that non-sports journalists envy and are eager to consider "corrupt." The beat sports reporter and his club's information director have, in reality, little reason for an adversary relationship, because the essential material the reporter must deal with is accessible to him directly: he can see the game, talk to the coach, study the statistics, and — when necessary — go over the head of the PR department to the club owner or the league, both of whom recognize the fact that they are in the business of making news, and want coverage more than they want any specific content.

There are, of course, situations that call for suppression or manipulation. If the ticket manager is stealing receipts, or the star halfback is involved in a paternity suit, or the team doctor is accused of prescribing drugs too freely, or even if the general manager is simply tired of hearing about what an idiot he is, the publicity man (oops, information director) must try to make his friendly local media people see things the club's way.

But these are peripheral issues, and they come up infrequently in proportion to the amount of time the journalist spends on the beat. When they do come up, the situation is no different from that encountered by any other reporter covering any other subject. But whereas in most non-sports areas, stories become stories only when something remarkable or unpleasant has occurred, in sports the material being covered is routinely benign most of the time.

Thus the PR function in sports is heavily devoted to servicing the media. This means:

• Setting up and operating a comfortable working area for the press, with proper sight lines, table space, phones, electrical connections, television monitors, good lighting, and protection from rain and wind: the famous press box.

• Arranging and distributing credentials that give writers, photographers, and broadcasters access to press box, field, and club-house.

• Supplying factual information in the form of statistics, player biographies, play-by-play, out-of-town scores, and so forth. (The "official" play-by-play account, in football and basketball, is of great value to the reporter because it allows him to watch the action instead of getting bogged down in detailed notes.)

• Answering questions as they arise, and communicating with players, officials, and others during a game for on-the-spot clari-fication of injuries, controversial plays, and so forth.

• Helping line up transportation to and from arenas located where ordinary public transportation is not easily available.

All such things (and the list could be made much longer) are aimed at making it possible for the journalist to do his or her work effectively and to meet deadlines. Does this influence the journalist? Of course it does. In the most favorable way imaginable. It makes the journalist a "friend" of the organi-zation. Does this "friendship" undermine the independence or objectivity of the reporter? Sure, sometimes. That's up to the reporter.

But the real beneficiary of all these devices is not the reporter as a favored individual. It's the paper or station that gets his prod-uct on time and in good shape.

And the publisher and the promoter are allies, remember?

An unskillful information director who doesn't perform these functions smoothly makes enemies for his employer. Is that im-portant? Yes and no. It won't really affect the paper's decision about whether or not to cover the game, and it won't make the re-porter falsify the report. But in all those gray-area instances where a reporter may have a choice — whether or not to come up with an extra feature, or take a legitimately positive view of some-thing that's a little ambiguous, or take the trouble to understand more fully something that seems unfavorable on the surface — sloppy PR work can have a harmful effect.

Does such a setup enable a lazy reporter to drift? And how. Is this "managing the news?" Not if the reporter is conscientious.

At best, the sports reporter and sports publicity man develop mutual trust to a high degree. The reporter expects to be told the

truth when he pursues a subject, to be informed of all general announcements at the same time everyone else is, and to have his
own original ideas (his precious "exclusives") protected. (That is,
the PR man, aware of the story being developed, hasn't the right
to pass it on to someone else — although he can't deny or protect
the story if someone else gets the same idea and asks for information about it.) A sports beat is a twenty-four-hour-a-day proposition, and it would be unreasonable to call the coach or general
manager on the hour every hour to ask if anything is new. The reporter must be able to rely on the PR department to let him know
when anything important happens (a trade, an injury report, a
schedule change), so that he can go about his real task of learning
all he can and reporting what's appropriate.

The PR man, at the same time, has to be able to trust the reporter. He has the right to expect that the reporter won't break
release dates on routine items, that he won't take advantage of
confidences, or of access to private areas, in order to take cheap
shots or sensationalize situations, that he'll treat whatever happens with a reasonable sense of proportion, and that he'll be accurate.

But doesn't all this sound just too, too idealistic and cozy?
What about the free drinks and press-room food? The parties on
the road? The Christmas gifts? The off-the-record revelations that
tie the reporter's hands? The actual bribes and social favors one
hears mentioned so slyly? They all exist. But they are no more or
less common than thievery and venality in other businesses. It
depends entirely on the people involved. The ethics involved will
be discussed in the next chapter, but what should be noted here is
that in all journalist-PR relationships, the primary responsibility
for respectable behavior lies with the journalist. You can't cheat
an honest man, the saying goes, although you can rob him; and
you can't bribe or influence an honest reporter, although you can
certainly mislead and outsmart him. The PR person who lies, tells
half-truths, or lets a reporter get something wrong that could be
corrected is a fool. And the reporter who adulterates information,
for whatever reason, is a knave.

The very aspect of this relationship that non-sports people attack most often is actually its saving grace: its continuity. Because
the beat reporter (and others from his paper) are in daily contact

with the team, there is ample opportunity for either side to get even for any betrayal. He who lies today won't be believed tomorrow. It's similar to the unwritten law that keeps players from purposely maiming dangerous opponents: if you do it to them, they can do it to you. No better formula for reasonable enforceable honesty has yet been devised. In our federal government, it's called checks and balances; in international affairs, it's called mutual deterrence.

CONFIDENTIALITY

The right of a newspaper reporter to refuse to reveal sources has been argued to be a First Amendment right. It follows from the principle we saw earlier, that the only way a reporter can obtain information is through someone else, and if that someone doesn't want to be known, identifying the source will freeze up all possible future sources.

Sports reporters seldom run into situations that require them to face jail to protect a source. But for the reason already stressed — the continuity of beat relationships — observation of the rules of confidentiality is essential.

People have all sorts of ideas, opinions, judgments and intentions that they don't want to see attributed to them in print or on the air. As a reporter, you want to know as many of these things as you can, to increase your understanding of what goes on around you. So you must follow strictly two self-imposed limitations: confidentiality and relevance.

Some of the varieties of confidentiality are:

1. Off the record. Don't say I told you, but use the information if you can substantiate it some other way.
2. Know but don't use. Be aware that such-and-such is the situation, but don't make it public until I say O.K.
3. Not for attribution. Go ahead and use the information the way I'm giving it to you, but don't say it came from me.
4. Private. Here's what happened, but does it really have to be made public?
5. Top secret. If this gets out, I'm finished; let your conscience be your guide.

Every sportswriter knows that the longer he's around, the more people he knows, and the more access he gains to reliable information, the more certain it is that every once in a while he'll be beaten on a story. Someone else will write about something he has known in confidence. That's tough, but the tradeoff is worth it — to the reporter's paper as well as to the reporter personally. He will gain far more, and get more good stories, by maintaining his reputation for integrity than he will lose from occasional embarrassments.

In his relationship to news sources, the ideal journalist observes four "don'ts" along with stubborn devotion to the principles of confidentiality and relevance:

1. Don't take cheap shots.
2. Don't form close friendships.
3. Don't be afraid of arousing anger, but don't pick on people just to show you're not afraid.
4. Don't deny an error, or compound it by looking for justification.

RELATIONSHIP TO EMPLOYERS

Here reporters in the different media are in very different situations. Newspaper reporters have great job security and relatively low pay. They are pretty much on their own within the scope of their assignments, and are at a low level in the publishing hierarchy. Most of their contact is with copy-desk editors and sub-editors, and they get relatively few letters from readers. (Columnists get more.)

Television announcers get high pay and practically no job security. They deal with higher-echelon broadcast executives, advertising people, and sponsors. They are in the volatile world of show business, and can't escape the high-stakes corporate games that come under the heading of office politics. They are guided, restricted, and judged in every word and gesture. They reflect the policies of networks, sponsors, and ball clubs, rather than their own views. They draw large mail response and published criticism.

Radio announcers are somewhere in between, but much closer to television announcers than to newspaper reporters.

Magazines are run by committees. Writers either fit the pre-conceptions of the editor to a high degree or are edited merci-lessly to conform. Most magazine writers are free-lancers, which means that they sell each of their articles independently, wher-ever they can, so they are completely subject to editorial whim.

RELATIONSHIP TO COLLEAGUES

The same differences apply here. Newspaper sports reporters generally share routine information, spend much of the year in the company of a few others on the same beat, and have less con-tact with other members of their own staffs than with fellow beat reporters from other papers. There is some competition for fresh angles and unrevealed information, but not much, because the PR system sees to it that everybody gets everything, and because most cities don't have truly competitive papers. There is more pressure to avoid missing what others have than there is to de-velop something others don't. (A writer who has the knack and stomach for consistently sensationalizing whatever is available, however, can build a fast-rising career, if he has employers who want that.)

Television people are usually transients, moving from one weekend or major event to another. They have no competition with each other, because most televised events are the exclusive property of a particular network or station. They spend much more time with their own technical and business people, and with the athletes they cover, than with newspaper reporters.

Radio play-by-play announcers also have no internal competi-tion, but are closely related to beat writers in working patterns and social contacts. Like newspaper writers and unlike television people, they have to live with their mistakes.

Jealousy and ego are prominent in all fields, and the six-month season on any beat gives more opportunity for low-level irritabil-ity with one's fellows than is present in other journalistic as-signments. But the print and broadcast media have some areas of true conflict.

One such source of conflict is time, where the electronics media win, hands down. The play-by-play is live. But postgame interviews, on tape, are aired within minutes. If a writer and a broadcaster get the same statement from a player at the same instant, it is fairly useless to the writer. And if the writer wants to pursue an idea that he doesn't want the broadcaster to pick up for free, he must wait until he can get the player away from a microphone. He may or may not have time to do that, depending on his deadlines.

Another area of conflict involves time in a different sense. The interviewer with the microphone has only so long to record the interviewee's voice and can't really follow up on any complex idea. The newspaper reporter can (at least the PM paper's reporter can), and thus can develop a more thorough and more enlightening story, moving from one source to another.

At the really big events — Super Bowl, World Series, Kentucky Derby, Olympics — the conflicting needs of the various media lead to real bitterness: shoving and pushing, bad language, and ill feeling that settles into a permanent animosity. Not only the mechanics but the purposes are in conflict. The print people want material for a good story when the event is over. The electronic world needs a good show now. The newspaper wants the hero's words; radio and television need his voice. The optimum value of a story in print lies in how much it can explain; radio and television depend on delivering "conflict."

At this point, jealousy and ego enter the picture. Newspaper reporters envy the money made by broadcasters, on the false premise that they are doing the same job. Broadcasters envy the freedom and image of objectivity newspaper journalists enjoy, on the false premise that they, like the newspaper journalists, are reporters. The truth is, reporters report and broadcasters sell products. Each gets paid accordingly.

RELATIONSHIP TO THE PUBLIC

The journalist — newspaper, magazine, radio news show, or even television news show — has one thing to offer: a reputation for integrity. He or she is the fan's surrogate, going where the fan can't go, telling the fan what the fan can't find out for himself.

The play-by-play or network broadcaster offers personality and performer star quality.

The print reporter is relatively anonymous, even when his by-line is familiar to regular readers. He is his *paper* rather than himself. The institution outshines the individual. People say "The *New York Times* said . . ." or *"Sports Illustrated* said . . ." more often than they attribute a story to a particular reporter by name. But in radio and television, the individual outshines the institution. People say "Howard Cosell said . . ." or "Lindsey Nelson said . . ." rather than "ABC said . . ." or "KNBR said . . ."

So it is not surprising that the autograph seekers clustered around a ballpark's clubhouse hound broadcasters as often and as intensely as athletes, while few recognize, or care, which writers walk past. The same is true in restaurants, airports, hotels, and on the street. Broadcasters are celebrities. That is their burden. Reporters are unidentifiable working stiffs. That is their glory.

RELATIONSHIP TO PROFIT

Personal careers, as well as working habits, differ from one medium to another because of the different sources of profit involved. Newspapers are ranked according to circulation, which can be measured accurately and objectively. They get circulation by carrying out a strategy of touching all bases — satisfying the relatively small contituencies devoted to each different section of the paper, in order to attract a large aggregate readership. A clear line is drawn between advertising (even house ads) and editorial matter. Any one writer, no matter how brilliant, is not terribly important in the scheme of things (with rare exceptions). The real payoff, in newspapers, is for managerial skills. These are necessary to ensure the profitability of the enterprise and are the path to higher-level careers. Few sportswriters climb that path.

Radio and television programs are judged by ratings, which are statistical projections of small samples and are notoriously unreliable, despite the fact that executives stubbornly adhere to the self-serving excuse that "it's all we have." To get high ratings requires promotional skills and attention-getting on-the-air "tal-

ent," so celebrity status pays off. Networks can hire a celebrity
(Joe Namath, as soon as his playing career ends) or create their
own (Vin Scully), but only a personality that in some way turns
on the public will win in the ratings war. Meanwhile, countless
plugs blur the line between advertising and program content, so
that the announcer's personality affects both.

•

What does all this mean to the sports consumer? A newspaper
woos the readership with reliability and thoroughness, and hires
people who strive in that direction. A broadcast tries to dazzle
and fascinate the audience enough to keep it glued to the set, and
hires people who can help create that effect. Both are remarkably
successful.

16. Ethics

"Thou shalt not bear false witness against thy neighbor."
— Exodus 20:16

SINCE WATERGATE, a wave of indiscriminate ethical consciousness has swept through America, and Journalism, with a capital J, has been inundated. Sensitive to attacks on the press openly orchestrated by the first Nixon administration, and accordingly feeling a trifle guilty at their successful role in Nixon's downfall, publishers and newspaper executives hastened to assure the public that the high moral standards their editorials demanded of others would be observed in their own business.

In sports, however, the holier-than-thou pursuit of ethical purity had earlier beginnings. In the original publisher-promoter alliance, the idea of fair exchange developed early. The promoter wanted stories on his road games to appear in his hometown papers because these constituted free advertising for future home games (and were much better than ads, because they were more interesting and credible than blurbs about tickets). The papers (there were usually at least five or six in a major-league city, and as many as twelve in New York) wanted to cover road games because their readers were equally interested in the team's activities wherever a game happened to be played.

But traveling for six months with a baseball team is an expensive proposition for a newspaper sports department's budget. Some papers were hesitant, some flat-out couldn't afford it, and some were pefectly content to do without. The club, however, was only too happy to pick up the tab. Few papers, during the World War I era, saw any ethical problem in this. They could have forced or subtly pressured the ball club into buying ads at regular rates, and earmarked that money for writers' travel expenses. But they recognized the barter that was involved: the club, by paying for the traveling, was in effect paying for some of the free news space it would not otherwise get.

This was obviously more important to the less affluent papers, but in a competitive situation it was that much more important not to let coverage (and circulation) be entirely at the mercy of the budget. So picking up the tab was an accepted practice.

As new sports began to fight for newspaper space, new promoters followed baseball's lead. They offered trips, free tickets, and even supplied stories — anything to get their piece of the sports-page space. They could also use outright bribery. A few bucks to the make-up man, or the sports editor, assured an item about next Tuesday's boxing card, or a picture from the racetrack. Hiring a writer to do "publicity" or statistics or to edit a program made him an ally. In small towns, and on smaller papers in larger towns, this kind of side income for sports editors was cynically winked at as part of the package, no more honorable but no less common than local political graft.

But there's an important difference between bribes and expenses. The bribe, in one way or another, goes directly to the writer or editor who makes a decision about what will appear in the paper. The travel costs are a matter between two corporations, and of no real concern to the person choosing today's paper's content.

Stanley Woodward was one of the legendary sports editors of the mid-century era. At the *New York Herald Tribune* during the 1940s, he was the most respected man in his profession. In 1948, after being fired at the *Tribune* over policy conflicts with higher brass about what should be covered and what shouldn't, he wrote a book entitled *Sports Page.* Here's what he had to say about travel expenses:

> For years it was the custom of newspapers to accept the hospitality of baseball clubs ... Many still permit it ... Others pay full

expenses wherever the baseball writer goes ... It is certainly bad practice ... Most papers don't do it any more and I'm glad of it, but the deal was, or is, between the newspaper and the ball club and therefore should have no effect on the work of the reporter ...

I have always rationalized the deal as follows: You are not the guest of the ball club. You have nothing whatever to do with the deal. The arrangement is between your newspaper and the club. There are no strings on you, so write anything you want. You are a free agent.

When we changed policy and started paying our own expenses, it made no difference to the writer. He went on as before, only now the ball club sent a bill to his office, which the sports editor okayed and passed on for payment ... Everything was the same except the bookkeeping. I can't say that the departure has changed baseball writing an iota. It was always generally honest and critical. It has become neither more honest nor more critical. Long ago the ball clubs stopped trying to control the writers they transported.

I suppose that we have advanced the principles of our profession, but I was always fearful that the management would cite the tremendous expense of covering baseball as a reason for not spending money for covering something else.

That was more than thirty years ago, but the description is as true as ever. As a writer on the road, I couldn't care less who paid my bills, as long as it wasn't me: my thought did not go beyond the fact that *my paper sent me.* Which corporation eventually deducted the expense from profits made no difference to my attitudes.

And in the paragraph following those quoted above, Woodward put his finger on the real problem:

The baseball writer's danger never was that he would find himself under obligations to a bookkeeping system — rather that he would become so attached to an athletic organization and so close to its performing members that he would get out of focus on the picture he was trying to make.

In journalism, ethics and morality must be judged by *content:* what is published. In politics and business, it is reasonable enough to assume that "He who pays, influences; he who accepts payment acquires obligation." But this is not a reasonable or even relevant standard to apply to news coverage. In news coverage, what is at issue is independence of judgment and accuracy of reportage, and money is seldom the medium of control.

What the journalist reports is out in the open for all to read and hear and see, and to check on every day against other sources of information — especially in the case of sports. What's written is correct or it isn't, within the natural limits of ambiguity.

A writer who roots too hard for his favorite player, or vents his spleen at a manager he doesn't like, is not made more objective or ethical by having the ball club bill his paper for his expenses. But the danger that the report will be biased in favor of the people the writer lives among, and gets to like, is very real. It must be guarded against and counteracted by a change of assignment or an explicit warning, if there is a basis for such action in what the writer says in print.

Here we have the built-in, perpetual dilemma. To know more, you have to be around more; but the more you're around, the more you come to share the viewpoint of the people you cover. Up to a certain point, sharing that viewpoint *increases* the accuracy of your information: ignorance is no proof of impartiality. But beyond that point, being too close to the trees to see the forest can warp your judgment in three ways: by engaging your emotions on a sympathetic level, by lulling you into taking for granted a familiar situation that is not so familiar to outsiders, and by making you reluctant or afraid to give offense to those who have become long-time companions.

There is absolutely no solution to this problem, in theory. It is the ethical analogue of Heisenberg's uncertainty principle in physics: the act of observation alters the event observed. To the extent that you can exactly measure one quantity (position), you make accordingly vague some other quantity (momentum). You can maximize access to information at the cost of some fuzziness in objectivity, and you can achieve complete objectivity with total absence of information. The practical answer is vigilance and intelligent choices about which element — information or noninvolvement — is more important to the subject at hand.

I believe, therefore, that the *ethics* of journalism are not closely connected to sources of money. The same high-ranking editorial officials who refuse free plane rides to events their readers would like to know about, and who bar their employees from writing "program pieces," boast that their paper's editorial integrity is not affected by millions of dollars worth of advertising. If they can resist being corrupted by oil companies and department stores, why should they worry that one of their sportswriters — whose product they can examine every day and who can be discharged or disciplined any time they choose — will be corrupted by a free hot dog or a beer?

The same applies to all the questions raised about press-box and press-room food, complimentary tickets, and other modest perks the beat reporter acquires. As customs, they arose naturally from the working conditions. (A baseball writer, for instance, often spends eight or more consecutive hours in a ballpark and couldn't go out to lunch if he wanted to.) As a practical matter, ball clubs use the respectable title of "press room" (with its tax-deduction legitimacy) to cover what is really a hospitality room for club employees, nonjournalistic visitors, business associates, advertising executives, celebrities, and so on — a mix of people, incidentally, that is very valuable to the reporter's information-gathering process.

But on *ethical* grounds, the damage is done as soon as a paper accepts a working press ticket, a parking pass, the physical layout of a press box, the installation of communications wires, and so forth. To be *ethically* pure, a paper would have to send its reporter to stand in line, get a general admission ticket (which may be behind a post), keep all his own statistical records, interview players at their homes, and always return to the office (or at least leave the ballpark) to file his story. No integrity-crazed newspaper executive has yet demanded that. But a sports promoter spends much more money on building, staffing, and policing "working facilities" than on "entertaining the press."

Similar considerations apply to signed articles that appear in programs (since the writer's integrity is on the line for what he or she says) and, in what has become a major bugaboo during the last twenty years, having writers serve as official scorers. This practice, in major-league baseball, goes back almost a century. It is rooted in the idea that a club or league employee can't be trusted to make impartial decisions about hits and errors affecting his club. From the league's point of view, it would be better to hire unaffiliated scorers, such as umpires; but that would be much more expensive than paying a few dollars to a writer who's already on the scene. (What the league really needs, and is paying for, is the form that has to be filled out and filed; it is much more important than actual decisions about hits and errors.) But the paper should be only too happy to have its representative publicly certified as objective enough to do the job. The source of payment — from the league office through the Baseball Writers Association of America to the writer — is of even less relevance than travel expenses. In fact, the writers, through their association, make the scoring assignments, not the clubs or leagues, so even the writer whose prime motive is to get the money must satisfy his *colleagues* rather than the people he covers.

When the money question is put aside, however, a legitimate ethical point arises. We have already noted that good journalism demands staying out of the story you're covering. A writer as official scorer is part of the story of every potential no-hit game, and every controversial call on a key play. For that reason alone, it is best not to have him score. But that's not the reason given by papers that forbid their employees to score. (This particular problem of maintaining proper distance from the event being covered could be solved by having the writer score only on days when he or she is not covering that game.)

So false issues abound in the ethical areas of sports coverage, because so little attention is paid to the way things really work. A play-by-play broadcaster is often paid, and invariably approved, by the club whose games he covers. Does he, for that reason, say the team won when it lost, or call an enemy home run out? Of course not. But he doesn't endlessly second-guess the manager, either, unless the club management wants him to (to stimulate interest). Could it be any other way? The club has sold an *exclusive* right to broadcast its games. Would it allow this special weapon to be used against its interests? Would you, in that position? By the same token, newspaper reporters aren't likely to write, "This paper had an outrageously misleading headline and two terrible typographical errors in yesterday's sports page" — and no one expects them to.

What, then, are the authentic ethical obligations in journalism, specifically in sports journalism?

• Getting it right is the first and foremost obligation, in every sense, at every level.

• Observing confidentiality.

• Recognizing privacy, by applying the test of relevance.

• Rejecting real, as distinct from *pro forma,* conflict of interest. Doing publicity work, accepting gifts of significant value, taking bribes, and going on payrolls for "advisory" duties are examples of true conflicts of interest. Selling the products of your expertise — program stories, statistical services, public-speaking appearances, official-scoring services — honestly and openly, to legitimate purchasers, is not a conflict of interest in any meaningful sense.

• Striving for honest evaluation, regardless of who may be hurt.

• Avoiding damage to anyone by careless, inaccurate, or vindictive evaluation.

• Weighing as seriously and as solemnly as you can the relative claims of the public's right to know against common decency and the subject's individual rights. In journalism, the decision will often go against common decency, and certainly a professional entertainer has chosen to waive many private rights. But failure to *consider* the issue, or hiding behind "the right to know" and using it as an automatic cop-out, is unethical.

Finally, there is a significant difference between sports news and general news in societal terms. The American journalistic tradition of adversary relationship between reporter and subject grew out of dealings with government. It is a cornerstone of democracy, and the idea behind the First Amendment's free-press provisions. People in political office, and those seeking it, are in a position to misuse public funds, misapply coercive power, manipulate legislation, and alter people's lives. The press is the public's watchdog, a protection against abuses not only when it uncovers them but also by its threat to do so. Those who represent the press in this task *must* have, to a degree at least, an adversary relationship with their subjects.

But mass-entertainment professional sports are *not* a government activity. They aren't even a life-necessity product in the private sector. They are diversions, of value only to those who enjoy them and only so long as they provide enjoyment. This makes the adversary relationship less fundamental. It's still there, but it's not as important and not as frequently an issue. A bad decision by a football coach does not affect the body politic in the same way a bad decision by a judge or legislator does. Giving out a false story about what a star athlete gets paid is not the same as misappropriating school funds. A ball-field brawl between two teams is not the same as a ghetto riot, or police brutality, or picket-line violence. Monopolistic ticket prices are quite different from monopolistic fuel-oil prices. A bad call by a referee is not the same as sending an innocent person to prison.

Journalism's role in uncovering wrongdoing and deterring those in power from excess, by threat of exposure, gets precious little scope in sports entertainment. As we have seen, the sports business cannot even exist unless a large public accepts it as satisfying a voluntary pleasure-seeking impulse. After all, it *is,* when all is said and done, fun and games. And journalism, whether it likes it or not, is part of the fun.

As an ideal, the "ferret-out-wrongdoers" impulse is just as valid for sports as for anything else journalism treats. But in practice, and in the context of sports activity, how much "wrongdoing" can there be? When games are fixed, people steal, or an assault takes place, the occurrence becomes, almost by definition, a non-sports story, and it is certainly treated as such. But within the sports field, as we have defined it, outrageous revelations are hard to come by. The politician and the businessman want to use the press to tell their side of the story, and have a great deal more they want to keep secret. But the sports promoter (as distinct from any particular athlete) is in the business of giving people as much information as he can about his activities; and the press is his ally, not his enemy, in that pursuit.

To a great degree, then, sports journalists and sports promoters really do have a common interest: the generation of more and more entertaining material about something that doesn't *really* matter too much. Unlike his or her non-sports colleagues, the sports reporter is likely to be swamped with too much information, and must pay more attention to selecting sensibly than to digging out hidden facts. And that's where we find the ethical obligation that is valid in more areas of life than just journalism: keep a sense of proportion.

PART III

The Cultural Interaction

17. Reflection and Reinforcement

WIDESPREAD EXAMINATION of how our culture is affected by our interest in mass spectator sports began in the 1960s, in the climate of questioning and rebelliousness that coincided with the Vietnam era. Comment on this interaction has always been plentiful, and one can find it in the writings of Mark Twain, George Bernard Shaw, and countless other social critics. But these were invariably personal observations presented as such. They didn't attempt systematic sociological analysis or research, and they didn't relate their conclusions to current political and economic questions.

In the 1960s, however, many professional economists, sociologists, psychiatrists, psychologists, and historians turned their attention to "the impact of sports on society." College courses blossomed, seminars and panel discussions proliferated, congressional hearings and legal briefs produced mountains of material, journalists offered instant profundity, and men of important intellectual standing (such as philosopher Paul Weiss and novelist James Michener) took the time to write books on the subject.

Several distinct positions emerged. The political Left, by and large, believed that sports "caused" various attitudes and practices and "indoctrinated" the population (especially through children) in the acceptance of a status quo favored by the existing "power structure," which maintained this system consciously for its selfish purposes.

The logical consequence of this belief is: changing attitudes about sports can "cause" changes in society. The practical problem then becomes: how to marshal the attention-attracting capability of sports in order to espouse new and desired attitudes, once we decide exactly what changes we want.

The political Right, along with many nonpolitical sports fans, believed that sports represented one of the glories of American democracy. They considered competitiveness, team loyalty, preoccupation with success, insistence on fair play, and physical exertion to be basic virtues of free enterprise, traditional family morality, and the Puritan ethic. They saw the "character building" of athletes, the "complete equality" of players chosen on the basis of ability, the "healthy" interest of spectators, and the "keep boys out of trouble by playing ball instead of joining street gangs" syndrome as surviving virtues in a culture otherwise besieged by foreign and malevolent influences.

The logical consequence of this belief is: protection of this remnant of pure "Americanism" from adulteration by "political" considerations, and promotion, as much as possible, of participation in this preferable cultural activity.

Centrist liberalism, which was the country's majority view at that time, took an intermediate position. It acknowledged that, to a degree, spectator sports might be "an opiate of the people" when overemphasized. But the achievements of the post–World-War-II years — the breaking of the color line in professional sports, the opening of college opportunities to athletic blacks, the economic benefits of major-league expansion, the free entertainment supplied by television — were worth the risk, and outweighed any damage. The logical consequence here is: a successful system is allowed to operate and keep growing in the "right" direction, as it has done for twenty years. Sports attitudes *do* "cause" social change, but they don't need conscious leadership because they are contributing to the gradual change that is coming about anyhow.

Religious fundamentalists (overwhelmingly Christian, but with a significant segment of Moslem converts in the black community) found in sports a "sin-free" recreational environment that did not conflict as much with morality as the sex-and-drugs elements that were emerging so openly in other forms of entertainment. The logical consequence: support and protection from change of this island of acceptability in an otherwise deteriorating world and use of it as a wedge for evangelical messages if possible.

And advocates of "personal fulfillment," in whatever form, saw widespread interest in sports as a wedge of another kind: watchers could be persuaded to become participants. The consequence: such groups probe for and expound the mystical elements of everything from jogging to batting averages, and thereby find a handle to "turn on" converts to whichever mysticism they're selling.

All these views were flawed in at least one important respect. Sports *reflect* social conditions; they don't *cause* them. They certainly *reinforce* various attitudes that society has built into them, but those attitudes originate in what the public is responsive to. Sports have the form they have because they satisfy that response; they don't *impose* or *invent* a response, conspiratorially or otherwise. What's more, sports have the form they have because they were shaped by the society in which they developed — and in which they continue to develop, day by day.

The distinction between cause and reinforcement is important. Whenever society changes, sports change, but while both changes are slowed down by the forces of tradition, of which spectator sports is one powerful example, sports don't *initiate* change.

Evidence of this is not hard to find. Half a century ago, in 1930, such events as the Intercollegiate Rowing Regatta at Poughkeepsie (for eight-oared crew), international polo matches, the U.S. amateur golf championship, yacht races other than the America's Cup, and championship prize fights in the lighter weight divisions got major sports-page attention. They no longer do, but not because a cabal of plutocratic manipulators decided against them, or because their inherent virtues lessened, or because they were undemocratic in theory, or because they were more sinful than the sports that did maintain preeminence (such as baseball, college football, heavyweight boxing, horse racing, and track and field). They faded in importance because the total social fabric in which they functioned changed.

There are still eight-oared crews competing for the college

championship (and in the Olympics), but there is no longer a special society glamour attached to Eastern college families. The social class that could maintain and master polo ponies has disappeared. Golf (like tennis) has become dominated by professionals. The ghetto life that produced thousands of boxers is gone, replaced by another type of ghetto that turns out basketball players. And the very fact that there are many more people who today can afford to enjoy sailing and boating reflects the economic changes that robbed yachting of its special status.

At the same time, in 1930, there was no intersectional college basketball, no stable professional basketball, no generally accepted professional football, no golf or tennis tour, and no harness racing beyond the county-fair level. That was because the social and economic conditions for their development had not yet evolved. Basketball needed large arenas (which the introduction of ice hockey and the popularity of boxing brought about in a few key cities). The explosion of the college population after World War II, a consequence of the GI bill, set the stage for the flow of basketball and football talent into the pros. Golf became tied to real-estate promotion. Pari-mutuel betting on thoroughbreds, which showed states how much tax money they could collect, led to similar arrangements, and the construction of tracks, for harness racing. Then of course, came television.

We have seen, in Parts I and II, what the true *conscious* purposes of sports promoters and media marketers are: to turn an honest profit in an entrepreneurial context, and to help it along with as much monopoly as they can obtain. But we have also seen that sports entertainment, in particular, is enormously sensitive to public whim, and is entirely at the mercy of the ticket-buyers of a *non-necessity*. Newspapers aren't quite as sensitive, but broadcasters are at the mercy of the ratings system even more than sports promoters. And we have seen what alliances these interests form.

To argue that sports lead, rather than follow, public fashion simply ignores reality. The "all-powerful networks" have not been able to sell soccer to a wide enough public, in three tries during the course of a dozen years; and the death of baseball, so widely predicted and even declared a decade ago, has not materialized. Powerful as the media are, they are powerful as amplifiers, not originators.

Yet, there is also some validity in each of the positions we have mentioned, once the cause-and-effect relationship is put in proper perspective. Sports are a tremendous force for the status quo, because continuity and coherence are so large a part of the enjoyment involved (for reasons we'll explore in the next chapter). They *do* distract millions from more serious thoughts — as do murder mysteries, sexy movies, rock music, science fiction, and all other "escape" entertainments. As mass entertainment, they are definitely an antirevolutionary force.

Why be surprised, then, that established institutions and the nonrevolutionary mass of the population support and reinforce sports? After all, most of the continuing mechanisms of any society — schools, churches, governments, courts, businesses — are *intended* to stabilize, reindoctrinate, and keep change within the bounds of gradualism. If it's revolution you want, don't expect these institutions to help you.

Now it's true that if you can seize control of such institutions, you can direct them toward the changes you want. You can seize newspapers, radio stations, military bases, and legislatures; but you can't seize a *voluntary* entertainment as long as it remains voluntary. First you have to establish a system of coercion; then you can dictate attitudes and activities. And in such an eventuality, sports entertainment will serve the new status quo as efficiently as it did the old. In Nazi Germany and the Soviet Union, no less than in America or Britain or Japan, sports have served and reinforced whatever society they inhabit.

As propaganda, then, the attachment of political causes to sports events is usually self-defeating in American society. The sports fan's attitude is, "Don't mess up my entertainment with your message." Whether it's a black-power salute in the 1968 Olympics, a boycott of South Africa, a United States boycott of the Moscow Olympics, an assertion of women's rights, or objection to the use of an American Indian as a team emblem, it is likely to be counterproductive as a means of getting a sympathetic hearing from the mass of sports fans and the general public, even among many who agree with the cause in question.

Does this mean such activity is futile? Not at all. It may well be one step in a larger process of shaping opinion, and may have other political benefits. Sports are no more immune than other areas of life to being used as *weapons,* and crusaders habitually use whatever comes to hand. What should be noted, however, is the limited utility of sports as an instrument. Crusaders shouldn't expect too much from it, and noncrusaders should not overreact in their irritation or fear.

Does that imply, in turn, that efforts at sociological analysis are wasted, pointless, or misguided? Quite the opposite. They can be valuable indeed, if they deal accurately with how things work, because understanding how we operate can tell us what we are. Precisely because mass-entertainment sports do reflect our social values, their highly visible manifestations can illuminate the true nature of those values.

But journalism — daily or weekly journalism, that is — can't perform that analytic function to any appreciable depth. Journalism is a craft, not a science. Its practitioners are analogous to carpenters rather than atomic engineers, ward nurses rather than brain surgeons, cops on the beat rather than general-staff military planners, plumbers rather than designers of hydroelectric plants.

As such, journalists are part of the establishment's reinforcement process when they deal with sports; they can't be otherwise. A skilled machanic is expected to keep your automobile in running order; you don't go to him if you want to redesign the public transportation system. When and if the social structure does get redesigned, however, it will take electricians, carpenters, and mechanics to make it work — just as they make what we have now work.

So theoreticians, academics, political activists, and social critics have their proper roles in dealing with spectator sports, as with anything else — but not on the daily level. And they can't be effective by accepting superficial myths. The accuracy of their conclusions can't be any greater than the thoroughness and accuracy of their observations.

18. The Sources of Appeal

IF OUR DESCRIPTIONS of the sports and journalism businesses are correct, and our approach to their functions valid, what can be said about the power of this entertainment's appeal? Why do sports spectacles get such a large share of America's attention?

At the very start, we enumerated the elements that make fandom attractive, but we did that from the promoter's point of view. The promoter seeks to use these to maximize his success, or at least to coast along on their by-products.

Now let's examine the same elements to determine their effect on our society, from the consumer's vantage point. Essentially, they fill vacuums. They supply satisfactions that are not only difficult to come by in other ways, but deeply craved. If the kind of sports establishment we're familiar with didn't exist, we would have to invent something else to supply the same satisfactions. The fact is, we *did* invent this.

Let's rearrange our list of appealing elements this way:

1. Rooting interest
2. Hero worship
3. Reliving earlier pleasure
4. Participation in mass (or even mob) activity
5. Medium for common discourse

These elements have a common thread. They are the stuff that goes into the formation of "community consciousness," "consensus," or "shared values." Every society has mechanisms to generate such feelings, and discharge them. Among such mechanisms are a native language, religion, national identity, caste, historical tradition, common danger or other intense experience, uniform schooling and folk culture, and well-defined political structure.

American life has been notably deficient in such customary cultural glue since the middle 1800s. That deficiency has had numerous beneficial consequences, and accounts for the diversity, pluralism, upward mobility, intellectual freedom, and other characteristics that have made American life notably different from European and other older cultures. But it is a deficiency, and sports has turned out to be a peculiarly appropriate artificial binding agent.

The British are highly conscious of themselves as an "island people." The French language forms an exceptionally strong bond for the French. The Russians, once so unambiguously bound to the czar, have no less doubt about their exact relationship to the soviet state. In the emerging nations of Africa, the suppression of cultural identifications in the past, and the struggle to build them now, are recognized as fundamental problems.

But Americans, as they poured across the ocean and spread westward through the wilderness, did not come with one language, one religion, one history, one ethnic stock, or one outlook. And as they settled, they did so in fantastically different environments, confronting differences in climate, terrain, crops, economic necessities, establishments of law and order, and political organizations. Nor did they seek homogeneity in these respects. The "melting pot" concept prevailed to a point, but Americans also took pride in local control and independence. Schools were determinedly secular and localized. High fashion and high culture had little impact (and therefore little unifying force) on the frontier or in areas of explosive urban industrialization.

The founding fathers, predominately English, had a common bond to the throne, even in their opposition to it. But a couple of generations later, even that was gone. The things that were America's own, and distinctive, became incomparably diverse. Something had to fill the gap. And what could do so more easily than a town ball game against a neighboring town, or racing one horse against another, or a wrestling match or sharpshooting contest?

To a nineteenth-century Englishman, being English had deeper meaning than being from Yorkshire or Cornwall, even though local pride existed. But to Americans, local and regional ties had more reality than the rather abstract idea of nationhood, which impinged on daily life to a lesser degree. Rooting for a local contestant, then, was an ideal outlet for feelings that had relatively little else to attach themselves to.

It is probably not a coincidence that baseball, the first mass-entertainment sport, blossomed right after the Civil War. That war made nationhood a central issue, but it also cemented regionalism. When it ended, the restored Union entered an era of unprecedented growth and power, totally free of any outside threat, that lasted two generations (until World War I). In that context, the newly organized baseball games offered a perfect balance. In rules and strategy, the game itself was "universal," accepted and understood in exactly the same terms in every corner of the country; and it was uniquely American. But the individual teams and leagues served as ideal focal points for local loyalties and the harmless discharge of regional rivalry. So, to put it badly, rooting interest took root.

And shortly after 1900, when our old friend Albert G. Spalding, as an elder statesman, felt that a formal historical record of baseball's origins had to be established, he threw his influence behind a flimsy myth about one Abner Doubleday as a teenager in Cooperstown, New York, in 1839. The myth went virtually unchallenged until the 1950s, and it accounts for the location of the Baseball Hall of Fame in Cooperstown today. Baseball actually derives from various English bat-and-ball games, including rounders and cricket, and was acquiring distinctive characteristics in New England in the 1700s. But to Spalding and many of his contemporaries, it seemed essential, emotionally, to establish for baseball a nationalistic pedigree free of "foreign" derivation.

Attached to school teams as well as club and town-name teams, this variation of patriotic passions can be exercised in a nation that has no royal family, no threatening neighbors, and a steady influx of immigrants who can pick up this point of reference quickly and easily.

A similar dynamic exists with respect to heroes and role models. Many countries have a centuries-old supply of kings, sol-

diers, holy men, artists, and scientists to draw upon, and a literature about them that is familiar from childhood on. Only a few
emerge as legendary figures in the national imagination (as
George Washington is in ours), but let's consider some dates:
King Arthur (real or not), 600; Charlemagne, 800; Robin Hood,
1200; Luther, 1500; Shakespeare, 1600; Newton, 1700; or even
Bach, who died in 1750. The United States didn't even exist while
these men were alive.

What's more, our political leaders have always been proudly
painted as "ordinary" men: any boy could grow up to be president. Our only important military actions were against over-
matched Indians or Mexicans and against ourselves (in the Civil
War), except for the War of 1812 (which gave us our "Star-Span-
gled Banner"). Not until Thomas Edison do we find a civilian
admiration figure widely perceived as such. The pool from which
to draw heroes was a small one.

Again, sports easily and naturally filled the vacuum. The activity was plentiful. The newspapers and telegraph wires spread
fame. Success was clearly defined. Attachment to a sports figure
involved little conflict with other identifications (national origin,
religion, political affiliation) that might cause discomfort in one
region or another. And the achievements of the hero could be accepted on the impeccably high plane of sportsmanship, without
any touchy philosophic questions about war, property, or relation
to God.

Next we come to a bonanza: the ability to grasp and enjoy
sports while still a child. If sports are pleasurable then, they not
only can remain pleasurable later, but, when experienced later,
they set up echoes of earlier happy times. Every person has some
pleasant experiences from childhood that are remembered and
idealized, and other unpleasant experiences that are suppressed.
Unpleasant ones may become attached to a sports activity, but
then that person is not likely to grow up to be a fan. For the vast
majority of fans, sports memories are the self-selected pleasant
ones.

When a promoter sells you a ticket to tomorrow's ball game, he
is also selling you a three-hour segment of a replay of some former personal happiness. On the conscious level, this comes from
memory, thanks to the built-in continuity and coherence of

sports; but it may be that the subconscious effect, the aura felt by a ten-year-old taken by a parent or grandparent to an exciting place full of hot dogs and popcorn, is even stronger.

And this touches upon another ever-present human feeling: togetherness. People enjoy gathering in large groups for a common purpose. Apart from their spiritual content, religious services satisfy this urge. At various times in various places, parades, political rallies, conventions, coronations, and street festivals also cater to this desire. In American history, the pomp of royalty and militarism, the elaborate pageants of papal Catholicism, and other forms of traditional ritual have taken a relatively small position. The sports event — especially the Saturday afternoon high school or college football game, and the season-ending climaxes like the World Series — provided the occasion for such social interaction. And it had the added advantage of requiring no disciplined, studied response from the assembled crowd, as a religious ritual might. Instead, the sports event provided the opportunity to yell and scream and feel strongly, in a perfectly acceptable setting. If you doubt the power of such feelings, look at a newsreel of some of Hitler's speech/rallies. The similarities — and differences — between such a rally and a football cheering section are worth pondering.

All this, of course, contributes to a reservoir of conversation. Talking about sports is a topic of common interest in essentially impersonal social contacts. Every culture must have such a medium of exchange. In farming areas, it might be the weather. In England, it might be some gossipy item about the royal family. In literary circles, it might be a quote from Shakespeare (or, in Italy, a quote from Dante or an opera).

In America, thanks to the journalistic machine and the shortage of other guaranteed "safe" topics, spectator sports have become this subject of common discourse, of icebreaking or time-passing conversation, even among those who do not care deeply about the sports themselves. "Don't argue politics or religion" is a time-honored guideline for arm's-length etiquette. A literary allusion may be taken, in some circles, as an attempt at a put-down by an intellectual elitist. An inappropriate comment may reveal the speaker to be a clod. But rarely will anyone be insulted by "Do you think the Yankees will win the Series again?" or seriously embarrassed upon learning they've already been eliminated.

Incidentally, just how tenuous the relationship can be between the content of a conversation and the actual words uttered was demonstrated by a young baseball writer named Vic Ziegel, when he made his first trip with the Yankees in the late 1960s. Having heard stories, he was eager to get his share of the high living suggested by the words "on the road" — especially with the Yankees.

The first stop was Kansas City. There was a bar across the street from the hotel. That was the bar to go to for action, Vic was told. Sure enough, seated on a stool, unquestionably unaccompanied, was a lovely girl.

Vic searched his mind for exactly the right approach. It had to be casual, neutral, and polite, yet it had to require an answer and be intriguing enough to lead to longer discussion. He remembered that he had just seen, on a newsstand, that day's Kansas City paper, with a headline saying "Vote Today on Water Fluoridation." So he said: "What do you think of fluoridation?" And she said: "I'm sorry, I'm waiting for someone." She understood perfectly. He did too.

Opening with "Do you think the Yankees will win?" would not have got him any further, but since few Americans have as lively an imagination as Vic Ziegel, many rely on remarks about sports for harmless openers.

With so much going for it, the sports establishment's power and stability should not surprise anyone. It would be astounding if things were otherwise. All the tendencies just discussed are heightened by national television for the major events, and are subtly altered by it for more local events, but the roots go so deep that only the direction of the outer branches is seriously affected.

As our society changes, the detailed map of the sports scene will change. But there is no indication that the extent or intensity of America's interest in this type of entertainment will diminish in any way, nor is there the slightest sign that the "entrenched" sports — major-league baseball, professional and major-college football, horse racing, championship boxing, and, at a lower level, basketball and hockey — will yield their preeminence.

19. The Poison of Amateurism

ONE CONCEPT peculiar to sports deserves condemnation.

It is called *amateurism*. Amateurism has been pumping a poisonous hypocrisy through American society for more than a century, and continues to do so. Almost all the harmful effects of the sports establishment can be traced to this misnamed "ideal." And it's a virus that touches everyone everywhere, even those who have no apparent connection to sports.

Amateurism, as it has come to be defined and interpreted by the worldwide sports community, is evil *in principle*. That amateur "rules" are widely violated in practice is generally accepted, with a wink, or a sigh, or indignation, or indifference. And it is also well understood that tolerating these violations is hypocritical. What is rarely considered, however, is that the amateur ideal — if perfectly observed and policed — is incompatible with any decent modern society, especially American society. In many twentieth-century cultures, it is simply an inapplicable term. In others, where its definition can be put into some sort of correspondence with reality, it reflects and promotes concepts those very societies renounce.

In short, amateurism doesn't work anywhere; if it did work, it would be a bad thing; and since it can't work and shouldn't, institutionalizing its respectability (through the American school system, primarily) corrupts the intellect as well as the ethical sense.

If the above ferocious charges are true (and we'll try, of course, to substantiate them), how come amateurism has survived so long and is so seldom attacked even today?

Because it is an exceptionally effective mechanism for the production of:

1. Cheap labor.

2. Positions of power and control that offer significant rewards to those who hold them.

3. An illusion of idealism that ranks among the best devices available for the illusion-making process that fuels spectator interest.

Can such allegations be sustained? Let's see. We'll begin with the definition of amateurism used through most of this century by the International Olympic Committee (IOC), the ruling body of that competition. Because all nations and athletes (in the sports covered) look upon Olympic participation as their highest goal, the IOC definition is the one everyone must come to terms with. And that definition, in turn, grew out of the accepted ideas in nineteenth-century Europe, especially Victorian England. In the last decade, this definition has been altered in significant respects, but it's the older form that's relevant to us, because we're talking about its effect on the thinking and practices that became standard under it.

The older definition said:

> An amateur is one who participates and always has participated in sport as an avocation without material gain of any kind. He cannot avail himself of this qualification: (a) if he has not a basic occupation designed to insure his present and future livelihood; (b) if he receives or has received a remuneration for participation in sport; (c) if he does not comply with the rules of the International Federation concerned, and the official interpretations of this rule.

Parts *a* and *b* are abhorrent concepts when analyzed, but they're really just verbiage ignored in practice. The part that counts is part *c*, and especially the last clause. A "non-amateur" (which is more inclusive than a "professional") isn't eligible for the Olympics, and will be barred from all the smaller competitions that lead to the Olympics.

And who is an amateur? Anybody the "International Federation concerned" says is an amateur. And who isn't? Anybody it decides is not.

The abuses and tortured logic used by such bodies are self-evident, and before we belabor the point with examples (which we will), let's ask another question. Why? Why make such a designation as "amateur" in the first place? And why consider it a virtue?

In ordinary usage, *amateur,* as distinguished from *professional,* connotes less proficiency. As Tevye says about poverty in *Fiddler on the Roof,* it's no disgrace, but it's no great honor, either. When we speak of a musician (or any artist) as an amateur, we don't imply moral superiority, or even praise. We are explaining the artist's status, either as a justification for lack of skill or as something to marvel at, if the skill is of professional quality. Do you know of anyone who prefers to be treated by an amateur doctor? Or defended by an amateur lawyer, before an amateur judge?

Note, incidentally, that this demarcation has nothing to do with talent. Professionalism is the cultivation of a talent through time, training, and dedication. An amateur may actually be more talented, in native aptitude, than a polished professional, but he or she hasn't developed that talent to the same degree.

In sports, unlike the arts, medicine, or law, the activity consists of pitting one competitor against another, for the express purpose of finding out which one will win. It would make admirable sense, therefore, to ensure fair competition by grading the participants, so that only those of reasonably equal abilities are brought together. And that's exactly what's done with weight classes in boxing or wrestling, age designations in Little League, major-league and minor-league affiliations among professional teams, and varsity and intramural distinctions in schools.

But what is the essential ingredient in developing athletic talent to the highest, world-class levels of proficiency? Time. Time to train, practice, concentrate, and gain competitive experience. So it would make perfect sense to separate amateurs from professionals on the basis of time and effort devoted to becoming proficient. The term *professional* itself signifies someone who has completed a rigorous, accepted program of preparation, and who makes the practiced activity his chief occupation.

But that is not how sports amateurism is defined. It is defined exclusively in terms of *remuneration.* Why? Why should it matter how an athlete is financed? Why is a millionaire's son, who can

practice golf eight hours a day for ten years, put in the same category with an office worker who shoots one round a month (both
are classified as amateurs), instead of being grouped with another golfer who practices eight hours a day but makes his living
by teaching golf or winning prizes for his play? The very illogic of
this example contains the clue: the fiscal definition of amateurism
protects the privileged from competition.

This concept of sports organization, which didn't exist before
the 1800s, and evolved in the England of Queen Victoria, wasn't
pointless in the culture of that time. That was a time when "gentlemen" still didn't soil their hands with "commerce," if they
could help it; when hereditary privilege was still the backbone of
social status; when work performed for pay was considered
vaguely degrading, if sometimes necessary; when affiliation to
club or caste or family was still considered more important than
personal worth or eccentricity.

It was also a time when the facilities and leisure time for sports
activity were generally unavailable to ordinary or working-class
people. The golf course, the running oval, the polo field, the
cricket ground, the newly designed tennis court were the prov-
inces of the upper class. (The working-class game was football —
soccer — and it became openly professional without much fuss,
throughout Europe and soon throughout the world.)

But athletic games are mastered by muscle, determination, re-
flexes, and alertness — commodities not restricted to "nice" people. In fact, since the lower classes were so much more numerous
and generally less inhibited, they could certainly overwhelm club
members if they could compete under equal conditions for any
extended period of time. So elevating the lack of remuneration to
a symbol of moral purity was in tune with the social climate; and
it was very, very convenient. In plain language, it kept the riff-
raff out. For a while, that is.

At this point, someone is sure to ask about the ancient Greeks
and their ideals. The ancient Olympics, which inspired the modern Games, had no cash prizes and were also our model for democracy and citizen participation, weren't they? No, they
weren't. Ancient Greek "democracy," where it did exist briefly,
was a slave-based society that supported a small upper layer of

citizens. Professionalism was plentiful in the ancient Olympics, and prizes of great value were heaped upon winners by their communities. (Even at Olympia, the promoters knew how to avoid putting up expensive awards themselves.)

In any case, the social forces of mid-Victorianism had nothing to do with American life, even then. But the practices and frames of reference that became codified in the financial definition of amateurism were grafted on to American culture too.

The messages embedded in such concepts can be paraphrased thus:

• Since athletic excellence can be achieved only through full-time application, and since tangible rewards for the fruits of this effort are forbidden, there must be something wrong with honest pay for honest work.

• Since superior achievement is honored but cannot be rewarded directly (as it can for the artist or the surgeon), and since part-time effort can't achieve the goal, it must be all right to accept sponsorship, openly or covertly.

• Since everyone has to eat, and since only the "authorities" can determine whether you have complied with rules only the independently wealthy could live up to, it must be proper to lie (at worst) or pervert logic (at best) and stay eligible.

But what if every single individual in America were a paragon of integrity, and lies and subterfuge did not exist? Would we want a system that restricts competition to amateurs drawn only from a leisure class? That brands compensation for honest work as somehow dirty? That cheats a performer of a decent share of the tangible rewards his performances generate for those authorities who sell tickets and television rights, have salaried staffs, and share profits with ancillary businesses?

We would not want it, and we don't have it. In practice, everyone sees that value is given for value received in amateur sports. The high school athlete is rewarded with college admission he might not get otherwise — a ticket to upward mobility. The college athlete gets a free ride (worth thousands of dollars a year) and is in a position to obtain advantageous postgraduate opportunities through alumni and publicity.

The independent amateur who has crowd appeal — in track

and field now, in tennis in the past — gets under-the-table money in the form of "expenses" and other *legal* gimmicks. And the professional, who quite properly and honorably dominates the American scene, gets paid whatever he can negotiate for his services — and is barred from most world-class events.

Here we have a larger and living application of the competition-reducing principle that gave birth to the financial definition of amateurism. No totalitarian society, however mild, has difficulty with the Olympic definition. All its people, in every activity, are acknowledged to be in the service of the state, earning their keep in an assigned task. If the state decides to assign you to play hockey, because you're good at it and will bring glory to your country, you're not getting paid to play. You're getting paid to be a good citizen, whatever it is you do. This attitude applies to most of the world today, starting with the USSR and China.

In the so-called free-enterprise societies, of whatever degree, individuals market their skills. The best athletes, in order to be the best, must sell these skills. They therefore cannot meet the Olympic standard. So the rest of the world doesn't have to compete with the best free-enterprise athletes, and at the same time can use its own best athletes. Is it so surprising, then, that the current definition of amateurism has wide support?

By subscribing to this definition, uncritically, American society has been infected with a debilitating disease. The entire school system, which forms the backbone of America's athletic programs, insists on an amateur posture. But the high school football or basketball star is perfectly aware of the tangible reward he is playing for: a free college education. And the college player knows he is getting it. His coaches know. And his teachers. And the school administrators. And his parents and family. And his nonplaying classmates. And his out-of-school friends. And all the neighbors and local businessmen who congratulate him on his athletic success. And he knows they know. And they know he knows.

A more pervasive institutionalization of hypocrisy is hard to imagine, and it is at work every single day, in millions of cases. The lesson is inescapable: It is all right to do one thing while professing its opposite. It's not only all right, it is warmly endorsed and fostered by the leaders of society and all the authority figures who fashion a child's values: parents, clergy, teachers, and government officials.

If you accept the idea that remuneration is O.K. when it is properly disguised, you cripple your moral sensibilities. If you accept the disguises at face value and say they are not really remuneration, you cripple your capacity to think straight. And for three generations, *everyone* who has been to school in America, not just the athletes, has been exposed to this moral flabbiness and intellectual dishonesty. The athlete, at least, earns his keep by actual effort, but everyone else sees — and enjoys and profits from, in many cases — the hypocrisy that is being accepted.

None of this, please note, involves *violations* of the serpentine rules. Those also abound, come to the attention of millions, and are usually accepted. When, in some particular instance, punishment is inflicted and self-righteous horror is expressed, the rarity and quixotic nature of the incident merely heightens everyone's perception of injustice. The violations, which can't be kept secret from those who participate in them, even if they are never uncovered officially, compound the problem but don't alter its basic nature.

The problem is that upholding amateurism as an ideal in an industrialized world guarantees daily indoctrination in false values. Work *should* be rewarded. World-class athletic performance, for the entertainment of millions of paying customers, is *work*. A privileged leisure class, which could afford to play just for the love of it, is what Western civilization has been rejecting for the last two hundred years, in capitalistic countries no less than in socialistic ones.

In reality, there are millions of true amateurs playing sports everywhere — but not in front of ticket-buying audiences, for the purpose of mass entertainment. It's the deliberate confusion of two distinct functions — play and entertainment — that does the damage.

Why, then, does modern democratic society cling to the old definition? Cheap labor. The professional is controlled by whoever pays him: he must perform when and where and how the employer decides. But before he agrees, he can command a high

price for his services (that is, a significant fraction of the income
he generates for the promoter). The amateur, on the other hand,
is controlled by *eligibility*. And that can't be negotiated. It's completely in the hands of the promoter — the school, club, IOC, or
whatever. To stay eligible, the amateur must accept what's offered: scholarship, books, room, training table, expense money,
free equipment, lionization, promises, or even the products of
cheating. These awards are substantial in themselves, but they
add up to a smaller fraction of the promoter's budget than negotiated fees would.

Just as it suits the socialist world to have a no-money definition
of amateurism imposed on market-exchange societies, it suits
school and amateur-sports authorities to have the same definition
imposed on the performers they "hire" so indirectly. You
couldn't get away with that if you presented it openly. If nothing
else, the antitrust laws would get in the way, but aside from that,
the illusion of glamour, which draws spectators, would be tar-
nished by acknowledged cheapness.

So the package is wrapped in high-sounding morality. Amateurs are presented as "pure," "noble," "disinterested in profit,"
and "motivated by love of sport." Professionals are grubby,
greedy, commerce-soiled mercenaries. And of course professionals must never, never, *never* be allowed to compete against
amateurs, because they would show up the amateurs for what
they really are — less proficient — and would destroy the amateurs' gate appeal.

There is only one appropriate word for such a system: *sick*.

20. Sports-think

BLURRED MORAL PERCEPTIONS and twisted logic aren't the only damage sports have done to American thought. Thinking itself has been adulterated because of the permeation of language by sports images and metaphors. We think and talk so much about games that we end up thinking about the real world as if it were a game, and even those who have paid no conscious attention to the sports mystique fall into the traps set by this kind of false reasoning.

Unlike the amateurism scam, this is an unplanned phenomenon from which no one benefits. The fact that it is unintended, however, does not make sports-think any less harmful; if anything, it makes it even more dangerous.

Reasoning by analogy is central to human thought. None of mankind's progress from the cave would have been possible without it. The mind struggles to grasp the unfamiliar in terms of its similarity to things that are already familiar; to find simple elements in the complex; to identify a few reference points among many; to reduce to language — that is, to code — concepts too multifaceted to be communicated directly.

Sports have been purposely, if not always consciously, designed to stress the familiar, the simple, the narrow in scope and definite in meaning. We noted at the beginning of this book how comprehensibility plays a large role in making sports popular. Sports language thus becomes a ready-made medium for simplified simile formation, and its users become preconditioned to thinking in such channels.

But inappropriate analogies lead to wrong answers. And sports delude us into accepting all sorts of inappropriate analogies. To speak of "the game of life" as a poetic expression is harmless enough. But to make decisions in business, in politics, and, above all, in war, as if real life were a game can be disastrous. When we reach the point where we can't tell (or don't bother to tell) where the simile leaves off and reality begins, our troubles multiply.

To the statement "Life (or politics or war) is not just a game," most people would answer "Of course," and shrug such a suggestion aside as belaboring the obvious. But how often do we stop to consider exactly how games (in the sense of athletic games staged for entertainment) differ from real life?

Let's look at this in tabular form:

Category	Sports	Real life
Rules	1. Few and simple	1. Many and complex
	2. Explicit	2. Usually not explicit
	3. No serious dispute about interpretation	3. Interpretation always subject to doubt and argument
	4. Must be observed or game can't continue	4. Can always be ignored (at some risk) without ending "contest"
Referee	1. Always present and in charge	1. Rarely present
	2. Cannot be overruled by a contestant	2. Can be ignored (with risk)
Result	1. Ends at a definite point in time	1. Open-ended, always goes on
	2. Final score always defines outcome	2. No score, and outcome is often vague
	3. New game always starts even	3. All activity grows continuously out of preceding "result"
	4. Only "affordable" stakes are agreed to	4. Stakes can be life and death
Strategy	1. Few choices, well defined	1. Many choices, hard to define
	2. Parameters known	2. Parameters indefinite
	3. Tomorrow's conditions like today's	3. Tomorrow's conditions unknown
	4. Fairly equal matchups arranged	4. Mismatches are legion
	5. Us vs. Them clearly identified	5. Competing interests often unclear

This table is intended to be suggestive, not definitive. (We wouldn't want to make the mistake of pushing an analogy too far.) It does show how profound the differences between games and life are, however. And, sometimes, how subtle. We should not expect the formulas in one column to hold true for the other.

Thus when we say, "He can't get to first base with that customer," the metaphor is vivid and useful to anyone who understands baseball. But if we add, in reference to the salesman's intention to keep trying, "A ball game is never over until the last man is out," we switch to a different level of comparison; and this one introduces inconsistencies. In a baseball game, the rules guarantee each team the chance to score enough to win before making twenty-seven outs in nine innings. In life, that salesman's game may be over long before he realizes it, for any number of reasons: recession, racial prejudice, a poor product, body odor, whim, coincidence, unknown competition — anything. In a game, therefore, the contestants and the spectators know exactly where things stand with two out in the ninth, whether the score is 1–1 or 12–3. In real life, the contestant must *decide* at which point he "still has a chance," and at what point he has embarked on a costly waste of time that might deprive him of other sales (the "next game").

Still, inaccurate metaphors about third parties are hardly fatal. Sports-think does its serious damage when it colors our decision-making processes, and it does that by fostering two specific attitudes: the win-lose idea, and an excessive faith in numbers.

We begin to equate winning with "success," and losing with "failure," although quite different concepts are involved. Winning or losing is inseparable from the defeat of a specific opponent. Success or failure belongs in the vastly larger dimension of attaining or not attaining a goal. In sports, they become identical (even though they shouldn't) because, after all, beating an opponent is the acknowledged goal of any game. In real life, though, countless successes (and failures) occur in contexts that have nothing to do with beating anyone.

Sports-think, however, subliminally narrows our focus. We talk of "victory over disease," as if some properly devised strategy that fits within definable rules will guarantee that "success."

If the success isn't achieved, within a time frame that depends on our patience and attention span, it automatically becomes "failure" and therefore a "defeat." And a defeat must be somebody's fault, because if all the plays were made correctly, victory would result, wouldn't it? If we were more precise about our images, we would use the phrase *victory over disease* to describe a particular patient with a strong will to live, who achieves recovery from pneumonia.

Most of all, though, the win-lose syndrome hurts in politics and international affairs, including war. Every political system can be reduced to "ins" and "outs." The "outs" try to get into the positions of power, and the "ins" try to stay in. This is, of course, a contest, and in bare outline it has a legitimate similarity to a game. But the real issue, in every society, is what the "ins" do as governors while they are in office. The contest is a periodical preliminary to the serious business of running things: it decides who the governors will be, but it has nothing to do with the function of governing.

In sports, of course, victory in the contest is an end in itself: there is nothing beyond it, except the next game or the next season. So a sports-loving culture, steeped in sports-think, starts to follow the contest for power in contest terms, rather than in terms of what the winner will do later. And all the mechanisms of journalism, especially television, stimulate this response. Those very techniques and alliances that journalism found so effective and profitable for sports coverage are applied to the coverage of political contests.

On the eve of the 1980 Democratic National Convention, the hot issue was whether or not President Carter should release the delegates committed to him during months of state primaries, and create an "open convention" so that someone else might be nominated if the delegates preferred. Former governor Abe Ribicoff, of Connecticut, spoke in support of sticking by the results of the primaries, and said (on a national-news telecast): "Why should the convention turn to someone else, who didn't go through the trouble of running in all those primaries, and give him the prize of the nomination?"

Note the word *prize*. To refer openly and publicly, in advocacy of a contested position, to the presidential nomination as a "prize" is, I submit, sports-think in action. That politicians privately see it as a prize shouldn't shock anyone. But that they now believe that the *public* sees it as a prize, rather than as an honor or an obligation or an opportunity or some other suitably idealistic word, is a relatively new development. Here was a supporter of the president, offering "He won the game fair and square according to the rules, so don't deprive him of his trophy" as a persuasive argument for making a choice about the future welfare of the nation.

And when the convention took place, the misapplication of sports-think was made more explicit. In front of a nationwide audience, for almost two days, the argument put forth on behalf of Carter was "Don't change the rules in the middle of the game," in just those words.

If, as those involved kept insisting, momentous decisions about the future of this country and the entire world had to be made by choosing a candidate, such reasoning was appalling. If sincere, it showed total inability to distinguish the important from the trivial; if not, it displayed a conviction that those who were to be persuaded were incapable of making that distinction.

Needless to say, the merits of President Carter and the open-convention controversy are irrelevant to this discussion. It's the degree to which the contest is perceived as *primarily a game* that's important.

I leave it to qualified social scientists to explore the following questions:

• Was this emphasis the same in America (on a national scale) before sports-think was circulated more widely through the general population by television, after 1950?

• Is the proportion of attention given to election contests, as opposed to policies in power, the same in America as in countries that have less institutionalized interest in spectator sports?

• Are individuals in other cultures as remorselessly branded as "winners" and "losers" in non-sports activities as people are in America?

In regard to all these questions, my guess is no.

It doesn't take a social scientist, however, to realize that calling a contest a race conjures up sports associations, while calling it a campaign suggests military connections. Anyone who followed the news each Tuesday through the first half of 1980, as the series of primaries unfolded, knows that journalists kept calling the campaign a race, whereas years ago it was called a campaign for nomination.

Even the most advanced achievement of mankind's history, the landing of humans on the moon, was presented to Americans as a race: we had to beat the Russians to the moon. We did, in 1969. But built into the idea of a race, remember, is the acknowledgment that when it is won, it's over. There's nothing more to do about it. Is it a coincidence, then, that since that race was won, we have stopped going to the moon? One can wonder.

The winner-loser psychology has endless facets. It is fostered by advertising techniques ("Hertz is Number 1"), public-opinion polls, marketing surveys, and countless contests. (In the late 1950s, on the heels of the Cold War, a young pianist named Van Cliburn became an American hero because he won a competition in Moscow; not because he did or did not play well as an artist, since many of those who cheered him knew and cared nothing about his type of music, but simply because he beat the Russians — exactly the reaction we saw when the U.S. hockey team did the same thing a generation later.) In this way, the skilled practitioners of opinion molding have cashed in, knowingly or unknowingly, on the sports-think mentality.

Sensitivity to numbers has also been a marvelous tool. Sports fans are conditioned to accept numbers as objective measures of undisputed fact. A 5–3 score is just that, 5–3, nothing else. A won-lost record, a batting average, the number of yards gained, the amount of prize money, the number of players allowed on a team's roster, the figures that appear in a box score — all of these are to be believed. Sure, there may be a typographical error or some other mistake, but the *meaning* of accurately reproduced numbers is not to be questioned. The team with the best record wins the championship. If you make 10 baskets in 20 tries, you're a 50 percent shooter. Someone may say you hold the golf club all wrong, but if you shot a 73, it's still a 73.

Opinions and value judgments can be disputed (and sports

fans love to dispute them). Celebrities can be misquoted. Descriptions of a play can vary according to different observers. But the box score can't lie: it records exactly what happened. We saw what a fundamental role statistics play in sports interest, and how they can be misinterpreted for forecasting and analysis; but as *information*, sports statistics have an air of inviolable validity.

In games, of course, we've agreed beforehand on exactly what will be counted, and how, and what each number will signify. Great care is taken to record things in a uniform manner. There is no ambiguity about the input. In the larger world, that's not true at all. Even so basic a constitutional requirement as the decennial census produced lawsuits, arguments, angry charges, and political conflict in 1980. The validity of the input was challenged vehemently.

So every day the American public swallows statistics on unemployment and the cost of living, popularity polls, and advertising slogans ("five out of six dentists," "half the calories," "800 grams of pain-relieving ingredients"), with no possibility of questioning or comprehending the input. (Experts and specialists question these things constantly, but the public does not.)

The issue here is not *manipulation* of figures, which is a separate subject. Assume the numbers mentioned are correct. It's the illusion that numbers, *because they are numbers,* are somehow more objective and believable than words.

One can say that this prejudice in favor of quantification has been characteristic of Western civilization since the Scientific Revolution began during the time of Galileo. And of course it is partly because of this frame of mind that entertainment sports, in their developing stages, latched on to the use of numbers in the form familiar to us. But in the America of the last fifty years, more people have developed the feel for numbers, more deeply, through following sports than through the influence of math and physics courses. The faith in journalistic statistics is rooted at least partly in sports-think (and partly in the reliability of stock-market tables, temperature readings, and election tallies).

Uncritical acceptance of numerically expressed information,

without attention to the source or significance of the numbers themselves, decreases our ability to think clearly and arrive at sensible decisions about the real world. Sports habits cultivate this particular flaw in sound thinking.

What's more, sports statistics accustom us to surface simplicity. A passionate Yankee fan wants every detail of last night's game, but most of those who watch the eleven o'clock news are content with just the score. There are fans who pore over the league standings, but many more are content simply to know who's in first place.

In the 1980 presidential primaries, this approach was nearly universal. Headlines in major newspapers were as telegraphic as radio and television newscasts in reporting "Carter Wins Florida" or "Reagan wins California." For any remotely sensible understanding of the relationship between the latest returns and a particular candidate's political prospects, one had to consider the percentages involved, the number of voters, the size and importance of the state, and the nature of the particular delegate process — matters that the political reporters went into conscientiously enough. But the sports-think–conditioned mass of the population (and many less inspired journalists) settled for the simplistic "So-and-so won another." When, on the same day, Senator Kennedy won a large number of delegates in Massachusetts while President Carter won a few (but a majority) in Maine, the *San Francisco Chronicle*'s headline read, "Carter, Kennedy, Each Win One" — exactly the same thing it might have said about a double-header ("Giants and Cubs Split," for instance). A win is a win, right?

But perhaps the most misleading sports similies of all have to do with war, a subject for which they seem so apt, on the face of things. Didn't we say that games are an "idealization" of warfare, not to mention a sublimation of warlike instincts, and that football in particular is an analogue of military tactics in a "territorial war game"?

Ah, but the operative word here is *idealization*. Losing the capacity to distinguish between an abstraction and the real thing is the whole point. Let's look at another table:

Category	Game	War
Goal	Record a victory	Impose your will on the enemy
Means	Score points	Kill, destroy, and disable
Context	What the rules allow	No rules
Effort	Only during game, in context of rules	Total mobilization of all resources, all the time
Result	Victory or defeat	Control or surrender
Consequence	Next game	Survival or death

The win-lose concept has always been inapplicable to real wars between nations. The motive in war is always to make the vanquished do what you want: provide slaves, wealth, conscripts, territory, or whatever. You may succeed to any degree — the Romans wiped out Carthage forever, the American colonies broke away from England without touching England itself, and Napoleon was able to burn Moscow but could not stay there — but battles are only one of the instruments used to make the enemy yield. This has nothing in common with winning a game, where the presupposition is that you and your opponent will play again.

Since atomic weapons were developed, the idea that no one can win a war has been the basis for "mutual deterrence." In one sense, this was always true; in another, it still isn't. Was France one of the "winners" in World War I? Was Japan a "loser" in World War II? What about Poland? On the other hand, during the thirty years that the United States and the Soviet Union have refrained from bombing the planet into oblivion, have they failed to try to impose their wills on each other (and others) by one means or another, including the employment of large military forces?

Sports-think is totally inadequate to deal with such questions — or any serious questions about the real world. But all too often, and probably at an increasing rate, Americans try to apply it. That they often apply it without being aware that they are doing so makes life that much scarier. So here are some more questions for qualified sociologists to pursue:

• Was the television-induced excitement about a Reagan-Ford

ticket at the 1980 Republican Convention an example of sports-think response by network news executives and some political aides?

• Is there a connection between decreased productivity and other problems of American business, and the sports-think mentality that ambitious executives apply to climbing corporate ladders?

• Was sports-think oversimplification one of the elements that helped muddle the thoughts of some of those who made the thousands of decisions during our Vietnam era?

None of which is intended to suggest that all the ills of society can be blamed on habits of thought drummed into us daily as a result of our absorption with spectator sports. There are plenty of other culprits. But the fallout from sports-think is present, and it is increasing, and it is disturbing.

21. Racism

THE CLASSICAL MYTHS about race relations in mass-entertainment sports are:

1. Sports are a shining example of triumph over prejudice, since both players and spectators consider only the playing ability of the individual.

2. This development in sports has led American society to higher moral ground in the struggle against discrimination.

3. The emergence of black stars is at the cutting edge of the advances made by the black community as a whole.

4. At the same time, the white establishment has carefully kept things under control by systematically exploiting and underpaying black athletes, subjecting them to quota limitations, and keeping them out of key positions.

Like all myths, these have an element of truth (or they wouldn't become myths), but they provide a totally inadequate picture of the real world. The fact is, racism in the realm of sports to a remarkable degree reflects the relationships of the larger culture. At any given time, it isn't much ahead or behind the prevailing attitudes of America as a whole.

Upon reflection, this shouldn't seem remarkable at all. Sports entertainment, we have seen, is a commodity most sensitive to the immediate preferences of a large public. Anything that's really unacceptable, or runs counter to mainstream tastes, quickly fails in the marketplace. The central fact, that this particular diversion is a non-necessity based on illusions that must be kept alive in the mind of a potentially fickle public, dominates all other considerations.

The myths, therefore, must be adjusted for different historical eras and must be reduced to less-sweeping generalities. In very rough form, we can divide the eras this way:

• From 1945 (end of World War II) to the mid-1950s. Breaking of traditional barriers in previously all-white framework.

• From the 1950s to approximately 1970. Conscious application of quotas and tokenism in many (but not all) circumstances.

• Since 1970. Institutionalization of *subconscious* prejudice (expressed through rationalized value judgments rather than explicit quotas or tokenism), and some backlash against growing militancy on the black side.

These closely parallel developments in the larger world.

As for generalities about the 1980s, we can say that on-the-field, during-the-game discrimination is virtually nonexistent (even in the reverse form, so widespread a generation ago, of congratulating ourselves that black men and white men are playing so well together). Off the field, black-white hostility, low-key ethnic separation, and authentic camaraderie are as common, or as rare, as in any other American context, depending on place, time, surroundings, the course of events, and personality mix.

Two factors distinguish the sports field, however. Effective performance is clearly measurable, and the entire activity is exceptionally visible (and purposely so).

Therefore sports do tend, to a modest degree, to accentuate equality of opportunity and acceptance, and to stimulate public attitudes already leaning in that direction. When integration takes place in major-league baseball or in a southern university's football program, it obviously has more impact than when the same thing happens in an office or a neighborhood. And while people can purposely demean, carelessly ignore, or simply be honestly oblivious to special skill shown by an unwelcome minority in business or in intellectual activities that are judged subjectively, they can't blind themselves to the athletic accomplishments of a Jackie Robinson or an O. J. Simpson. At least not as easily. But it is tempting to overrate this effect. It's real enough, but it flourishes only in a fertile environment created by external forces.

The Branch Rickey-Jackie Robinson story, seen in historical perspective and with the advantage of hindsight, offers some insight. Rickey was a brilliant, exceptional executive. He developed baseball's farm system in the 1920s and 1930s, turning the minor leagues into wholly owned subsidiaries of major-league teams. When he moved from St. Louis to Brooklyn in 1943, he brought his methods with him, but this was in the middle of a world war, of course, and not much could be done immediately.

When the war ended in 1945, Rickey could see, as a businessman, that a new supply of baseball talent would have to be tapped. His farm operation, imitated and expanded by others with greater financial resources, was now standard. There was a large group of high-quality players in the Negro leagues who had been systematically barred from "organized baseball" for more than fifty years. Tapping that pool would not only give his team an immediate competitive advantage but would also open the door to future black players who, under existing custom, would have to remain outside the system. That was the economic motivation for signing Robinson.

It is important to realize that the above explanation doesn't diminish Rickey's personal sincerity about racial justice, or the courage it took to carry out the breakthrough, or the serious moral values involved. Rickey has received, and fully deserves, the greatest respect for his leadership role in this extremely significant piece of social engineering. But the climate had to be right. After all, Rickey had operated for three decades within the lily-white baseball system and had made no attempt to challenge it, while the social climate wasn't right.

By 1946, two things had changed. Because World War II had required the first total mobilization of American manpower since the Civil War, blacks in military service and the defense industry acquired more opportunity and more equal interaction with at least some whites than they had had before. They were also accorded more equal treatment under various federal laws. And in the white society, four Roosevelt administrations on the heels of the traumatic Great Depression, and a desperate war against Nazi super-race mentality, created willingness to confront discrimination as an issue.

Without the right climate, and without the economic need for new talent, Rickey (or anyone else) might have done nothing more in 1946 than was done in 1936. And it is interesting to note how similar the underlying forces that encouraged integration were. During World War II, blacks were "let in" to some areas of productivity because they were needed (everybody was needed). And they were allowed in major-league sports when they became needed there.

On the college level, different but equally practical factors emerged. The GI bill, which financed the college education of war veterans, transformed America's colleges from essentially elite institutions, populated largely by those who could afford them, into more "open" schools to which larger segments of society could aspire. What's more, the military draft didn't end when the war ended, so the expansion of college admissions, begun to accommodate the first wave of GIs, continued into the 1960s.

College population, in America, means college sports programs (especially football and basketball) that have high entertainment content. The fact that a black GI was entitled to the same opportunity as a white GI proved less important, in the long run, than the overall expansion of athletic programs, and the aspirations of individual colleges. The GI bill created a different outlook on scholarship funding and on the size of undergraduate population, and it opened the door to new levels of recruiting college athletes. At that point, college recruiters turned to black athletes the same way Branch Rickey had turned to the Negro leagues: as an untapped pool of talent in a highly competitive activity.

Because sports are so explicitly competitive, even those with the deepest prejudices had to go along eventually — or get beat. Just as Rickey's steps with the Dodgers (with Don Newcombe, Roy Campanella, and others who quickly followed Robinson) forced the rest of baseball to admit blacks, so all colleges, even in Alabama and Mississippi, sooner or later had to try to keep pace or give up.

Again, none of this negates the moral impact of what those who led in the shattering of color-bar custom did. Nor does it ignore the fact that in many cases, especially in southern colleges, integration came only after laws had been changed. (In fact, that's the whole point: a social climate that leads to legislation against discrimination simultaneously affects the sports scene.)

But the need to win *on the field* hastened and intensified the barrier removal to a degree not felt in business and other endeavors.

The next stage of racial relations in sports also reflected events in the outside world. As it became necessary to disavow prejudice (which of course did not disappear), the common sublimations appeared. To a white audience, even one black player could be proof of antidiscrimination virtue, so tokenism flourished. Would a white audience be able to "identify" with too many black players? Or — a less lofty, strictly business consideration — would too many black customers make white customers uncomfortable? Such questions led to the establishment of definite (but not publicly acknowledged) quotas, and were still being asked in 1980 about the National Basketball Association and its 75 percent proportion of black players. An outstanding black player who could help you win was clearly desirable and proudly acknowledged as proof of your fairness. But the marginal black player, whose talent was on a level with that of a white player competing for the same job, was a nuisance and a threat to some perceived "racial balance." The black players who made it, therefore, had to be better than anyone else.

None of this is new or startling. Any group subjected to discrimination in any society knows the process. The glib rationalizations began to abound: blacks lacked courage under pressure; they weren't as quick mentally; they were showboats who couldn't be relied upon; they didn't develop deep enough team loyalty; they couldn't play "with pain" — or, conversely, they could withstand pain better; they matured earlier, implying that they wouldn't improve as much with experience; they didn't have leadership qualities — or at least could not expect whites to respond to them; they lacked ambition once they reached a certain level.

An individual, black or white, who illustrates any or all of those characteristics can always be found. A thorough program of psychological testing and long-term observation might show that one segment of the population has a different profile in these respects than another — or it might not. But no such program has been attempted or advocated, and as generalizations (less openly expressed these days, but by no means eradicated), these charac-

terizations remain biased. Such opinions have great utility, however, as copouts. If attendance is disappointing, and this can be
blamed on public prejudice (which the promoter deplores, of
course), the promoter is held less responsible for the failure.
(Since a large portion of the population does share the subliminal
prejudice, the argument is easy to sell and the promoter can believe himself totally sincere.) And if all or some of those stereotypes about black players are true, then a prejudiced scout or administrator can justify his reluctance to deal with too many of
"them."

Meanwhile, in the late 1960s, another phase in racial relations
emerged. Black militancy, devoted to political and even revolutionary goals, became an excellent lightning rod for resentment
many whites were unwilling to express otherwise. It enabled them
to condemn a group of black athletes for their behavior rather
than for their existence. The overreaction to the black-power salute at the 1968 Olympic Games in Mexico City, to Muhammad
Ali, to Afro hair styles and facial hair, and to black-culture man-
nerisms such as special handshakes and one-handed catches,
manifested this deflected distaste. Of course one can legitimately
feel that sports and politics shouldn't mix, and be annoyed at the
intrusion of political messages into entertainment. But in most
cases, it turns out to be a one-way objection. The political activity
of starting every game with the national anthem, or having a
mayor throw out the first ball, or raising the flag at an international victory is swallowed whole by many who get furious at the
presence of other "politics." As always, it makes a difference
whose ox is being gored.

And, as always, actions breed reactions. There arose just as
overblown a counterreaction, in which making Muhammad Ali a
transcendental hero and espousing numerous black concerns became a test of liberal faith for those who didn't care all that much
about the sport of boxing itself. (In similar fashion, much of the
professional-football mystique became associated with right-wing
jingoism, during the Vietnam era.) Just as white prejudice found
ways to express itself obliquely in the perpetual spotlight of spectator sports, so black activists (as well as anti-Castro Cubans,
Puerto Rican nationalists, and other groups) sought to use this

stage for their message. What mattered, in sports, was not the content of the message but the scope of the stage.

When all is said and done, however, sport in America in the 1980s has come a little further toward true integration, with less ongoing turmoil, than, let us say, central-city school systems or the nationwide job market. This is because specific and measurable performance is built into the activity itself, and neither excellence nor incompetence can be hidden. The shibboleths of the 1970s — the absence of black baseball managers and executives, black quarterbacks in pro football, and black coaches in football and basketball — are evaporating, slowly but perceptibly. Studies about disparities in pay scale between black and white stars, a hot academic subject in the 1960s, are pointless now (and didn't really reflect prejudice then, as much as they reflected what blacks would accept on the market).

The largest area of black exploitation in sports today is at the college level. Black athletes are recruited intensively, then slipped through the system with forged grades, nonexistent credits, and other gimmicks, and cut adrift without degrees in much greater numbers than white athletes, and for a familiar reason: they are the pool of cheap labor. This is not because some sports promoter or college arranged it that way, but because the society as a whole has done so. And neither coaches nor athletic directors nor college presidents seem terribly reluctant to take advantage of whatever grist they can find for their mills.

In two important respects, however, black athletes themselves have acquired a leadership role, as a group. First, they have made white athletes more militant on issues of importance to them. Gains made by professional player unions, and resistance to college-coaching tyrannies, owe their existence to the consciousness-raising experienced by whites who come in contact with black teammates. Blacks, through their own life experiences, arrived on a team quite sensitive to what constitutes abuse of authority and subtle (and not-so-subtle) put-downs. Belonging to a generation that was starting to fight back against such mistreatments on every front, they recognized it easily in a sadistic coach or a skinflint general manager. Athletes, for the most part, are not heavily endowed with social consciousness; their attention, usually from childhood on, is focused on athletics. A white athlete, who is not subjected to prejudice in daily life, often may not realize how he is being exploited or treated unfairly by a coach: He's had little experience with systematic mistreatment. The black athlete, although just as absorbed with sports while growing up, has been sensitized by the non-sports portion of life, and has a stronger emotional stake in self-assertion beyond the realm of the athletic field. Within the sports world, blacks have been teaching whites what dignified equal treatment means.

The second way in which black athletes have assumed a leadership role, oddly enough, has to do with integration from black to white, instead of the other way around. The political militancy of the last twenty years, in all parts of the world, has tended toward ethnic fragmentation, and that has been happening in America. But in sports, black athletes (and not only the stars) are a force *against* fragmentation — not because their ideas are different from anyone else's, but because cohesion is the nature of sports.

Socially, the separation is still strong. On most ball clubs, away from work, whites tend to go one way and blacks another — just as in the rest of American life. (What's equally important to recognize is that *within* each group, there are just as many subgroups and individual preferences as in the other.)

And social separation, more than anything else, accounts for how little progress blacks have made in obtaining positions of authority in sports organizations. The business structure of teams is exactly the opposite of the field structure: there are no obvious won-lost records and batting averages by which to judge an executive's performance. There aren't even sales figures, unlike in other businesses, because of the monopolistic nature of league organization. So these positions are basically filled by means of the buddy system, which is not necessarily illegitimate. In the absence of objective guidelines, people tend to hire people they know. In sports, this means the people you socialize with or have some family connection with. Not until more blacks have social contact with more club owners and general managers will there be a larger flow of blacks into the lower levels of the corporate ladder that lead eventually to the higher levels.

Finally, there is one aspect of race that remains taboo. Are there genetic or other biological differences that make black athletes better in some sports than in others? This question has been left remarkably unexplored. It smacks too much of "blacks-are-inferior" concepts, which are used as put-downs along with IQ tests and other "standards" that are too easily misapplied. To joke, in an admiring way, "Of course that basketball team can't win — it's got four white guys" is commonplace and acceptable. But to examine seriously what sort of body structure or chemistry might be the result of a particular genealogy is not. To assert, gratuitously, that blacks have certain physical superiorities can be as insulting as to claim they are mentally inferior. (That's the "They've-got-natural-rhythm" syndrome.) For one thing, such assertions lump individuals together by race, which is the very stereotype being fought against. For another, there is the tacit implication that athletic success due to *genetic* endowment somehow discounts the more honored achievements of skill, intelligence, and determination.

It is an observable fact that dark-skinned individuals dominate such sports as basketball, track, and boxing in America, and are disproportionately outstanding in football and baseball. At the same time, they are disproportionately few in hockey, swimming, tennis, golf, and soccer. In track, they dominate the shorter distances and jumps, but not longer distances, weights, and pole vault. There are mountains of evidence to explain these distributions on cultural grounds. Reference is made to the kinds of early choices, opportunities, and preferences that are built into American society and channel individuals into their chosen events during formative years. But after all the environmental factors and pressures are sifted through, are there physical proclivities?

The sample here, remember, is taken from the highest levels of major professional sports. *Every* individual who reaches the majors is already exceptional, so sorting out characteristics in this population should not have spillover ethnic connotations. Are there discernible differences in physical endowment between, say, the very best athletes of African descent and the very best athletes of Norwegian or Italian descent? If there are, they won't prove anything *general* about all blacks or all whites or all Europeans or all Asians, but they might reveal something about human physiology that wouldn't show up in other ways.

Whether or not such studies would have any scientific value, none of significant scale have been made. Or if they have, they have not been publicized. Perhaps the necessary techniques for meaningful investigation have only recently been developed. But up to now, this has been too sensitive a subject in social dynamics to be fully explored. And that is one more example of how race relations in sports are locked into, and inseparable from, the fabric of a particular time.

To say "Sports create better race relations" is not entirely untrue, but it is certainly an exaggeration. To say "Race prejudice still characterizes the sports scene" is also an exaggeration, although bias certainly exists. But to say "In sports, we come closer to the democratic ideal of objective judgment than in most other things we do" is to come pretty close to the mark.

22. The Role of Women

WHILE QUESTIONS of equal rights with respect to race mirror the larger society, the situation is entirely different with respect to women. To begin with, there are real biological differences between men and women. And the psychological and cultural differences between the sexes, formed in infancy and even before that through the attitudes of prospective parents, also take a different form than do differences between races. Discrimination along racial or religious lines is always applied as class distinction: the objects of the discrimination are a numerical minority, invariably imprisoned in a particular economic class, and society's constraints upon them are enforced against the class as a whole.

But women are not a numerical minority, and discrimination against them has always been applied *within* class boundaries. That is, males of an upper class treat males of a lower class as inferior, but they also treat females of the *same* class as inferior; and males of the lower class treat females of *their* class as inferior. In fact, insofar as they are male, lower-class males have considered themselves superior to upper-class females in one-to-one confrontations when free of socially enforced class restraints. The literature of the last three thousand years is full of examples.

For sports, and for the women's-rights movement of the 1980s, these differences in the nature of the discrimination (as distinct from the fact of discrimination) have consequences that have been only sketchily explored so far.

When blacks were being excluded, it was plain to see that perfectly proficient practitioners of the sport were being barred for an extraneous reason. Satchel Paige and Josh Gibson were out there facing Babe Ruth and Bob Feller in baseball exhibitions, yet playing in their own leagues. While establishment promoters and the white public succeeded in keeping black athletes out of their consciousness, they could not deny their existence when circumstances brought black athletes into the limelight. Correcting the abuse, therefore, and creating equality of opportunity, required nothing more than dropping the barriers. This is not to say that all barriers have been dropped, or that many individual blacks haven't started from a position of disadvantage, but *conceptually* no other step is needed to achieve equality.

With women, however, the exclusion from sports is rooted in centuries of attitudes about males and females that have created, in reality and not just in theory or in response to oppression, different viewpoints and different desires. To redress the balance, if that is the goal, simply dropping barriers or being *willing* to treat women equally is not enough. The pool from which to draw women players and spectators is disproportionately small. Put it this way: If an all-inclusive survey of American males in the year 1937 had asked, "Would you like yourself, or your son, to be a star athlete?" the proportion of "yes" answers from black and white respondents probably would have been the same. The blacks, fully aware of discrimination at that time (after Jesse Owens had triumphed in the Berlin Olympics, but before color lines in baseball and other sports had been breached), nevertheless had the same athletic aspirations white males did.

But if you had asked all American women in 1970, "Would you like yourself, or your daughter, to be a star athlete?" the proportion of "yes" answers would be staggeringly smaller than among all men. That's the crux of the difference, and it won't be lessened by civil-rights legislation, equal-time provisions in the media, militancy on one side, or eagerness to be fair on the other.

Male-female equality in mass-spectator-sports entertainment — the activity we've taken such pains to define narrowly — is far, far off. But it is not as far off in some respects as others. In recent years, the women-in-sports issue has been much discussed in three regards: women as participants, women as fans, and women as journalists.

Women as sports reporters, magazine writers, and broadcasters made dramatic gains in opportunity during the 1970s, and this trend will accelerate in the 1980s. Women will have equal access, if not equal numbers, quite soon.

Women as fans are also increasing rapidly in number, but remain a minority of the *dedicated* sports audience (about 15 percent, according to some surveys). Thanks to television, they now have equal opportunity to watch sports. They do not have comparable motivation. How long will it be before their spectator motivation numerically equals that of American men? Three generations, of which the second has already begun.

Women as participants, at major-league levels in the kind of sports we're talking about, will never attain equality. That's right, never.

Is there a basis for the three dogmatic assertions just made? Concerning journalism, the issue boils down to employer willingness. In my classes at Stanford, from 1976 to 1980, the number of women who chose to enroll in a sports-subject course approached half the total number of students. Only a small fraction of any class had any serious intention of making sports journalism a career; but within that fraction, there were almost as many women as men.

No great mystery is involved here. When male-female stereotypes were different from what they are today, little girls were rarely exposed to major-league sports as spectators. It was traditional for a father, grandfather, or uncle to take a boy to the ballpark, thus helping to establish the layers of complex joy to be relived by the adult male fan. Rarely (in proportion to the whole population, that is) would an adult take a little girl. (Part of the ballpark ritual, of course, was to bring the little male into an all-male adult environment — a facet of the ballpark experience not available to the little female.) So when the primary exposure to spectator sports in childhood involved live attendance at a sports event, the cards were stacked in favor of the male.

It was this key experience that stimulated the male to read sports pages, listen to the radio, and argue about sports with friends. By mid-high school, he was a fully trained, expert sports fan. But by mid-high school, when girls began going to football games as "dates," most of them had little sports knowledge and less emotional attachment. If they then became interested and, as college freshmen, went out for the school newspaper to cover sports, they were hopelessly behind the boys in accumulated background.

Over the last twenty years, this situation has changed. At home, young girls can see sports on television as easily as their brothers, and those females who do become interested begin accumulating as much background as males. By college age, the boy who became a fan at ten is no better prepared than the girl. And if the woman, at that point, wants to pursue the subject further, she is just as well equipped as her male classmate. Meanwhile, newspapers and television stations are eager to improve their male-female balance, so the well-prepared woman is more likely to get a chance today than ten years ago.

But serious obstacles remain. The existing editorial departments, which are overwhelmingly male, retain their prejudices. Many women, even according to old-fashioned male-chauvinist views, have excellent characteristics for reporting: eye for detail, gift for language, sensitivity to surroundings, people-orientation, and sharp minds. And year for year, at school age, they have greater maturity. What they do not have, of course, is precisely the macho mystique that made so many boys sports fans in the first place, and that the middle-aged professionals in the field still cherish. But the obstacles are entirely (and literally) manmade, and they are crumbling.

As for the noisiest question of all, a woman reporter's access to male dressing rooms, the controversy is simply silly. Of course a woman is entitled to exactly the same professional access as any man, and if a male athlete is disturbed by this, all he has to do is keep his shorts on until he enters the shower. Male reporters don't follow athletes there, either. (In practice, many sports organizations would love to keep *all* reporters out of locker rooms but don't dare because of the promotional necessities we outlined in Part I. So they are only too happy to seize upon the modesty issue as an excuse to keep women out. They can then argue, on the grounds of equality, for a "separate press-interview facility" for all reporters, male and female. Where they can get away with this kind of thing (in golf and tennis, for example, where "tickets-are-available" notes are not a daily necessity), they do; where the press doesn't let them, as in baseball and football, they don't. But the battle goes on.

At any rate, we will see more and more major-sports reporting done by women, with little effect on either sports or journalism. But it will take much longer before the majority of women become sports fans. Any woman interested enough to pursue a sports-reporting career automatically demonstrates her commitment, but the vast majority of American women don't feel that way. Even the ones who develop great loyalty and knowledge with respect to a particular sport seldom have the childhood-initiation emotion to build on that boys do. Women are, by and large, less intensely trained in the special joys of spectating. (Television people can tell you that many women become fanatic followers of a particular team or sport, and are just as fascinated by the Olympics as men; but men, in large numbers, will turn on the set and watch *whatever* sports program is offered, within a reasonable range of subjects, while women won't.)

This evolution will take three generations. Today's twenty-year-old woman may be a sports fan, but she is not, very often, the daughter of a mother who is a sports fan. Her mother has accepted the fact that it's all right for girls to be sports fans (something her mother's mother did not accept); but only when today's twenty-year-old has a daughter, who can experience with her mother the shared-interest process we described as taking place with boys, will that daughter grow up to be a truly generalized sports fan. And only at that point will the demographics of television viewers and ticket buyers start to balance off at 50–50 male-female.

Which brings us to women as participants. Many women can beat many men at any game. A few women can beat almost any man. But the best woman player cannot compete with the best men players.

It's not only that women have different physiques. It's that the games we're talking about were *designed and developed* to reward exceptionally gifted *male* physiques. And it's not a question of "toughness," or mental outlook (which is the product of upbringing, and could change), or acquired skills. In World War II, the Russians found that women made better tank drivers than men, because, in a machine where muscle power didn't count, they were more comfortable, being smaller, and could remain alert longer. And no male ever burned with fiercer competitive spirit than Billie Jean King.

But the fact is that men are bigger and stronger, have longer muscles, and have different distributions of fat to muscle than women do. They also have different angles of movement in some joints (hips, pelvis, and probably shoulders). These characteristics would not necessarily be advantageous in every athletic activity one could devise; but in the mass-interest games we are dealing with, they are advantageous. Rooted in male activities, hunting and personal combat, the games we know emphasize precisely those muscular proficiencies that are specifically male: How hard can you throw a ball (or a spear)? How fast can you run? How hard can you hit?

Women may exceed men in terms of stamina, we now know. They excel in long-distance swimming, for instance. They can move around a tennis court and lob and volley as well as men, but they can't serve as hard. They can putt as well as men, but they can't drive as far off the tee. They can dribble and shoot a basketball, but they can't rebound against bigger men. Of course, smaller men can't rebound against bigger men either. And that's the point.

Back at the beginning of this book, we listed the elements that go into the illusion that makes sports entertainment commercially viable. One facet of the illusion is indispensable at the major-league level: the spectator's conviction that he is seeing *the best players available.*

The heavyweight division has always dominated professional boxing because it is tacitly accepted that the best heavyweight would beat all the smaller champions. (He might not, in a particular case, but we assume he would.) We can't prove, scientifically, that the two teams in the World Series or the Super Bowl are the best in the world. But we accept the idea that their season's progress to that point *defines* them as the best. And since basketball is a game in which exceptional height is indispensable to victory, we sacrifice some of our feelings of personal identification (with a Wilt Chamberlain or a Kareem Abdul-Jabbar) for the sake of the more important belief that lesser players couldn't beat them.

On this rock, all hopes that top women's sports can be promoted on the same level as top men's sports will founder. The Olympics, with their emphasis on measurement sports, will only solidify the awareness that the best women can't match the best men. The world record-holder at 100 meters, traditionally hailed as the world's fastest human, will always be male. Given absolute equality of opportunity, facilities, coaching, and motivation, the female half of the human population will not produce the best runner, the highest jumper, the best baseball player, the best football player, the best hockey or basketball player, or the best fighter — nor even one who ranks among the top twenty males.

In other activities yet to be designed, or not yet so popular, women may very well equal male performance some day. But we have, in America, an established commercial sports scene, with its intricate alliances to the media, advertising, politics, and so forth. It will not yield its grip. The "best-in-the-world" syndrome is too vital a part of its appeal to be subverted.

None of which means, it goes without saying, that women's sports won't carve out their own large, substantial, prosperous enclaves (as they have already done in tennis and golf). But they won't attain overall *equality*. Nor will that third generation of true-bred women fans alter the situation when they come of age. To the extent that they become *mass* fans (and therefore important factors in television ratings and ticket sales), they will develop the tastes males already have, and become just as captivated by the "best" illusion.

All of these arguments apply only to the top layer of sports activity, however: the multimillion-dollar, tens-of-million-spectator extravaganzas, and the league games that lead up to them. Below that level, the classification of competitors by equitable standards is entirely acceptable to sports fans.

College and high school teams, most of all, are perceived in a different way. Whoever roots for Harvard or East Side High or

Notre Dame is not *primarily* concerned with seeing the best. The focus is on the identity of the institution (which, it is hoped, will emerge best in its class). As more colleges, under prodding by federal legislation, set up full-scale programs for women's varsity teams, it is quite possible that spectators will become as interested in those bearers of the school colors as in the men. Notre Dame football is not about to be eclipsed by women fencers; but it is entirely conceivable that at a place like Stanford, a women's basketball team playing for the national women's title will get more attention than a men's team that finishes last in its conference.

In other words, since we accept male classification by ability — weight classes in boxing and wrestling, college teams as distinct from pro, amateur runners as distinct from pro — we should have no difficulty with male-female classifications as well. Here the existing difference in impact *is* correctable, at least in theory, by promotion and by added female motivation. In theory, yes; but in practice, it will still be a long haul. For women, sports have two powerful counterrevolutionary forces built in. One is the principle that we discussed at the beginning of this section, that sports reflect rather than form social attitudes. Allied to this is the conservatism of the media, devoted to satisfying existing audiences rather than trying to develop new ones. Women will get full equality in sports activity when they achieve it on other levels.

The other factor is that male chauvinism, macho mystique, and sexism are integral parts of the sports entertainment men support. To a very large extent, sports is the subject American men turn to when they want to feel *separate* from women. (Because when they went out to play ball as boys they escaped mother's supervision? Don't ask me.) This is incompatible with equality. Can equality be imposed on something so entirely voluntary as rooting for the Red Sox with the passion of a Jonathan Schwartz? One wonders.

It is possible, then, to stipulate all sorts of changes in society that would lead to more equal status for women in sports. But only after such changes take full effect would they filter down to the sports scene. In the America of 1980, for all the talk, there is very little indication that mass sports entertainment won't remain a male-oriented activity for a very long time.

23. The Special Status of Children

CHILDREN ARE the first sports audience. This fact is so fundamental, and so obvious, that it is virtually ignored in learned analyses of sports, in opinion surveys, in journalistic planning, and in the minds of countless sports officials who should know better.

Let's define, arbitrarily but not unreasonably, children as those between the ages of eight and fourteen. Before eight, children are too young to grasp the complexity of the various popular games, and don't read well enough to expand their interest (allowing for precocious exceptions). Around fourteen, children are transformed into an entirely different life form called "teenager," which may well belong to an alternate universe, and from whence some individuals return to earthly existence and some do not.

But in that pre–high school segment of child development, sports fandom usually begins. The infection is by no means all-inclusive: many children escape it altogether, the degree of virulence varies greatly from case to case, some shake it off after a fairly brief confinement, and, as we have just seen, it is highly male-selective, in its present form. Still, in millions upon millions of cases it becomes a lifelong addiction of a type rarely contracted for the first time in adulthood. There are people who develop fan interest later in life, but they are relatively few, and many of those do so through contact with an interested child.

Promoters are perfectly aware of this state of affairs. They have long known that children who root grow up to be adults who buy. "Knothole Gang" plans in baseball, which offer children free admission in some way, go back half a century. From the time games were first played within enclosed grounds, the return of a ball knocked over the stands or fence (usually foul) meant free admission, and it wasn't adults who stood around outside the park to chase down and retrieve baseballs. Al Schacht, whose pitching career was later eclipsed by his fame as a baseball clown and New York restaurateur, loved to tell of watching games in the Polo Grounds, before World War I, by climbing a tree outside the left field fence. Today, the cultivation of young fans is systematized with great sophistication: bat days, ball days, cap days, T-shirt days, and batting-helmet days are staples of the baseball schedule. Similar souvenirs, in greater variety, are marketed by football and other sports. Groups of children are brought to games by charitable organizations, day camps, school units, and so forth, and one of the popular devices is to have schools distribute free tickets as a reward for good grades. Habit formation is the name of the promoter's game.

And sports entertainment is particularly suitable to children at this impressionable stage. The illusion of importance, the comprehensibility, and continuity, the thrill of unthreatening hazard, the built-in story line of us-versus-them-equals-good-versus-evil, are well within the capacity of the child to understand and to enjoy. The surroundings are noisy, exciting, colorful, dramatic — even if seen only on television or conjured up in the imagination. Actual attendance includes the availability of delicious junk foods frowned upon at home. What going to the circus or carnival meant to rural America in the nineteenth century, going to the ballpark has meant to urban America in the twentieth.

What's more, children are better equipped than adults to appreciate two basic aspects of spectator sports. First, they can develop rooting loyalty in a purer form than grownups, because it is unadulterated by more complicated considerations. The home town's name on the uniform is reason enough, and the ups and downs of joy and despair can be focused on each game's outcome. A man or woman with a job to worry about and a family to care for may get a momentary boost in morale from knowing that "their" team won, but it's not enough to blot out the harsher realities of life. The entertainment is a respite from serious life, not life itself. For a child, however, a victory by the home team can quite legitimately form his or her mood for the entire day or week, since there is so little else (other than schoolwork) on life's scorecard at that age.

Related to children's sharper reactions to the game's outcome is a second aspect of spectator sports, the "now" syndrome. Time runs at a different rate for children than for adults. The younger you are, the longer and more vivid the present moment seems. Sports, by their nature, stress the "now": this play, this inning, this game, this final score; and there will be a fresh start tomorrow. Even the most dedicated adult fan may find his midseason sensibilities dulled by perspective, by knowledge of what has happened in the past, by awareness of future probabilities, and by the realization that today's melodrama may easily be canceled by tomorrow's. Children haven't learned that yet, about anything, and therefore are that much more in tune with the artificial cosmic finality of each event.

Finally, of course, children play these games themselves, both informally and under school or other adult auspices, and are therefore especially ripe for the hero-identification and vicarious-thrill elements of sports promotion. The Walter Mitty type of adult, who can imagine himself running for a touchdown, rarely loses touch with reality to the point that he doesn't recognize his dream is a dream. But the child who imagines the same thing is projecting himself into a personal future that has not yet been proved unrealistic. The universal habit of children in baseball games yelling "Look, I'm Willie Mays!" while imitating a basket catch, represents a real difference in emotional experience. Adults who play weekend softball can't do that without self-consciousness. Pretending is a child's natural activity.

One practical consequence of this process is the creation of a personal Golden Age for every fan. The sports happenings of these impressionable years acquire an intensity and nostalgia value never again attained. As the fan grows older, all new events are measured, consciously or not, against those earlier events that were most deeply felt. If nothing else, the passage of years piles up more and more detail, more and more of which is recognizably repetitive. The "first" or "only" exceptional occurrence in a

World Series has greater impact on the fan than the twentieth instance of that event (a ninth-inning game-winning hit, for instance), and the longer the historical sequence goes on, the less
exceptional any single incident seems. But for the individual fan,
"history" begins when interest is first aroused.

Allowing for some overlap, therefore, sports "eras" turn out to
be segments less than ten years long, not neatly in step with
calendar decades. Those who become fans at a certain stage —
say, the late 1940s in Brooklyn, or the early 1960s in Los Angeles — emerge with a common heritage. They will respond, forever afterward, to the same resonances, memories, inside jokes,
and serious comparisons. To those who grow away from fandom
in later life, that period becomes merely nostalgia, like an old
movie or a junior prom. But to those who remain fans, memory of
the old days enriches and colors everything that follows, and im-
parts a distinct flavor to that fan's ongoing experience. Hence the
popularity of old-timer days and halls of fame.

This helps account for the innate conservativism of the sports
scene, the fans' resistance to change, the ever-strengthening grip
of the establishment sports, and the alliances we have discussed.
People may yearn for the past on many levels, and deplore
changing fashions in movies, books, clothing, or lifestyles; but
that yearning for the past *must* be satisfied to a reasonable degree
by the sports promoter, because it touches on the deepest level of
spectator enjoyment.

Such attachment, in turn, means great vulnerability in the impressionable child. If the prevailing tone of sports comment is
cynical, sarcastic, or excessively concerned with "only winning
counts," point spreads, or contract negotiations, a certain segment
of the adult public may be titillated or even honestly concerned.
But children will accept these views as normal, and make them
their models for thought and behavior. If there is one thing children do more thoroughly than anything else, it is imitate.

Until about twenty years ago, it was customary to present
sports in a predominantly idealistic light. At least three generations grew up in an atmosphere in which sports implied sportsmanship, the virtues of team loyalty (that is, patriotism), and ad-
herence to rules. Even children noticed, fairly early on, that such

things as cheating and selfishness existed, and that people didn't always live up to their professed codes of behavior. But established authority, in the form of newspapers, magazines, books, and radio broadcasts, clearly conveyed the idea that departures from the theoretical standards of virtue were exceptions to be deplored.

The athletes, by and large, were presented as admirable heroic persons, not simply as talented performers who might or might not have bad character. Stars were rarely quoted, and even more rarely with photographic accuracy. Babe Ruth's animalistic appetites and crude behavior, so well documented in various biographies after his death, were well hidden from the public — including children — during his heyday. Ring Lardner's famous short story "Champion," which contrasts the depraved character of a boxer with his public image, shocked people when published in 1916, precisely because it was so out of step with prevailing mores. The end of that story is pertinent here, because the ugly facts would never have passed a hypothetical "sporting editor." "Suppose you can prove it," Lardner has the editor say. "It wouldn't get us anything but abuse to print it. The people don't want to see him knocked. He's champion."

Basically, that sentiment remains valid. Despite all the success and notoriety, during the last twenty years, of books debunking sports heroes, the day-to-day, bread-and-butter interest of sports fans depends on being able to maintain a benign view of the heroes and the activity. On this level, realism, as the antonym of romanticism, is unwelcome and the enemy of enjoyable identification.

But times and fashions change, and since World War II our culture has moved in an antihero direction on many fronts, at an accelerated pace after Korea and Vietnam. It would be simpleminded to expect attitudes toward sports, especially journalistic attitudes, to escape so strong a tide. When we feel less reverence for presidents, military leaders, churchmen, and educators, and are bombarded with reports of their inadequacies and venality, we should not be surprised that sports figures also get stripped of their heroic veneer.

For children, however, this has a different effect than for

adults, with consequences for society that need more attention than they get. Sports used to be one of the primary conduits for idealistic messages, particularly suitable to a child's comprehension, and since other conduits (church, classroom, respect for authority, political prestige) are also less efficient, how will idealism be instilled? We recognize that some activities tolerable for adults are damaging to children: drinking alcohol, smoking, working in coal mines, and driving cars. In the same way, the "truth" about the private lives of sports figures, or the business practices of teams and colleges, can have a different effect on a child than equivalent exposures about movie stars or congressmen.

What role does a deromanticized presentation of highly publicized sports, which are followed avidly by children, play in creating an altered social fabric? Do attitudes toward morals, ethics, pleasure, work, and honesty develop differently when this vivid portion of childhood imagination is pointed in a different direction? Do journalists and sports promoters have some responsibility to take account of these effects?

To ask such questions is not to raise the specter of censorship or self-censorship, or to advocate a return to an earlier idealism, or to reject "reality," or to extol hypocrisy. It simply means we should realize that the effects do exist. A half-truth about a player's "depravity" or a team's "greed" is no more honest than a half-truth about exaggerated nobility, but it leads to a different conclusion in young minds and emotions. *Absolute* truth is rarely, if ever, available to journalists. Exaggeration of any sort, in any direction, is an unforgivable flaw in objective reporting. The test of relevance, therefore, has special significance for the childhood audience. For instance, we should ask ourselves whether it is the hero's playing ability or his drinking habit that is the proper focus for attention, and in what proportion.

So journalism's perpetual wavering between Pollyannaish and accusatory half-truths comes down on the Pollyannaish side most of the time in sports reporting. Nowadays, this is not so much because editors consciously worry about children in the audience as because their own subliminal sports viewpoints were formed as children. This is changing, slowly. Dirty words, which have always formed the standard vocabulary of athletes even more than of soldiers (because of their power to release tension), were unprintable until very recently, and weren't associated with sports until one came across them at an older age. Now even eight-year-olds know they are commonplace (and not only in sports, of course). What such a change means is for psychologists, philosophers, social scientists, and moralists to determine, but it is impossible to pretend that it isn't a change and that it won't mean *something*.

In the 1980s, the child's approach to sports will be colored by two serious subjects, gambling and drugs. The push for legalization of gambling inevitably shifts the winning-losing emphasis from vicarious loyalty to personal gain. Increased publicity about the use of drugs (beyond mere alcohol) by glamorous sports figures will alter the role models they represent, just as drug use by musicians altered perceptions of popular music in the 1960s and 1970s. Wherever all this leads, it's hard to believe it won't do enormous harm.

Carried to a logical conclusion, however, stripping sports of their romantic and idealistic elements and making them less appealing to children would be a form of fairly quick suicide for the mass-entertainment sports establishment. The industry's sense of self-preservation is rather strong, and so is that of its numerous allies, so the resistance to muckraking is both powerful and effective. If you can't keep converting children into new fans, you can't stay in business. In this respect, children, who form the purest element of sports-watching enjoyment, may be the means, simply by their existence, of that enjoyment's preservation.

24. Gambling

SPECTATOR SPORTS and gambling are inseparable. My favorite sports gambling story concerns the stereotypical New York businessman who loves to bet on basketball. He calls his bookie on Thursday and says, "What's the basketball tonight?"

"There's three pro games and five college games," says the bookie, and reads him the point spread on each game.

"I'll take 'em all," says the bettor, and makes selections for all eight games.

He loses all eight.

Friday, he calls and says, "What's the basketball tonight?"

"Five pro and thirteen college," says the bookie.

"I'll take 'em all," says the bettor.

He loses all eighteen.

Saturday: "What's the basketball?"

"Eight pro, sixteen college."

"Gimme all."

He loses all twenty-four bets. He is now 0-for-50 in three days, and has lost $5000.

Sunday: "What's the basketball tonight?"

"No basketball tonight."

"Whaddayamean, no basketball?"

"It's Sunday. There's no basketball games scheduled Sunday. On Sunday it's hockey. You want to bet some hockey games?"

"Hockey?" screams the bettor, outraged and incredulous, "What do I know from hockey?"

The joke contains profound psychological truth. In betting, the hope of gain is secondary. The main satisfaction comes from the feeling that you "know" something, that you outsmarted the cosmos by guessing right. When a bettor wins, he ascribes it to his superior power of analysis. When he loses, it's bad luck.

Financial gain, of course, is the underlying desire. But there are many avenues to financial gain: work, theft, investment, invention. The habitual gambler who hopes to strike it rich, and for whom the money to be won is the primary motivation, can turn to inanimate objects like cards, dice, roulette wheels, or even elections. Bingo and lotteries thrive everywhere. But the sports bettor is a hybrid. He loves to bet, but he enjoys the game too. It's because he thinks he can figure out the game that he chooses sports as an outlet for his gambling urge.

That's the "real" sports bettor, a minority of the sports audience but an appreciable fraction of it, and a disproportionate fraction of those who constitute the passionate following. More numerous are those who want a little stimulant to their involvement, analogous to a cocktail before dinner. If you can make a small side bet with a friend, the game in front of you becomes more interesting. Anyone who has ever tried to play poker without chips understands how insipid a game can be if you have nothing at stake. Let's call the first type the habitual bettor, and the second type the casual bettor. Between them, they form the backbone of the adult sports audience.

These two kinds of gamblers fall into subgroups. Thoroughbred and harness horse racing exist entirely as devices for legal betting, and the two-dollar bettor is no more interested in the horse as an animal than in a playing card as an artistic illustration. There are, to be sure, people interested in horses who breed, train, and race them, to "improve the breed." But if only those people were involved, horse races would be as frequent — and as expensive and exclusive — as yacht races of the America's Cup class. The democracy of horse racing, which draws more customers through its turnstiles each year than any other sport in America, is based completely on the equal opportunity to cash a bet.

Horse players may be expert judges of horseflesh, followers of some arcane numbering system, or anything in between. They may be interested in other sports too, although many are not. Whether they study the form charts, buy tip sheets, seek inside information, or simply woo blind luck (deciding, for instance, to "bet their age" by choosing those two digits for their daily-double ticket), the result of the race is meaningful only in personal terms: "their" horse won or lost, and no other aspect of the score counts. Dog racing and jai alai, as developed in Florida, are other sports that fall into this category.

Without the opportunity to bet, openly, under supervision that guarantees the winners will be paid off, and ensures a fair contest, these events would not draw crowds. A few historic events, such as the Kentucky Derby, transcend betting interest and become fascinating, competitive sports events for millions who do not bet. But these are exceptions to the rule, and survive only in a context that day-to-day betting provides.

In other sports, betting is less fundamental but not necessarily less present. Horse racing, dog racing, and jai alai are legalized and licensed by some states, and don't exist where they are not. Other sports are automatically legal and need no licensing, while betting on them is illegal (except in Nevada). Boxing requires licensing for a different reason — to protect the health and safety of the contestants, at least in theory — but does not entail legalized betting.

The reasons for this distinction become apparent as soon as we list the requirements for attracting bettors. First, the event being wagered on must be sufficiently complex to provide suspense and mental stimulation, but sufficiently simple to be followed easily. But that, we have seen, is exactly what entertainment sports are designed to be.

Second, there must be the conviction that the contest is truly unpredictable: that is, that the outcome is not prearranged. (A high-wire act in the circus may arouse suspense and a sense of hazard, but it is most definitely rehearsed. An improvisation by an actor or musician may be unrehearsed, but it is not a contest. Neither is suitable material for betting. But a visibly lopsided pair of dice would also be seen as unsuitable, as would a tennis match between Bjorn Borg and an eleven-year-old boy. The concepts of doubt and "fair shake" must be present.) But entertainment sports have been designed for that too.

Third, the subject of the betting must happen frequently, and its result must be easily accessible to all interested parties. Presidential elections are occasions for many private bets, some trivial, some immense; but they seldom occur. Casinos, legal and otherwise, are often difficult or expensive to reach, and the result of the bet is not broadcast beyond the immediate area of the table. Theoretically, one could bet on the number of sunspots recorded by major telescopes every day, but how would one go about getting the results? But that's exactly what entertainment sports are, for their own purposes: frequent and accessible, with every result promptly publicized.

Fourth, a bettor needs continuity — repeated instances of the same basic circumstances. The comparable event must keep happening, time after time, to give you a chance to get even when you're losing. And it has to be recognizably similar each time, so you can feel you are accumulating knowledge that will increase your chance of winning. And that, too, is exactly what entertainment sports provide.

Finally, there has to be someone to bet with. A large body of other bettors, with similar interests, must exist to create a "market" — in the sense of the floor of the stock market — where pools of winnings can be formed by collecting from losers. Gambling is not practical without someone to function as a broker, whether it's an illegal bookmaker, a legal one, the operator of a pool, or the state. Entertainment sports, by generating a large public for their activities, create just such a market for betting.

Now we can see how different sports, with their different characteristics, create different contexts for betting. Horse racing is a competition of elemental simplicity: the only "score" is the order of finish. That's why it's not much fun to follow the results of races, over a long period of time, without betting at all. It's *too* simple.

As soon as one wants to bet, however, marvelous complications appear. Past performances, lineage, records of jockeys, trainers, and owners, weather conditions, fractional times, gender, and just plain hunches can all be taken into account. Since the complications lie almost entirely in the area of predicting rather than in complex rules or tactics during the event itself, only betting sustains interest.

The second point, reliance on an "honest" race, is a two-edged sword. Horses, being unable to talk, cannot be persuaded to fix a race for personal gain; but the people who handle them can, secure in the knowledge that the horse can't snitch even if suspicion is aroused. The animals themselves, therefore, are admirably above suspicion, and have been bred for the urge to run fast. Their human handlers, on the other hand, must be surrounded by elaborate security machinery, so that belief in *their* honesty can be sustained.

That's why state governments (and, in earlier times, "the best people" from "high society") accept responsibility for running a fair game. The central problem of this industry is to prevent a fix, or uncover one if it occurs, and therefore horse racing is organized to reassure the public. The power of the state (through licensing and other regulations) is used to this end, and the state acquires a stake in its effectiveness because so much tax revenue is generated by the betting. The horse becomes little more than an animate roulette ball or a pair of dice.

As for frequency, continuity, and a constituency of interested persons, the racetrack is ideal. The daily program consists of eight to eleven races, most tracks operate six days a week during a meeting, and racing goes on somewhere every day of the year. In the largest metropolitan areas, there may be "flat" racing (the thoroughbreds) in the daytime and harness racing at night, with sixteen or more chances to lose your money.

Off-track betting dwarfs on-track betting in volume. The private (and illegal) bookie's big advantage is flexibility. He can extend credit, accept complicated "if" bets ("if I win on the first race, bet so much of it on the second," for example), and take bets on any race anywhere. Legalized off-track betting shops (as in New York City) are usually just extensions of the pari-mutuel windows at the track.

Pari-mutuels are the ultimate community-of-bettors system: they form a market exchange. The payoff odds are automatically determined by the proportion of money, out of the total pool, that backs any particular horse. No opinion goes into setting the odds. And the state share (taxes) and track share (operational expenses) can be taken out of the pool directly, like a withholding tax. If $100,000 is bet on a race, and the takeout is 17 percent, that means $83,000 is available to be distributed among the winners. If $41,500 was bet on that horse, the payoff becomes even money: for each $2 risked, you win $2 (in addition to the return of the $2 you paid for the ticket).

All the innovations in racing come in the form of exotic betting patterns. Daily doubles, exactas, quinellas, pick-six, perfectas, trifectas — all are methods of picking sequences of winners. The races themselves have changed little since the days of Ben Hur. Why not, then, bet on "people" races? Why wouldn't human track and field events draw just as avid a clientele?

Because the key element of credibility can't be maintained. Human racers can talk — and bet for themselves. To those who don't think in terms of betting, this makes no difference at all, and track competition thrives worldwide. But those who do bet have, or quickly acquire, sensitivity to the possibility of manipulating results. No one doubts that human runners could manipulate without detection, if they were so inclined.

Manipulation is also easy in boxing. There are only two people in the ring, and if one doesn't hit quite as hard as he could, or falls down when he is hit, it's pretty difficult to prove he did so on purpose. Yet boxing is one of the biggest betting sports, because it meets the other four necessary conditions so well: it is elemental yet complex in technique; accessible; frequent, with individuals having long careers; and followed by plenty of fellow fans. There is, moreover, some feeling that most major fights are honest, because the stakes are high (not only in terms of the winning purse, but also in terms of status for future earnings), and because each fighter faces real physical danger.

In racing and boxing, as in dice and roulette, odds are expressed as probabilities: 3 to 1 or 10 to 1 or 5 to 2 or whatever, which means you win more in proportion to the unlikelihood of your choice. In casino gambling, these are straight mathematical probabilities, adjusted to favor the house. In racing, probabilities were originally a matter of opinion on the part of the bookmaker who offered the odds, but pari-mutuels reduced this to automatic expression of collective opinion. In boxing, it remains strictly a matter of the oddsmaker's opinion.

In general, people bet, person-to-person or more elaborately, by setting odds. When the odds in a two-choice bet (such as a fight) are 5–2, you risk losing five dollars to win two dollars if you bet on the favorite, while you risk only two dollars to win five dollars if you bet on the underdog. That was the way people bet on team sports as well, until the 1940s. Then point betting came into the picture, and it now dominates football and basketball.

This was a marvelous invention. In a closely contested game, there is no shortage of suspense, since the decision (and your bet) remains in doubt. But most games produce a decisive margin in the score well before the closing moments, and many are perceived as mismatches before they start (whether or not they actually turn out that way). In odds betting, more often than not it's clear that you have won or lost long before the game actually ends. But point betting changes all that. To bet on the favorite, you have to "give" points, a stipulated number that will be added to the actual score of the underdog. If you bet on the underdog, you "get" the points. The payoff, then, will be on the outcome "with the points," not simply on the winner or the loser.

With point betting, the suspense can become even greater, and more prolonged, in a one-sided game. Suppose Michigan is a fifteen-point favorite over Indiana, a fact that has already established the belief that Michigan is most likely to win and is considered a much stronger team. Sure enough, Michigan dominates the football game, and is leading 21–0 in the fourth quarter, content to have the game end that way, not going out of its way to embarrass the loser unnecessarily. But right down to the last play, an Indiana touchdown and extra point can decide the bet, one way or the other: A 21–7 Michigan victory, every bit as good in the league standings and in the hallowed history of the school as a 21–0 victory, would be a 15-point bettor's defeat (or an underdog bettor's triumph). The element of hazard has been prolonged and intensified. In the old system, if Michigan were a 4 to 1 favorite, it wouldn't matter that there was a late touchdown, and the issue would have been clear long before the game ended.

Also, many practical betting benefits arise from point betting. The illusion of figuring things out, so fundamental to sports betting (and so appealing to the horse player), is enhanced when one tries to calculate the margin of victory, not merely the identity of the winner. For the broker, whose profit lies in balancing his books by having equal amounts bet on each contestant, changing the point spread in one direction or the other as bets are placed is a much more efficient and accurate fine-tuning device than changing the odds. And the bettor, by watching the scoreboard, can follow the fluctuation of his chances moment by moment, instead of being frozen into pregame odds.

Point-spread betting is even better for basketball than for football, since so many points are scored so quickly, and since late-game margins fluctuate so rapidly.

This system has made pool betting the standard "small-time" type of sports betting in America. In schools, offices, and daily newspapers, lists of games are offered with point-margin favorites. You pick a certain number of games, pay accordingly, and get paid in odds if you get them all right (or some stipulated percentage of them). Picking six out of six might be worth 10 to 1 (a $10 payoff for a $1 bet), and picking 15 out of 15 might be worth 200 to 1. The investment seems tiny, the "action," as you follow your fortunes, is plentiful, and the fact that the payoff is far short of the "true" odds in terms of likelihood doesn't diminish the sense of triumph.

It would be fatuous to deny that point-spread betting did a great deal to popularize sports in the 1950–1970 era, coincident with the spread of television. The success of Monday Night Football owed much to the extra chance it gave millions of casual bettors to get — and watch — one more shot after their Saturday-Sunday indulgences. And it's the casual bettor who counts, as far as the sports promoter is concerned. Serious bettors, whether they're professionals, emotionally ill addicts, or wealthy high rollers, are not numerous enough to affect ratings and ticket sales — although they are valued customers for luxury boxes, season tickets, and comparable amenities.

But every benefit contains its drawbacks. Point-spread betting makes manipulation — crookedness, to be blunt — much easier.

To make good their deal with gamblers to throw the 1919 World Series, the Chicago Black Sox actually had to lose the games. Sixty years and millions of investigative words later, it still isn't clear which player did exactly what on the playing field. To play badly enough to lose deliberately to an inferior team not only requires a callous moral sense but also involves substantial risk of arousing suspicion.

But if a favorite can guarantee that a bet on the underdog will pay off, without having to give up his own victory, the moral question is much fuzzier and the risks are less. All he has to do is win by a margin smaller than the point spread — which was set illegally in the first place. Why not? Who will be hurt, except those illegal bettors who are in no position to complain?

Such rationale lay behind the fix scandals that gutted college basketball in the postwar years and were exposed in 1951 and again in 1961. The favored team tried to do enough wrong to win "under the points" without actually losing. If things got out of hand and the game was actually lost, that was a shame — but it didn't alter the success of the bet.

Who was hurt? Well, the bookies, for starters. Illegal or not, a bookie is simply a banker, insofar as he performs only the bookmaking function. He needs approximately equal amounts bet each way, to have enough money to pay off the winners. His profit is his commission, which he usually collects by paying only ten dollars for every eleven dollars bettors put up, just as the house gets its cut from roulette-wheel odds by using zero and double-zero and paying off 35 to 1 for what is mathematically a 37 to 1 proposition.

If a fix is in, and the bookie doesn't know it, he'll get burned. Those arranging the fix will bet large amounts in the right direction. So America's bookies became the first line of defense against indiscriminate fixing. The fans, the club managements, the press, and the excluded players may not know "business" is being done; but the bookmaking community is alerted instantly to money flowing in an unexpected direction. It doesn't need conclusive proof that something funny is up: it just needs to feel some unexplained influence, and it can take that game off the boards. Widespread refusal to take bets is not evidence that a fix is being attempted. Any uncertainty — an injured player, a lack of form, a rumor, a whim by a big bettor — can cause that. But it is very difficult to carry out a fix, for a substantial payoff, without making the bookmaking community aware of the strange movement of money. (And if substantial money weren't involved, it wouldn't be worth fixing the event.)

Of course, a bookmaker can try to profit from a fix by betting along with it, and this happens. There are also cases of embezzlement by bank officers. Thievery pops up in many human affairs. But to the degree that a bookie functions as a broker alone, he needs an honest game as much as the promoter does, not only to avoid being sandbagged by a particular event but to maintain a clientele of customers, who would be turned off by any serious doubts about the fairness of the event they bet on.

In the 1970s, the issue of legalized betting got much attention in Congress and in state legislatures. If such an enormous amount of tax money could be collected from the racetracks, and if so many states could institute lotteries, why not accept — and tax — legal bets on "people" games?

We come here full circle to the need for belief in the integrity of the competition. The nonbettor must have this simply to be entertained; the bettor must have it to get a fair shake; and the promoter (and all his allies in the media, business, and politics) must have it to keep the business viable. It's the *belief* that's crucial.

In legislative hearings and countless public statements, all the established sports have gone on record against legalized betting. What do they fear? The gradual spread of a belief that games are worth fixing, and that fixers can go undiscovered. The argument runs this way: As long as betting is illegal, even though socially acceptable, it takes at least an ounce of lawbreaking spirit to do it. No one minimizes how much bootleg liquor circulated during Prohibition; but no one denies that far more has been consumed since Repeal. So at least some athletes who feel a certain amount of compunction against betting (on themselves to win, let's say) might not feel it if society, through governmental action, put a stamp of approval on it. (What's wrong with betting on yourself to win? Sooner or later you lose, and you have to get even, and the only result you can guarantee is that you will lose next time out.)

Now regardless of impulses, when betting is illegal (or legal only in an isolated place like Nevada), the prospectively dishonest athlete must have a "connection" in order to arrange a bet. Such connections are subject to monitoring by the rather elaborate security forces possessed by all major professional and college sports organizations and all illegal bookmakers (who have underworld ties, of course). The protection is imperfect, but, in the real world, fairly effective, and the two groups cooperate. When sizable amounts of money are involved, illegal bookmakers know their customers or they won't deal with them, as a matter of self-protection.

But if betting is legal, as off-track betting is, for example, anyone — the star quarterback, his wife, his brother-in-law, his business partner, his agent — can walk into any betting shop with total anonymity and bet any amount. In fact, civil-rights questions would probably arise if such a bet were refused. And this doesn't have to actually happen, ever, to undermine public belief. Simply being reminded through constant advertising — which legalized betting entails — that this is possible will make many people wonder.

Already, bettors tend to cry "fix" when a result goes against them unexpectedly, but they have nowhere to turn to demand investigation. And by and large, they understand the unpredictability of sports enough to accept upsets as natural. But when state-approved betting increases the number of unsophisticated bettors, provides a plausible context for fixers to profit secretly, and implies certification of honest effort by accepting bets, the intensity of the outcry at an upset will be increased. And with something to feed on every day, the worm of suspicion can grow very large very quickly, with or without objective justification.

All this, it seems to me, is a realistic enough appraisal of what would result from legalized betting, but it is open to the charge of being an exaggerated fear. I believe there are two stronger arguments against legalization, both of which are rooted in the old-fashioned idea that private businesses have some rights, and in the more recent idea that governmental supervision implies governmental guarantees to the citizen.

The first point has to do with children. It is their romanticized attachment to sports, through the media (as described in parts I and II), that produces adult customers down the line. The fundamental illusion of importance, which is all the promoter really has to sell, is nurtured by attitudes and reports about sports as they have evolved over a century, and the bedrock assumption in those attitudes is that *winning the contest* is what counts. Under legalized betting, this will change subtly to *winning the bet,* and the media will inevitably begin to reflect this view, as they now do in the coverage of racing.

Children will then just as inevitably learn to become betting fans rather than sports fans, and very quickly. Whether this is desirable, harmful, or insignificant from the standpoint of society, morality, mental health, economics, and idealism may be debated. But it will certainly stop the growth of those particular subliminal associations that make sports marketable as a reliving of early-life joy.

The sports establishment, however, is a collection of private businesses in what is called a free-enterprise system. It is taking all the financial risks. If it feels its basic market appeal will be threatened by being conscripted to serve as the state's roulette wheel, it is entitled to have that feeling honored. After all, if the state wants to run a gambling operation, let it finance the teams people will bet on, just as it finances its own lotteries. The state does not, in an arbitrary and discriminatory way, say to the producer of *My Fair Lady,* "You've got a great show there, and we'd like all our citizens to see it, so we're making a videotape of it and setting up showings in schools, libraries, and public squares, because we need the revenue we can get that way." In the case of a book or a movie, the state recognizes the proprietary rights of its creator. Likewise the state should leave alone an event staged by a private promoter for his own purposes in his own way, without using it, against his will, as a vehicle for a gambling activity he feels will damage it.

The second argument against the legalization of gambling is closely related. When the state taxes racetracks and runs off-track betting shops, it also licenses and supervises the races themselves. It makes a compact with the public, whose bets it takes, that it is playing some role in seeing to it that the events are honestly contested, just as it vouches for the safety of state roads and the integrity of state bonds. (Of course, thievery shows up here, too, occasionally; but the theoretical warranty is clear.) States do not, however, license or supervise ball clubs or tennis players; and no advocate of legalized betting is suggesting that they do so.

This, it seems to me, sets up the citizen-bettor to be victimized, because the private promoter and others who can influence the outcome — referees, coaches, players — are free to make bets (under state auspices) with no check on their backgrounds or qualifications.

One can, of course, in full sincerity, argue in favor of complete state supervision of all sports. The merits of such a system will be viewed differently by different people. But only after this has been advocated will it be fair to talk of legalized betting.

Finally, it should be pointed out that *legalized betting* is a misnomer. What is actually being suggested is "state-operated" betting, which the racetracks have. Strictly speaking, *legalized* betting would mean the abolition of laws against betting, and the issuance of licenses to those who wish to operate privately as bookmakers. If this were the case, bookmaking, like running a bar, a taxi, or a law office, would be a "legalized" private activity. But I haven't heard of any legislators suggesting that.

25. Addiction or Safety Valve? Politics, Drugs, and Violence

IN OUR DISCUSSION of gambling, we moved imperceptibly to a new level of interaction between sports and society. For the first time, we dealt with a situation in which the sport event is used *consciously* as a mere vehicle for achieving a type of satisfaction that is quite separate from the intended content of the event.

The basic idea of every contest, for spectator as well as participant, is to see who will win. But the bettor's attention is on the outcome of his or her bet, not on the outcome of the contest. Depending on which side he has backed, and under what conditions, his payoff may be tied to the loser of the contest, or to a certain margin in the score.

We use the word *win* for both activities — winning the game and winning the bet — and thereby blur a very important distinction. Stated most simply, the distinction is: Winning a game has meaning only in reference to the game itself, but a bet can be won on all sorts of things that aren't games or contests. The flip of a coin, or the amount of rainfall next month, is perfectly adequate material for making a bet. No complex rules and contexts need be created to carry out such a bet. But complex context is intrinsic to sports, and it is the substance of the interest they generate, whether or not there is any betting.

This difference is so important that it is worth one more example. One may use a book as a reader, to absorb its content. And one may use the same book, without opening it, to prop up the lid of a piano. The pure sports fan is analogous to the reader. The pure gambler is using the game as a prop. In real life, of course, nothing is "pure," and the fan-gambler combination can be found in every proportion. But the distinct nature of the opposite poles is not diminished by the fact that almost everyone falls somewhere between them.

Now, we have already seen in how many ways sports are used for other purposes: to make money, to exert influence, to satisfy ego, to supply diversion. We've noted the various institutional alliances that support the sports establishment. We have identified at least some of the indirect and subconscious effects the sports establishment has on children, on adult relationships, and on habits of thought. But in all those other "external" purposes for which sports are used, the integrity of the *concept* of the game is essential. Unless the identity of the winner of the contest is perceived as important for its own sake, all the ancillary effects lose their significance.

To the extent that an event is merely the occasion for a bet, however, the external purpose becomes different in kind. And the possibility of this extraneous use of the sports event brings us full circle to some basic questions:

• Are commercial spectator sports, in the American culture of this particular era, an opiate of the people, or an emotional safety valve, or both, or neither?

• Can they be used *consciously* for purposes divorced from the nature of the games themselves, by people not involved in the production or distribution of those games?

• Is it at all possible to consider sports sheer entertainment that does not somehow manipulate our cultural value system?

To the first question, the answer is a loud "Both." To the second, the answer is "Yes, but not very efficiently except in the special case of gambling." To the third, it is "Of course not, but not any more or less than with every other form of widely experienced entertainment."

Such dogmatic and clearly subjective answers can be justified in the following terms. If *opiate* implies deadening of the senses to the harsher realities of life, by providing a temporary state of satisfaction through illusion, then sports certainly fit the definition.

Creating such an illusion is what the sports business is all about. And if "safety valve" implies a relatively harmless release for accumulated emotional tension, then sports fit that definition just as well, since emotional tension and release form the very substance of the entertainment the sports illusion creates.

Both of these functions, however, tend to limit the effectiveness of all attempts to use sports for non-sports purposes. If the spectator perceives that external goals — such as support for a politician, or the promotion of good health, or some moral issue — have been attached to sports, the illusion evaporates, and with it the continuing interest. And to believe that hidden puppet masters are pulling the strings in a monster brainwashing operation that leaves most spectators unaware of manipulation but responsive to it — well, that's a degree of conspiracy theory entirely appropriate to mystery stories, but not to the real world being described here.

As for the subliminal conditioning sports followers receive, there is, it goes without saying, no escape. (In fact, that's exactly what we're examining in Part III.) But the messages transmitted are less explicit, and therefore have less direct effect, than those embedded in movies, books, and lyrics of popular songs, and daily non-sports journalism (in print and on the air). Precisely because a sports event must focus attention on its own artificial plot to have significance at all, it is a poor transmitter of abstract ideas.

Probing a little deeper, however, we can ask four more questions that can't be answered so easily.

1. To the extent that sports (especially on television) are sheer entertainment, have they reached a dangerous degree of obsession for too many Americans, as Henry Steele Commager, the historian, has suggested?

2. Since sports create, inevitably as well as deliberately, heroes and role models for the public, where will their tolerance of drug use and their permitted violence lead?

3. Does our sports interest, obsessive or not, really deflect attention from more important issues?

4. Are sports, in the international as well as national commercial sphere, only fodder for various propaganda machines?

The answers to these questions lie within the confines of the original premise of Part III, that sports are much more a reflection of the larger society than a cause of its characteristics, although, as reflecting agents, they have a strong reinforcing effect.

My answers, partial and unsatisfying, but at least useful starting points, can be framed this way:

1. Obsession is too extreme a word to describe our attitude toward sports, and that attitude is not a serious threat to our intellectual fabric, for a very simple reason. As entertainment, sports survive only if they compete successfully in the marketplace. We may not have true freedom of choice and a free-enterprise economy in many aspects of our society, but we come closer to it in the buying of tickets (and twisting of the dial) than in any other activity. The enormous expansion of major sports during the last two decades, both geographically and in television hours, is only the consequence of more time and money available to be spent on leisure activities. The fraction of the recreational dollar going to spectator sports is smaller, not larger, than it was half a century ago.

2. Sports heroes, like all heroes, have been devalued in American life, in so many ways and for so many reasons that trying to explore them here is unnecessary and would be outside the boundaries of this discussion. Nevertheless, prominent athletes, and their public images, exert enormous influence, especially on children and the parents of children. When heroes are revealed to be drug users, or extol violence, aren't they doing special harm? Harm, yes. Special? That's less clear.

First of all, the drug and violence issues have to be examined separately. Drug use, and abuse, falls into two categories: functional and social. Among the functional drugs are all the approved, questionable, and supposed painkillers and performance-enhancers. Athletes who make their living by subjecting their bodies to extraordinary strain (by definition) are naturally in the forefront of those who seek medical or extramedical aid in this regard. And the people who pay them to perform their exceptional feats encourage them to try such aids. The social drugs are those used for their emotional effect outside of actual athletic performance. These range from the almost totally acceptable tobacco and alcohol to cocaine and other powerful illegal agents.

Sports users of both types of drugs are entirely in step with the rest of society when economic class, living patterns, opportunities, and needs are taken into account. The performance-enhancing drugs, from Novocaine through anabolic steroids, were invariably prescribed *originally* by well-meaning doctors and trainers. (Athletes, after all, did not do their own pharmaceutical research.) That such drugs were overprescribed at one stage in our national life is now common knowledge. That athletes didn't give them up as rapidly as the medical establishment advised should surprise no one.

The athlete taking, or the coach permitting, such drugs is no different from the student who takes pep pills to get through exams, the housewife on tranquilizers or diet pills, the three-martini executive, or, for that matter, the nonstop coffee drinker. They all feel they need a particular drug to get through their tasks, and whether they are right or wrong, moral or immoral, misguided or reckless, there is nothing about their dependence that is intrinsic to sports.

What *is* intrinsic to sports is extreme nervous tension, of a sort shared by all professional performers (actors, musicians, politicians) and those who face physical hazards. Traditionally, such people have sought relaxation in social drugs to a greater degree than people who lead "ordinary" lives. Here the effect of the particular drug on the user can't be separated from the social context in which it is used. When speakeasies were "in" during prohibition, that's where sports figures — and actors, musicians, the wealthy, the prominent, and those who wanted to rub elbows with them — went. When marijuana became commonplace on college campuses, who could expect athletes coming out of four years of campus life not to view it as commonplace? When cocaine became the symbol of affluent indulgence, could we realistically expect every twenty-five-year-old suddenly earning $300,000 a year to be immune to the lure of flaunting his position and independence, and to avoid falling prey to very sophisticated drug marketers?

The point needn't be belabored. Those who live high-intensity lives in brief and hazardous careers, for great rewards, in businesses that require constant traveling and considerable loneliness and disorientation, will produce among their number a certain proportion of people who seek relief in drugs. Such people also have a higher rate of sexual promiscuity, divorce, tax problems, and gossip-column mentions than a similar number of middle-class office workers who seldom travel, have stable family lives, and tune in to Monday Night Football.

But what about their "special obligation"? Don't prominent athletes, by accepting the rewards of their position, assume an obligation to set good examples? The self-righteous answer is an uncompromising yes, and the fact is that a clear majority of pro-fessional athletes feel the obligation strongly and act on it. But a large number do not, and in the last decade these have been get-ting (legitimately) much more journalistic exposure than they used to.

To put things in proper perspective, however, one must com-pare athletes to other public entertainers. Does awareness that an athlete abuses drugs have more or less impact on more or fewer impressionable minds than the same knowledge about a movie star? The Beatles? A presidential assistant? A college professor? It would be nice if the sports world set spectacularly higher stan-dards of behavior than the rest of us. But it doesn't, and to read anything more into its mainstream imperfection is not the way to increase one's understanding of its place in the scheme of things.

Violence is a different matter. Violence *is* peculiar to sports, among the various kinds of entertainment. It's built in. Intimida-tion — physical intimidation — is a key element in athletics, and to deny that perfectly obvious truth is to miss the whole point of what wins and loses games. No player, coach, or executive fails to acknowledge this privately. Most try piously to minimize it in public remarks — and with good reason, since listeners who are not involved in such activity day-to-day interpret such talk as more vicious than it really is.

But the actuality is vicious enough. Anyone can see that the idea of a prize fight is to knock an opponent senseless, which means inflicting a brain concussion. Anyone with even rudimen-tary experience in football knows that, in most cases, the team that hits harder wins, and that most of the first-half hitting is de-voted to determining who will have less appetite for second-half hitting.

In baseball, at the professional level, it is a given idea that a ninety-mile-an-hour fast ball is a crippling weapon if the batter doesn't get out of the way, and that a runner sliding into a base will try to knock the fielder loose from the ball. Hockey permits collisions and body blocking at high speed, and basketball, near the basket, is no less physical, despite all the refined rules. Soccer has its share of kicking and body contact. And in a horse race, 100-pound jockeys crowd 1200-pound mounts against each other when coming around a turn, with occasionally lethal results.

Inflicting and withstanding pain are basic elements in sports. (In activities like track, the pain is self-inflicted.) But even more pervasive is the threat of pain. To perform the actions needed to win requires enormous concentration under pressure. Anything that breaks your opponent's concentration can help you. His expectation of pain — from memory of the last hit, or the last close pitch — can weaken his concentration on the flight of the ball. Intimidation is fundamental, and all sorts of psychological tricks are used to enhance it; but they wouldn't work if the credibility hadn't been established first by blows already delivered.

None of this, of course, is involved in other entertainments. A movie or drama may depict the most gory violence imaginable, but it's make-believe, and we know it. A dancer can suffer serious injury, and a high-wire acrobat can get killed, but these are incidental dangers. And very few writers get badly hurt while typing.

How, then, can such activity be justified? We turn our backs on bearbaiting and even dueling for a point of honor. How do we tolerate this violence in athletic sports? There are two saving graces. Rules are designed to limit the violence to acceptable levels (acceptable to the participants, that is). And participation is entirely voluntary.

The last point is often missed by editorial writers. No one is forced to become a boxer or a football player, or to remain one. It is true that dazzling rewards are dangled before the hopefuls, and that thousands make choices they later regret. That the economically disadvantaged classes produce more boxers and football players than golfers is not merely the consequence of a lack of golf courses in ghettos and poor rural areas. After all, those growing up in affluent suburbs could choose to fight or play football if they preferred, but few do, while those at society's bottom, whether from city streets or coal mines, are more willing to put their bodies on the line, to escape upward. But the fact remains, there is a choice.

It is also likely that only certain personality types choose to play such sports. Not every ghetto athlete turns to boxing, and many middle-class athletes play high-level college and pro football. But this is a psychoanalytic thicket we need not enter. It's enough to note that individuals who lack some taste for violence, and a tolerance for it, don't make it to the upper echelons of contact sports.

So violence *within the context of the game* is tacitly accepted, or the game wouldn't exist. Violence stimulated by the excitement of the game is another matter. Fights sometimes break out between players (in hockey nightly, in baseball rarely), and these are, with very few exceptions, "retaliation" encounters. They are a device — and an effective one, experience has shown — for keeping the general level of violence within agreed bounds. The players know the difference between a legitimate hit, however painful, and a cheap shot or an attempt to maim, even if spectators don't. Beyond any league rules, official actions, or verbal threats, the underlying practical law is, "You foul our player, and we'll foul yours just as hard." Retaliation and deterrence are essential features of the continuing relationships between competitors.

In such fights, serious injuries can occur, perhaps accidentally. When a weapon is used — a baseball bat, or a hockey stick — the internal civilized standards of sport are being violated, and severe disciplinary actions (or even criminal or civil charges) follow. But these incidents are not, in themselves, sports problems, any more than a fist fight between two office workers is a business problem.

Other fights involve spectators, either as an outgrowth of a fight among players (usually in indoor arenas), or within the crowd itself. This, too, is not really a sports problem per se, but a mob problem. Crowds often get out of control at rock concerts, political demonstrations, dance halls, and strike picket lines as well as at South American soccer games and Parisian race tracks. The history of Italian opera is replete with vandalism and even the burning down of theaters by disgruntled patrons.

Of course sports events inflame the passions of rooters: that's why they came. Of course selling beer for hours to excited fans is asking for trouble: but selling beer is one of the reasons for having the business in the first place. And of course hooligans tear up turf and seats in "celebration," knowing the television cameras are on them: that's a price we pay for worshiping television. (No one who has had occasion to ride a New York subway during the last fifteen years should be astonished that the population containing those who vandalized those cars contains individuals who wrecked part of Shea Stadium and Yankee Stadium when the excuse arose.)

Major sports events definitely provide an excuse for unruly crowd behavior. But so does anything else that gathers a crowd and stimulates excitement. To expect a promoter, whose financial existence depends on being able to stimulate excitement in large groups of people, to screen his ticket buyers for stable character and good manners is a wee bit unrealistic.

Violence, as a vicarious thrill, is part of the appeal of spectator sports. As an implement of play, it is fundamental to most games. As a by-product of crowd behavior, it's unavoidable. And as an underlying tendency in an activity that males developed as at least a partial expression of macho mystique, it is neither surprising nor eradicable. But no one is required by law to take part or watch, and if such violence seems objectionable, those sports can simply be ignored. The exercise of choice is always available.

3. The argument for deflection of attention, the opiate theory in its strongest form and a popular theme with left-of-center analysts, is usually cited in connection with racial questions. On the broadest front, this argument starts with the assumptions that revolutionary or at least drastic changes *must* be made in society as a whole, and that the powers defending the status quo are making good use of interest in sports as a soporific. According to the argument, intellects that ought to be confronting life-and-death issues are lulled into inactivity by the hypnotic entertainment. And the disadvantaged, who have the greatest stake in rising up to change the inequitable social structure, are not only lulled by the entertainment but seduced by a false impression that there is room at the top in the existing system, for those who can climb

the athletic ladder. The seduction concept has far more substance than the idea that intellects are being distracted from more serious endeavors.

In the black community, the false athletic goals presented to children are a serious problem. Latent (as distinct from overt) racial stereotyping, deceptive reports of open opportunity, exploitation of cheap labor, and efforts to keep blacks quiet come together with tragic results. Black children and their parents hear or read that 80 percent of the players in the National Basketball Association are black, and that their average salary is $200,000 a year. It's not hard for people whose consciousness of discrimination is alive every minute to think that there's a better chance in a field that's 80 percent black than in another (law, for instance) that's 5 percent black.

But the arithmetic, of course, is totally different. There are only 250 NBA players altogether, and 80 percent of that is 200 individuals. There are about 2,500,000 black males between the ages of five and seventeen who could be thinking about pursuing a path to pro basketball. The odds against any one of them are 12,500 to 1. There are, however, some 400,000 lawyers. Five percent of this is 20,000. If the same reservoir of black children set their sights on becoming lawyers, the odds would be 125 to 1 — a hundred times as good.

Arthur Ashe, the tennis star, has devoted his eloquent writing talents and much of his time to preaching nonathletic goals to black children and their parents. Insofar as the glamour sports, in which numerous individual blacks have excelled, have acted as a Pied Piper leading ordinary children astray, to that degree the sports establishment has had an enormously negative effect. It hasn't done so deliberately, but that doesn't soften the consequences.

This is one of the few instances where sports practice causes change more than it reflects it. The colleges, in particular, exploit the ghettos mercilessly. The more talented high school athletes are urged to concentrate on sports so that they'll be recruited. The colleges that recruit them use admission concessions designed to enhance opportunity for all blacks, so that they can stock up on athletes. Where snap courses and a bit of transcript falsification are necessary, they somehow happen. And the black athlete is rarely channeled into a worthwhile academic program (which would interfere with sports performance and risk ineligibility) and usually doesn't get a degree. Again, the top couple percent of minority athletes wind up in pro careers; the rest, cheated at worst and not helped enough at best, suffer.

The hypothesis that people would pay more attention to changing the world if they weren't zonked out by watching sports on television is highly questionable. First of all, there is no evidence that those who now think only of Monday Night Football would begin to think of monetary policy or electoral reform if football went off the air. It is at least equally conceivable that they would settle for "Laverne and Shirley" instead. Second, there is nothing to indicate that those who do contemplate serious problems have any difficulty in either enjoying or ignoring the sports scene, as their bent may be. Third, one could just as easily assume that if those rabid sports fans did decide to put aside their spectatoritis and become more active politically, they would throw their weight in the direction of the status quo, making revolution more difficult, not less.

We have here a special case of a larger argument that arises more often in connection with space exploration, military appropriations, and various pet congressional projects. People often say, "We spent fifty billion dollars going to the moon, for no good reason, while our cities rot and poverty remains unsolved." The implication is that if the $50 billion were not spent on space, it would be spent on schools, hospitals, and public housing. But nothing in our political experience indicates that this kind of either-or choice takes place. Amounts spent on welfare items seem to go up and down according to the public's enthusiasm (as estimated by officeholders and office seekers) for a particular program, whether or not some other expensive program also exists.

Similarly, it seems naive to look at the dollars being spent "frivolously" on sports — or cigarettes or beer or portable hi-fis — and assume that they would be spent on something worthwhile if the frivolity became unavailable. All indications are that some other frivolity would be found; and that if there were a real desire to finance worthwhile activities, frivolity would not stand in the way.

4. That sports are fodder for propaganda is an inescapable fact of life. Anything that holds attention is, and sports were created to hold attention. The Olympics, and all international competitions, are orgies of nationalism. How could they be otherwise? If you identify a competitor by his citizenship, what can his triumph or defeat reflect but that identity? Jimmy Connors, when he was the world's number-one tennis player a few years ago, complained that in the U.S. Open in New York, the crowd didn't root for him even though he was an American, while in every other country a native player had nearly 100 percent vocal support when he played. Connors, who was at the height of his bad-boy image then, was actually criticizing the spectators for being impartial enough to prefer a better-behaved foreigner on the grounds of sportsmanship. If such a feeling is present in so individualized a sport as tennis, in the mind of a citizen of the country that champions free enterprise and personal feedom, what must it be like in a team sport in a Socialist country that sees every activity as a service to the State?

The cultural struggle between West and East, since World War II, has been reflected in the struggle over the definition of *professional* and *amateur*. The winning and losing of games — as in the 1980 Winter Olympics — is happily accepted by the winners, and unhappily accepted by the losers, as a kind of rating of the value of their civilizations.

But the Olympic Games of 1948 and 1952 did not cause the Cold War, nor did the Berlin Games of 1936 launch World War II, nor did the American boycott of the 1980 Moscow Games demolish detente. Real-world events did that. Sports reflect, with surprising accuracy and considerable illumination, the societies in which they exist, but they are the mirror, not the light. And distorting the mirror won't change what the light shines upon.

26. Participation versus Spectating

PARTICIPATORY SPORTS, we said at the outset, are not part of our subject. Activities such as jogging, skiing, fishing, hunting, hiking, skating, various racquet games, boating, Little League and other youth-group programs, neighborhood bowling, weekend golf and tennis, and so on — all fall outside our definition of mass-spectator commercialized sports. A few points about them must be made, however, in relation to journalism and society.

Participatory sports are in no way inferior to the big-league sports we have dealt with. They engage, in the aggregate, millions of people — probably more than the total number of ticket buyers. They arouse passionate interest in their followers, are probably more beneficial to their practitioners than spectating can be, and more directly affect those involved. But they are irrelevant to fandom. And it is the fan phenomenon that dominates journalism's interest in spectator sports, for all the reasons already elaborated.

Many papers devote a good deal of space to participation sports, either in a special section or as a subsection of the sports section. In the book business, these subjects are the backbone of sports publishing success. But for day-to-day journalistic treatment, they are simply unsuitable.

The missing ingredient is exactly the thing participants value. They want doing, not watching. But thousands of doers, acting at different times and places, don't share a *simultaneous* reading interest in other doers. They want to read material — a lot of material — about things they can apply to their own doing. But they won't buy a paper every day to find out how far some jogger they don't know jogged yesterday.

Being a fan *is* spectating. It's an active, involved, absorbing form of watching, but it is not *doing*. So there is no contradiction between doing one thing and watching another, and many individuals enjoy both. But journalism and the sports establishment can't profit from the doing part. They depend entirely on watching interest. But that doesn't mean participatory sports aren't commercialized. They are, in some respects, even more commercialized than spectator sports. Their money is tied to equipment and facilities.

A sports promoter, as we pointed out at the beginning of this book, makes his money by drawing a crowd. He charges admission and also sells small items (hot dogs, beer, scorecards) to the captive audience while it's inside his enclosure. In participation sports, the middle man is eliminated. The participant has to buy a racquet, shoes, appropriately styled clothing, and balls. He has to rent a court, join a club, pay for lessons, and buy books.

The spectator-sports promoter toils to sell a ticket for $5 or $10, and he must sell it over and over again. A jogger can be sold a $200 all-weather suit and several pairs of $50 shoes, if the manufacturer plays his cards right. Anyone who skis, plays golf, or belongs to a health club knows how much money really goes out. And the standard formula for buying and operating a boat is: add up all the costs, then multiply by three to find out what you'll really spend. Golf courses and tennis courts are the centerpieces of real-estate developments. Profits made by hotels, motels, cabins, and campgrounds that are connected to the recreation business are hard to measure in dollars, but they dwarf those made by any major-league operation.

And this isn't really new. Remember Albert Spalding? In the early years of major-league baseball, Spalding, Al Reach, and Harry Wright went into the sporting-goods business. They understood that their highly skilled professional presentation of the game would automatically breed imitative participants by the millions — all of whom would need bats, balls, and gloves. After a certain point, it would have paid them to play major-league games without charging admission, just for the advertising value of attracting customers for their manufactured products. Later, golf clubs and tennis equipment became mainstays of their enterprise. But only in the last ten years or so have we seen the full flowering of participation gear on every level, from a hundred varieties of shoes to bicycle helmets. It's big business.

Let's return to fandom for a moment. In the case of baseball, fandom spurred participation. Does it do so now? For children, yes. For adults, not much. Children, natural fantasists that they are, want to imitate the glamour sports they see on television, and try basketball, baseball, football, and soccer themselves. A tremendous amount of equipment is sold to them and to the community and school organizations that serve them. Adults, on the other hand, recognize only too well that the professionals they see are doing something the spectator could never approximate. They may or may not be spectators, but they usually choose some other kind of activity to participate in.

What about the opposite? Does participation create potential fans? Not as much as you'd expect. Golfers form the bulk of the professional-golf audience, and to a lesser degree this is true of tennis. But joggers and long-distance runners have not flocked to standard track meets. People who are themselves passionately devoted to skiing, and who can spend all week wondering how good the snow will be at Tahoe or Stowe, rarely call newspaper offices to ask for the results of the latest Nordic cross-country competition held in Finland. Racers in a weekend sailing regatta are miffed if local papers don't carry their results, but very few care or ask about the yachting results in another harbor fifty miles away.

What we have here, then, is a very deep, very fundamental difference in values and goals. The basic attitudes of the participant and the spectator are on different wavelengths, even when both exist in the same person. Actually, the difference is between recreationalist and competitor. The recreationalist prizes exercise. The competitor craves dominance over an opponent. The former pursues excellence. The latter pursues triumph, and excellence is only a means to an end.

The spectator has been successfully conditioned to identify

with the competitor, and he can enjoy vicariously the dominance and triumph his chosen favorite provides. But he cannot vicariously experience exercise or excellence.

There is also a difference that does not involve the competitor at all. The participant wants a feeling of engagement, of being active, of doing. Taking part is more important than the scoreboard result (which may be important too). The spectator revels in a solitary, passive enjoyment, even if others are present. His private satisfaction (or bittersweet disappointment at losing) can't easily be put into words, although talking about the more superficial aspects of what happened is a large part of the fan's fun. But that passive pleasure can be obtained only by focusing on the win-lose result as the hub about which all other items of interest revolve.

A world of difference. And, we should note, the participant is better off. Since his focus is on doing, no change of fashion, physical surroundings, or circumstances can really cut him off from finding an alternate way to get satisfaction. If the path around the reservoir is closed off, the participant can run somewhere else. If there's no tennis court, switching to racquetball isn't all that traumatic. A sailboat without a race to enter is still a sailboat.

But the fan, once hooked on a particular sport or team, is stuck. His enjoyment stems from a strong commitment that is based on all sorts of resonances from childhood and depends on his emotions in response to the illusion. If the entity to which he attaches loyalty disappears — if the Dodgers leave Brooklyn, if the American Basketball Association folds, if his college drops football, or if Willie Mays retires — it is not easy to regenerate those intense feelings toward some substitute attachment. But enabling fans to renew such feelings perpetually, and keep them strong, is what the sports business is all about.

27. Good and Bad Influences

WE CAN NOW itemize and sum up some of the principal effects the sports establishment exerts on American life. On the positive side we get:

1. Reality testing
2. Democratization
3. Practical idealism
4. Acceptance of rules and discipline
5. Free entertainment
6. Cultural glue

Along with these benefits, we get such harmful influences as:

1. Institutionalized hypocrisy
2. Damage to players
3. Little League syndrome
4. Spectatoritis
5. Overemphasis on victory
6. Tolerance of abusive authority

Only a brief elaboration of each point is needed.

REALITY TESTING

This is by far the most important benefit sports have to offer. It may sound contradictory to ascribe reality testing to an activity we have persistently described as an illusion, but the acceptance of the illusion (that the result matters) is what brings reality into the picture.

The outcome of a single play or an entire game is not subject to differing interpretations. The score is the score, and it stands, regardless of what someone "deserves," and despite all the "what ifs." A ball is caught or it is not caught. A play either stays in bounds or it doesn't. One may disagree with an official's judgment about some physical fact, but the physical fact itself is unchallengeable.

Especially during school years, people have relatively little contact with uncompromising reality. Parents and teachers, by and large, are sources of aid and comfort (or should be) when something unpleasant or difficult transpires. A bad grade can be perceived as unfair or prejudiced. Lateness may be excused. A missed assignment can be made up at a later date. In almost any circumstance, mercy and forgiveness can be sought.

But a dropped pass is a dropped pass. It's incomplete and the next play starts. If the batted ball clears the fence for a home run, the pitcher can't undo the result by crying "I didn't mean it!" The clock keeps ticking, and when a game ends the score is final. And that, of course, is the way the physical universe we all live in works. Gravity doesn't care who we are or what our motives may be when we step out of a tenth-story window: it pulls down.

In our particular society, countless mechanisms protect us from the consequences of error (thank goodness). Those who grow up in comfortable surroundings get less experience with denial, and with the amount of effort needed to attain a goal, than their ancestors did two or three generations back. In the nineteenth century, life on a farm or in the central cities normally produced more encounters with something intractable than we are accustomed to today. Today, the things that frustrate us most — for instance, tangling with a bureaucracy or a computer — do so by means of the kind of stifling indefiniteness Franz Kafka described.

But everything in sports is definite, clear-cut, and unchangeable, once recorded. Everyone who plays in a game experiences this firsthand. But the same lesson is taught to all those who merely watch, once they make the commitment, as fans, to care about the result. This conditioning is of great value. Awareness of the immutability of results, and of how every step of a process may have a crucial effect on the outcome, is impressed on our minds more vividly, more often, and more permanently by exposure to sports than by most other means. This alone fully justifies sports programs at the school and college level, and is too seldom appreciated as a positive reminder to all.

DEMOCRATIZATION

A generation ago, when color lines were being broken, much nonsense was written about the liberty, equality, and fraternity of sport. Many who lived through the abandonment of overt bigotry felt they ought to be congratulated for accepting the enlightenment forced upon them, as if to say, "Boy, I sure live in a nicer neighborhood now that the guy next door has stopped beating up his children; good for me."

In the last decade or so, considerable research has been done on the persistence and subtlety of racial (and other forms of) discrimination. Very few blacks and Latinos have risen to positions of authority in sports organizations, despite their prominent roles as players, and this tiny proportion turns out to be strikingly similar to the proportion of blacks and Latinos at the higher levels of other American businesses.

So the "democracy" of sport has been called a myth, and a perniciously misleading one at that. In one sense, the criticism is perfectly correct. In the spheres of social position, power structure, and opportunity for advancement, the sports establishment clings to discriminatory attitudes no less than the rest of the American establishment. No more, but no less. In another sense, however, sports are profoundly democratizing influences that build up, layer by layer, much that is good and distinctive about American ideas of equality. The democracy shows up on the field, in the same way reality testing does. The ball doesn't care who catches or misses it, and does no favors for the privileged.

Again, those who play sports experience this directly, but the more important effect is on those who watch. By accepting the complex of emotional involvement that goes with rooting for a particular team, the fan becomes committed to the inescapable reality of the win-lose result, and develops, automatically, the habit of reacting to a player *as a player*. And he or she gets this training in the democracy of merit in a setting free of preaching, ideology, or political pressure.

It is an invaluable lesson that stimulates and reinforces our willingness to judge a person's actions by the results rather than by that person's irrelevant characteristics. It is much easier to ignore accomplishment (or failure) in less overtly measurable activities, and thereby keep stereotypes intact. But within the structure of a game, all players have equal rights, and all actions have equal effect. This does not eradicate internal prejudices in those who feel them, but it does give people early and abundant conditioning in accepting results unaltered by preference. It is the democracy of merit, of impartiality, of deeds over status. And it is worth something.

PRACTICAL IDEALISM

Closely related to the first two positive aspects is the daily exercise of idealistic concepts. The sports fan is immersed in ideas of team effort, victory for the sake of glory, determination, friendly strife, fair play, and so forth. And he or she sees the practical effects of these virtues, time after time. No matter how many particular cases arise where they are violated or ignored, the climate of high aspiration is always there, in a way that is seldom apparent in other daily pursuits.

Back in Part I, we defined patriotism as the loyalty a rooter attaches to a school team or any other object of affection he or she chooses. In other cultures, stimulation of the imagination in the direction of noble feelings stems most often from historical heroes and traditional folkways. In twentieth-century America, spectator sports serve this function, at least to some extent.

RULES AND DISCIPLINE

This society, with its refugee and frontier heritage and its worship of personal independence, has relatively few mechanisms for instilling respect for order. Sports do this very effectively, since the spectator as well as the player must accept unquestioningly the rules of a game, if there is to be a game. As for discipline (as distinct from authoritarianism), its virtues are made manifest by the performance of any winning team or player; and copious descriptions of the preparation and practice that go into making victory possible solidify our education in this necessary but often uncomfortable area.

FREE ENTERTAINMENT

Nothing is really free: someone somewhere always pays the costs. But spectator sports give more Americans more hours of diversion that are not paid for directly by the recipient than any other form of entertainment. Even if we define all non-sports radio and television presentations as "free," the fact remains that most of these programs have entertainment value only while actually in progress. They do not generate the entertainment a fan gets from talking, reading, wondering, hoping, agonizing, and speculating about a sports event before and after it occurs.

In this respect, sports entertainment is equally accessible to every economic stratum, to every social environment, to shut-ins and handicapped as well as the fully mobile. In a society tending toward more and more leisure time (often enforced on its older or underemployed members against their will), the existence of such cost-free recreation is a cultural plus.

CULTURAL GLUE

The democracy of merit, the idealism, the acceptance of rules, and the widely available free entertainment afforded by sports — these strands form a web of common interest, and every society needs such webs to stay intact. In other parts of the world, different histories and different customs have evolved other types of bonds. Many are based on a single dominant language, or religion, or economic pattern, or racial identity. America's famous pluralism makes such ties relatively less important, and increases the value of whatever activities do create a common currency of conversation, attitudes, emotions, and assumptions.

We don't have bonding agents with the power of a Shake-speare, a Pushkin, a royal family, a Verdi, a national church, or a two-thousand-year-old patch of identifiable soil. But it is aston-ishing the degree to which institutions like the New York Yan-kees, Notre Dame football, the World Series, and Muhammad Ali can supply a sense of common identity, no matter what our particular views may be toward any one of them.

The above benefits, I submit, are substantial and ongoing. But corrosive elements just as firmly embedded in this system are at work at the same time.

HYPOCRISY

The poisonous fumes emitted by amateurism and the self-serving activities of schools, colleges, and amateur officials have already been described. These abuses tower above other undesirable in-fluences by as much as reality testing towers above the other ben-efits.

But amateurism isn't the only source of indoctrination in hy-pocrisy. Professionals, and especially coaches, contribute system-atic lying. If idealism and rule observance are to be defined as be-nevolent influences, then all highly publicized and unmistakably obvious violations of those standards must have a harmful effect. When such violations happen and are tacitly condoned by those in authority, the message of hypocrisy hits home: "They tell us one thing, but they do another." It isn't the fact of cheating or dissembling that does the damage — we know nobody's perfect — but the *avoidable* tolerance of discovered cheating. Sports do more than their share to promote cynicism by winking at or denying all-too-evident corrupt practices.

DAMAGE TO PLAYERS

Granted that participation in sports is voluntary, that violence is endemic to competitive physical sport, and that the highest levels of performance necessarily involve unnatural strain on the human body, is the degree of physical injury and emotional dam-age inflicted on players entirely justifiable?

Playing rules are not etched in stone and are, in fact, altered every year. Do they really achieve the optimum balance between reasonable safety and attractive action? Is medical supervision all it should be? Is the player-control system, implemented through roster limits and monopolistic organization, which must exist in some form to ensure evenly matched opponents, used too freely to treat non-star performers as expendable cannon fodder, easily replaced? Are equipment and playing conditions as good as the state of the art can make them?

Are the myths of opportunity oversold to millions who won't make it? Is the pursue-flatter-pamper-protect-deify-denigrate-discard cycle so many athletes live through an unavoidable price of ambition, or something that operators of the system could humanize and improve? Is the thoroughly accepted obligation to provide medical aid less important than the obligation to provide appropriate help for the mental and emotional stress players are subjected to?

At major-league levels, these problems are dealt with to some degree (although often a very small degree), and the player's financial compensation is large. The real carnage takes place further down, where the number of victims is incalculably larger. Physical injuries with lifelong consequences abound in high school and college athletics and on sandlots and playgrounds, where thousands of the moderately gifted try to emulate the big leaguers who fascinate them. Yes, everyone is free to choose and must pay for the consequences of his choice. But can the glamorous professional and college sports provide better and more sensible examples to imitate? If not, how do we measure the true social cost of a thousand broken legs in the wake of Tony Dorsett's latest exciting touchdown run? Little attention is paid to this kind of fallout from our fascination as fans, but it constitutes a great big net minus.

LITTLE LEAGUE SYNDROME

Emulating the big leaguers becomes most objectionable when misguided adults use small children as animated dolls to play out their own grown-up fantasies of organizational power, local notoriety, and rooting interest. The children, who have no way of knowing better, are in turn seduced into playing their roles as microrobots.

In many places, Little League programs (and their counterparts in football, basketball, soccer, and hockey) are run with admirable balance, by kind and dedicated grownups sincerely interested in the welfare of the children. In many more places, they aren't. But the difficulty lies in the very concept, no matter how it is carried out. Little League sports call for a degree of organization that is simply inappropriate to that stage of child development. They stress formal competitive success at an age that should be reserved for play with *minimum* supervision, with no institutionalization of the identifications of "winner" and "loser." The better players are unfairly lionized, the poorer ones suffer devastating ego damage, and all concerned are subjected to pressures that have no saving grace.

Thousands of children emerge from these programs with an abiding hatred of the sport. Others duck out before they get started. But the very existence of such formal programs undermines the possibility of informal play for that age group in that neighborhood, partly by removing from circulation those who would be the most eager leaders of child-conducted games, and partly by branding as inferior and unworthy anything short of the sanctioned and uniformed leagues.

When the San Francisco 49ers arrived at the New Orleans Superdome for a workout the day before their opening game of the 1980 season, they found a series of Pee Wee football games in progress. The youngest group was composed of children six and seven years old. They wore full regalia — helmets with face masks, shoulder pads, artificial-turf cleated shoes, the works. They went through the regular (and totally wrong for their bodies) warm-up drills and calisthenics. They played with uniformed officials, a full team of ten-yard-chain caretakers, their coaches on the field calling formations, and six-year-old girl cheerleaders in typical costumes. The public-address system announced each play. They certainly looked cute. Several hardened professional players, some coaches, two team doctors, and two trainers watched for a while, and shook their heads. "Sick," was their consensus. I agree.

SPECTATORITIS

Anything to excess is harmful. I have called watching games "spectating," suggesting the whole interaction of involvement, attention, and rooting interest that creates a sports fan and accounts for the existence of the sports business. By adding "itis," I intend to suggest a diseased state, an excessive absorption with spectating.

We know how hard it is to fine-tune any kind of social engineering. If spectator sports have their benefits, they also lend themselves to creating addicts who lose all sense of proportion in their craving for more spectating.

One by-product of spectatoritis is the Little League syndrome — an attempt to transplant spectating values to local childhood contexts. Another is the invalid frame of reference we called "sports-think" a few chapters back. And in some cases, spectatoritis can lead to compulsive gambling (although some predilection must be there, no doubt).

Another by-product is passivity so ingrained that the capacity to participate in anything atrophies. In general, excessive passivity, with the accent on *excessive,* must be counted a social evil if it is widespread, and mass-entertainment sports do push in that direction.

OVEREMPHASIS ON VICTORY

Excess is the problem here too. It would be asinine to minimize the importance of winning in competitive games for high stakes — that's the whole idea. But the endlessly quoted Vince Lombardi remark that "winning isn't everything, it's the only thing" is even more asinine. Like Little League, sandlot injuries, amateurism, and spectatoritis, the issue here is applicability.

To define finishing first as the only acceptable goal in a major professional league is appropriate enough. That's what the team and its leadership are being paid to accomplish. To put the winning of a college conference championship above all other considerations is much less appropriate. It leads, among other things, to forged grades, false transcripts, illegal payments, and general corruption of what is supposed to be an educational institution. To exalt winning as the *only* goal in high school or Little League borders on the criminal. And to translate such ideas, through sports-think, into the realm of international relations, business, or domestic politics is an invitation to disaster.

But because the sports establishment is geared entirely to *professional* big leagues, with everyone down the line trying to imitate their pattern, the win-only psychology becomes pervasive. The urge to waggle a forefinger and shout "We're Number One," whipped up by television's ad-agency minds for their own purposes, has taken root and flowered beyond any apparent possibility of eradication. It is a harmful influence in our culture because it is unrealistic (there can be only one number one) and because it impoverishes us by downgrading so many other virtues: skill, courage, dedication, brilliance, satisfactory effort, improvement, honorable performance. All may be displayed without getting the ultimate victory as a reward. To *strive* for victory at all times is noble and proper. To reduce all values to whether you win or not is self-limiting and foolish. But it cannot be denied that the thrust of big-time commercial mass-entertainment sports is in this direction.

ABUSIVE AUTHORITY

Submission to rules and discipline is a social asset and a universal necessity. The exercise of *excessive* authority, on the other hand, is a social evil and a personal abuse.

How does one define *excessive?* The overemphasis on victory is a good starting point. What is appropriate whip-cracking on the part of a professional manager or coach is not appropriate for a college or high school coach. The idea filters down that iron-fisted command is the key to victory; and if victory is the only goal, then it must be all right to use this approach all the way down to Pee Wee football.

That's one common type of authoritarian abuse built into the otherwise antiauthoritarian American system: the coach is above the law. His edicts about diet, behavior, sex, length of hair, dress, and exhausting drills in ninety-degree heat, without water, are largely unquestioned (if he has a winning record). In practical terms, he outranks the faculty or the front office, until it is time to discharge him (because he didn't win enough).

The players who survive and succeed under this system adopt the same attitude and reproduce it when they become coaches. Not all coaches follow this path, but the majority do. And apart from the numerous individual cases of injustice or damage that arise, the climate of thought imparted to followers as well as subordinates is undesirable and out of step with the rest of our avowed social standards.

Does this mean a team should be run democratically, by committee vote, with an "open-classroom" approach that gives primary consideration to the whims and sensitivities of the players? Naturally not. That would simply be the opposite excess. A coach is and must be an authority figure, and players must submit to authority (as they do to rules and game officials). The question is one of degree, and in most cases at this time, the needle is in the dangerous-pressure portion of the gauge.

The other type of abuse of authority has nothing to do with coaching. It is administrative, and the process of amateur certification is the best example. The National Collegiate Athletic Association's investigative forays and television arrangements are also examples. Here it's a matter of selectivity, or arbitrary rulings favoring some and punishing others without making sufficiently clear distinctions. This autocracy is made possible by the combination of monopoly, entrenched bureaucracy, self-serving and self-devised regulatory codes, and the inherent brevity of the athlete's career as opposed to the official's span of service. Its chief harmful effect is the perpetuation of a structure that promotes hypocrisy.

•

How does the balance sheet add up? Is the sports establishment a net plus or a net minus, a little more than one hundred years after its evolution began? That's a legitimate question for sociologists, philosophers, psychologists, educators, and the clergy to explore. What we have reached is a starting point for such evaluations. If we now have some valid idea of how the sports business works, how its activities are transmitted to the public, how the public perceives it, and what some of the effects of those perceptions are, we are in a position to begin systematic investigations that can lead to firmly documented conclusions.

But not here, of course, and not by me. This is the end of the exposition I embarked on, and the limit of my competence. It is not, needless to say, the limit of my opinions. What is left is to express them.

My view is that the balance sheet comes out plus, not by a lot but by a discernible margin, because I think the six assets mentioned do their work a bit more efficiently and carry a bit more weight than the six drawbacks do. But that's strictly an opinion, and not a surprising one, since I wouldn't have pursued (and enjoyed) the sportswriting craft so long if I thought otherwise. And I have opinions about what could be done to tilt the scale further to the positive side in the next decade, as Part IV will show.

Immodest Proposals

28. Abolish Amateurism

ADOPTING FEASIBILITY as the first consideration in proposing remedies, it turns out that the change that sounds most radical is the one that's most practical and easy to carry out. Abolish amateurism. That is, cease classifying athletes by how much money they are paid, and by whom, as the means of determining who can take part in major competitions.

As we have emphasized all along, we're talking only about major commercial events — track meets in 15,000-seat arenas where tickets sell for ten dollars, college football programs that gross several million dollars a year in gate receipts, the Olympic Games, the Pan-American Games, international soccer matches, and so forth. That there are millions and millions of "true" amateurs engaging in activities that are not commercially promoted doesn't concern us here. It is the personal-finance aspect of amateur regulations that causes all the problems, both in fomenting hypocrisy and outright cheating, and in the practical application of certification.

Golf solved this problem long ago, simply by adopting an "open" system of classification. The difference between a player who gets paid and collects prize money and one who doesn't is still recognized, and some tournaments are limited to amateurs. But no attempt is made to segregate pros from open competition, and no amateur is punished for competing against a pro. Tennis solved the problem more recently, in the late 1960s, in exactly the same way. Both sports thrived, on a worldwide scale, as never before. Exactly the same thing can be done in any other sport that draws large crowds.

The main battleground in the 1980s will be track and field, the most important (in terms of spectator appeal) of the sports still firmly under amateur regulation (outside the college scene, to which we'll turn in a moment). As a matter of fact, movement toward open track began to gain momentum during 1980, and within the new structures that are gradually replacing the old Amateur Athletic Union and Olympic Committee arrangements, competitors, and promoters friendly to their needs, have a greater voice.

And the full force of the old amateur concept — that any contact with a pro forever contaminates an amateur — has been breached already. This boycott-and-blacklist system was at one time entirely analogous to the most restrictive forms of the reserve-clause system in professional sports, a method for retaining absolute control of everyone by threatening permanent exile for any unauthorized action or contact.

But today, a pro in one sport is already allowed to compete as an amateur in another — a development that has saved the college football and basketball careers of some who have signed pro baseball contracts, for instance. Nor does an amateur who takes part, as an amateur, in a golf or tennis tournament that is open to pros, risk his or her own amateur standing, as once would have been the case. To go the rest of the way doesn't require much more than a willingness to proceed.

But what about the vested interests already mentioned? If the college structure is devoted to the cheap-labor aspect of amateurism, and the Socialist countries are cognizant of the tactical advantage it gives them, how can they be impelled to change?

First of all, abolishing amateurism as a *requirement* for certification does not mean that every competitor *must* be paid. The permission to collect prize money when it's offered doesn't stop anyone from competing where prize money is not available. An example is Davis Cup competition in tennis, which was once a kingpin of amateur athletics. When the top players turned pro, this nationalistic enterprise — in which teams represent their countries — began to die, and saved itself by becoming "open." But it offers no prize money, and the same Bjorn Borg and Jimmy Connors who can command a $200,000 fee for merely appearing in a tournament or exhibition match, play Davis Cup for nothing but a modest expense fee, because of the other values involved. In the same way, the Olympics wouldn't have to offer anything more than the medals they now award, to retain their prestige and attract all the world's best athletes, because they are the Olympics.

For American colleges, therefore, the distinction between professional and amateur is largely irrelevant, and persists primarily as a means of preserving eligibility for countless international ties in track, swimming, gymnastics, wrestling, fencing, and other noncommercial sports. Putting aside for the moment these international complications, let's consider the college situation strictly as an internal American matter. Logically, amateurism has long since been dead. An athletic scholarship is compensation, substantial compensation, any way you look at it. Present regulations, by and large, make the maintenance of one's scholarship contingent on continued athletic participation (with exceptions, yes, but the pros also have guaranteed contracts that continue to pay players once deemed desirable, after they can no longer perform). And the whole thrust of equal-rights laws, in sports, is to extend to women and participants in "minor sports" the scholarship and recruiting practices made available for the major men's sports.

For colleges to agree, through their own leagues and national organization, to limit compensation to tuition, books, housing, and so forth, as they already do, is sufficient protection against raising the ante to the workers — that is, the student athletes. The mechanism of monitoring excesses would be the same as it is now, but the rationale for it would be sounder. The key requirement for certification in school and college athletics is *affiliation* with the particular institution, as a bona-fide student. Dropping the no-compensation requirement would make no difference whatever in that regard. And aside from the external ramifications, it would make little difference in any other practical way, while providing enormous moral benefits through the revival of intellectual honesty.

But what about those external ramifications? How can the non-American world be persuaded to give up what it sees as an advantageous system? Simply by unilateral declaration. In the commercial sports world, American athletes, American audiences, and American commercial television are so important to everyone else that *anything* our system really insists on must prevail. It's not unlike Hollywood's position in the movie industry before World War II (and to some extent still, if we broaden the definition of "Hollywood" to include television shows). The American market and American manufacturers and distribution are simply too large a fraction of the whole to be ignored.

If the United States (through the appropriate athletic bodies) simply declared it would no longer recognize the barring of professionals from major competitions, and stuck to it, the deed would be done. There would be, of course, a period of tremendous dislocation for a couple of years — but only for a few years, and maybe less, I'm convinced. This is because the benefits others perceive in amateurism would evaporate as soon as we refused to submit to the restriction.

For Socialist countries, there is no *theoretical* problem with open competition, since they claim to have no professionals in their societies, and since they have shown no reluctance to have their nonprofessionals compete in open tennis. And for everyone, commercial sports without American participation is a form of financial self-denial seldom maintained for long in the world as we know it.

The beauty of this approach is that it doesn't try to impose a set of values on anyone else. No foreign athlete would be barred *by us* from a Madison Square Garden track meet because of pro, amateur, or any other status he had at home. It would be up to all the other ruling bodies to decide whether they want to limit or punish such participation.

The further you look into the consequences of simply discarding the amateur requirement, the more you realize how little *practical* difference it would make. Most of the intermediate steps from the old rigid amateur ideals to true open competition have already been taken, and certainly public attitudes worldwide are notably different today from what they were half a century ago.

It is something that can be done merely by avowal. And the benefits would be enormous, on two fronts. In all the intangible areas, a festering fount of hypocrisy would be turned off. And in the commercial world, unfettered world championships in every conceivable sport, in an era of satellite television transmission, would have unlimited potential. It could be done tomorrow, by the stroke of several pens.

29. Restructure the Olympics

EVEN IF the amateur classification is not abolished, its power will continue to be significantly reduced in the near future, and this will gradually alter the nature of the Olympic Games, even if appearances stay the same. But the Olympics need overhaul from top to bottom. And any attempt to do so will run into massive obstacles in the form of entrenched interests (on the part of officials, not competitors) and practical problems. A structure that is in place is hard to modify, even when it loses efficiency, as American steel and automobile industries have discovered.

So we have to weaken, for the moment, our requirement feasibility, to spell out what changes would be desirable. Then we can estimate which ones are attainable.

The trouble spots are given below, along with good solutions, regardless of their attainability:

SITE

The problem: It has become prohibitively expensive to build new and complete Olympic facilities every four years in a different country, despite the hoped-for tourism benefits. The cost of the 1976 Games in Montreal is referred to as "scandalous" to this day, and there were so few bidders for the 1984 Games that Los Angeles got the nod after promising "austerity" and a minimum of government financing. (That's only the promise, of course; in reality, there will be plenty of government financing, hidden and otherwise.)

The solution: A permanent site in Greece is now being actively considered by the IOC. It is the obvious answer. The problem of determining a new location may be approached in several ways, however.

It can be a single place, used for a single simultaneous multi-sport festival, like the Olympics we are used to. This would eliminate the cost of building afresh every four years, and have the considerable advantage of familiarity and continuity. But it would not alleviate the horrible logistical problems that go with gigantism. It can be several places, each tailored to a certain set of compatible sports, which can be used either simultaneously or at different times during the Olympic year. (We have this separation already, of necessity, for the Winter and Summer Games.) It can be a single place, but with the competitions arranged sequentially rather than simultaneously. But it seems to me that a permanent site would have to have one additional feature. It must be an internationalized strip of territory, under something like United Nations jurisdiction.

Greece is certainly an appropriate location, for historical and sentimental reasons. But there can be no guarantee that Greece, or any other country, won't be in an adversary relationship to many other countries, at some future time. In fact, it is as close to certain as anything can be that at least one country will find some other country objectionable every Olympiad. In 1980, the big schism was between Russia and the United States, but Olympic boycotts took place in Canada in 1976 and in Mexico in 1968 for other political causes, involving Africa and China. The Nazi Olympics of 1936, in Berlin, are still the subject of books and vehemently expressed opinions. And how an Iranian team might be greeted in Los Angeles in 1984 is a good question.

No site on the national soil of any country can be divorced from that country's policies and laws at the time. It would be irresponsible and inconceivable for any government *not* to control events in its own territory. So for practical purposes, the chosen single site, in Greece or wherever, should be ceded to some international entity, for whatever compensation may be agreed to, in order to create a living expression of the Olympic ideal that the Games are a holy truce from other conflicts.

My own pet idea would take the following factors into consideration. Logistics come first, and the site should be one easy to reach by existing modes of transportation, for purposes of construction and supply as well as attendance by competitors and spectators. The playing facilities should be more studio than stadium, designed with maximum attention to television transmission yet large enough to accommodate noisy crowds, whose presence is essential to the ambiance of sports excitement. Housing and feeding accommodations have to be ample for spectators as well as for participants and officials.

Switzerland, it seems to me, has the experience with tourism to handle such a site if it is not internationalized, as well as a suitable climate for summer and winter competitions. Certainly the Winter Games could have a permanent home there. Some place along the Riviera, where France and Italy meet (and Monaco is located), might also work well, as might one of those spots around Switzerland's periphery that touches France, Italy, West Germany, or Austria.

The legal and fiscal details of establishing such an international enclave should not be staggering, once there is a willingness to put the plan into effect.

TEAM SPORTS

The problem: If excessive nationalistic fervor has become a political liability, which it was in 1980, how can single teams representing countries be reconciled with Olympic "brotherhood-of-man" idealism? In the original conception of the modern Olympics, there was no room for team games, and even the notion of combining a number of individual results to form a team score (as with a track team) was rejected. The team idea, in both senses, gradually grew as the result of pressure from officials and followers of team sports, who wanted a piece of the prestigious Olympic pie.

That, incidentally, is why no great effort has ever been mounted to push football (either soccer or American) and baseball into the Olympics. Their own successful commercial patterns were operating well enough to obviate the need for such recognition. Basketball and hockey, on the other hand, entered the

Olympic stream when they were still trying to establish full commercial viability.

Anyhow, it's hard to see how a team wearing a national uniform, composed of players brought together as all-stars exclusively on the grounds of citizenship, can help but inflame nationalism. The story of the 1980 U.S. hockey team is all the evidence anyone needs on this point.

The solution: Team sports should be separated, physically and theoretically, from individual sports. Whether or not we attach the word *Olympic* to what is actually perceived as a world championship is less important than making clear to all spectators and readers the distinction between team games and personal exploits.

If held at a different time and place from the individual events, Olympic team championships might even retain their nationalistic character without too much harm. In fact, world championships involving national teams (World Cup soccer, for example) are marvelous sports promotion. But if team sports are not totally separated from the other events, their national identities must be wiped out.

There is no reason why the basketball team must be *the* United States team. Let it be some existing team from within the United States (professional, if open competition comes about, as the Russian hockey team already is), and don't limit it to one team per country. Let the preliminary qualification process produce sixteen or thirty-two teams regardless of their national origin. Many countries would have only one team to enter, but many might have more than one (such as Canada, for hockey, or Germany, for soccer).

The essential requirement would be that the team's identity and basic composition has to be established for at least two years prior to the Olympics. A preferable minimum would be five years.

GIGANTISM

The problem: The pressure to get more and more officials into Olympic perquisites, not just for the quadrennial glory and excursions involved but for the continuing domestic power held by those who control access to the Olympics, has outstripped logic and any standard of general interest. The 1976 Summer Games listed twenty-three sports, including archery, canoeing, judo, modern pentathlon (take an A for the course if you can describe that event and its scoring), shooting, weightlifting, and yachting.

It doesn't constitute insult, provincialism, or arrogant value judgment to insist that such activities have different characteristics than track, basketball, boxing, or swimming — in number of practitioners worldwide, amount of commercial attention, and competitive format. To say that they don't fit well under a single umbrella is to state the obvious. A jazz group, a football marching band, and a grand opera all have notable and distinct virtues and devotees. But we do not try to arrange major entertainment festivals that involve all three at once, under the same format.

With or without team games, the size of the Olympic program has to be brought under control. Since it would contradict the very idea of the Games to restrict the number of countries that can take part, it will have to be the number of events that is limited.

(Meanwhile, I won't keep you in suspense: the modern pentathlon requires each contestant to run 4000 meters cross-country, ride a strange horse [that is, not one the rider trained on] over a steeplechase course, shoot with a rapid-fire pistol at a silhouette target, fence with a dueling sword, and swim 300 meters. Except for the fencing, the competitor is ranked by performance against time, not directly against other contestants. It's modeled on the requirements for a military courier before World War I.)

The solution: The only answer to gigantism is diffusion. It is unrealistic to believe that all those who enjoy the benefits of the Olympic label will give it up, or that those who haven't had it yet will stop pursuing it. But there is no need to try to do everything at once.

The problem is essentially one of scheduling. What we need is an Olympic Year, not simply Summer and Winter Games. If, in each year divisible by four, we had a series of Olympic segments — one each month, or almost that — involving four or five appropriately related events, all sorts of difficulties would disappear. Logistics would be easier. Each sport would get a better piece of the worldwide stage while on it. And every group could pinpoint its preparations better, without coming into conflict with the needs of too many other groups (at the U.S. Olympic Training Centers, for instance).

The newly built central-site facilities would not have to be as large as those now required (since no brief maximum-occupancy period would occur), and would function for the full year, which is more efficient for all concerned. Skiing in January, skating and hockey in February, team sports in June, water sports in July, track and field in August, boxing and wrestling in October — some such pattern would work like a charm.

Television would love it. The host site would love it. The contestants would love it. The public would love it. And nobody would get shut out of anything.

ADMINISTRATION

The problem: Most of the problems with the Olympics stem from the nature of the International Olympic Committee, a self-electing and self-perpetuating body that insists it has no obligations to any government or other group. It has a stranglehold on the world's National Olympic Committees and international sports federations because of its power to bar anyone from the Olympics.

The IOC is a singularly undemocratic, archaic, and secret body, unsuited in theory and in practice to the world of 1980. Some sort of reorganization, to make it more responsive to the will of competitors and of the governments who ultimately finance most Olympic activity, is inevitable.

The solution: Administrative problems boil down to problems of jurisdiction. As long as competitors (and officials) are classified according to citizenship, the problem of nationalism and its attendant political conflict cannot be dealt with.

But classifying entries according to citizenship is silly from the start. It's entirely possible that the four best sprinters in the world, all record-breakers, will turn out to be United States citizens —

or Jamaicans, or Nigerians, or Russians, or whatever. One of these would have to be left out, under present rules, while many lesser athletes would be included.

Furthermore, in today's world, people move from country to country — especially African and other non-American athletes recruited by American colleges. Citizenship hassles arise again and again, in all sorts of international competition, and many outstanding athletes have been victimized in the process. Why should the question of citizenship matter?

Then there are the political questions. If a competitor is certified as "representing" Great Britain, and the British government tells him not to go to Moscow, but the athlete (exercising his civil rights) does go, he has officially taken a position against his own government. (The punishment meted out to England's athletes consisted of being denied invitations to the queen's New Year's party. One can't help wondering what fate would await a Russian who managed to go to Los Angeles in 1984 against his government's wishes.) In each of the last three Olympics, at least some of the greatest athletes in the world did not compete because their governments were for some reason engaging in a boycott.

But if the athlete were certified as an individual, with no official mention of his nation of origin (as distinct from publicity mention, which is another matter), he would be taking a personal rather than a national stance. I don't suggest that this would help athletes from authoritarian states defy their governments, but it would certainly ease the situation in many countries.

So the proposal is to set up certification, and qualifying trials, by *regions,* not by national boundaries. Have all applications go directly through international special-purpose committees, treating each applicant as an individual.

It would then be the contestant's problem to get visas, satisfy the authorities at home, establish the proper public image, and arrange his or her own financing. These problems would have to be solved however they are solved in any particular society. But it would simplify the superstructure the contestant must now scale on the way to the Olympics.

•

Are these proposals practical and attainable within, let's say, ten years? I think so.

The central site will come about one way or another. A better-organized IOC, with more legitimacy in its composition and procedures, would also have a profitable business in leasing the Olympic facility to other competitions in non-Olympic years.

The team-sport question is closely tied to open competition, because the top world athletes in these activities are pros. I don't believe the present system will be changed much until the issue of amateurism is disposed of, but the separation will come quickly after it is.

Spreading out the Olympic program over the year requires absolutely no upheaval beyond that involved in an administrative decision to carry it out.

The divorce of Olympic certification from national identity is obviously difficult where authoritarian governments are involved. Here, however, the answer lies in the same direction as the issue of amateur standing: If the United States and other like-minded countries simply insist hard enough, the rest have no choice but to go along. It doesn't mean that citizens or representatives of countries that are "less free" will be any freer in their Olympic activities, but it does mean that those societies that don't demand governmental direction of sports activities will be freer of artificial restrictions.

Without some of these changes in one form or another, or equivalent reforms, the Olympics will die of their own weight.

30. Finance Medical Research

OPPOSITION TO governmental involvement in sports activities has been a consistent theme up to this point, with
respect to gambling, regulation, and Olympic control. But there is
another area in which the American government should be more
involved than it has been: financing medical research related to
sports.

The field of sports medicine is relatively new, and growing rapidly. Much of the work has been done voluntarily by doctors who
have organized their own groups, and some institutional support
has been offered by colleges, the U.S. Olympic Committee, manufacturers of protective sports equipment, and a few foundations.
But there is much more to do, and it can't be done without massive support. Other countries, such as East Germany and the Soviet Union, have supported such medical research in their own
contexts for their own purposes. Americans have been content to
accept as tough luck crippling injuries and even death, when they
could have been avoided.

There is a deficiency in this area on the part of the largest
sports promotional organizations — major-league baseball, the
National Football League, the National Basketball Association,
and the NCAA. They could do more themselves, in the way of financial support and internal regulations, but most of all they
could bring their persuasion machinery to bear on lobbying. One
reason they don't is that they are fighting against government in-
tervention in so many other areas of their operations. Nevertheless, their increased support is needed.

Medical issues concerning sports are categorized below.

TREATMENT OF INJURY

All the emphasis in spectator sports is on getting the valuable performer back into effective action as soon as possible. Team doctors and trainers have learned a good deal about this at the professional and high-college levels. But a vastly greater number of participants in organized athletics need repairs of a different order. They need healing that will produce the best possible life-long result, even if it means staying out of action longer now. For every big leaguer, there are thousands of school players. Beyond the fact that in many cases medical supervision of these young-sters is inadequate by any standard, not enough is known about the optimum treatment of all sorts of injuries that carry over in later life. And not nearly enough has been done to inform doctors who do not deal with athletes as a matter of course about how to handle athletic injuries that come to their attention only occa-sionally.

PREVENTION OF INJURY

The National Football League Players Association has been fighting with club owners for years about the injury-causing po-tential of artificial turf. This is a difficult negotiating point be-cause the clubs merely rent the stadiums that have it, and can't control its installation or specifications. And in baseball, the Major League Players Association has actually had to file griev-ances to get baseball teams to put padding on outfield fences. But beyond that, remarkably little is known about exactly what causes what kind of injury. Many limited studies have been done, but not the comprehensive full-scale analysis, over periods of years, that costs so much. Such investigation is needed.

PROTECTIVE EQUIPMENT

A recurrent problem in football has been the injury-causing po-tential, to opponents, of helmets and pads designed to protect the wearer. The number of baseball injuries ascribed, over the years, to "my spikes caught" is appalling. And a hockey player with all his own teeth is considered rarer than the dodo bird.

Special cases have received a lot of publicity. When Dan Pastorini suffered cracked ribs while playing quarterback for Houston, a "flak jacket" strong enough to protect the injury, but light enough to use, proved successful. In general, however, not enough has been done to develop truly light, truly flexible protective devices, especially for knees. It will take a great deal of money, scientific investigation, and motivation to make progress in this area.

The tendency in the athletic community is to shrug off such suggestions. The macho self-image is so ingrained, and so craved by coaches, that complaints of discomfort are viewed as excuses. When baseball batting helmets were first made mandatory, older players sneered and declared it was impossible to be so encumbered and still hit. But such resistance is quickly overcome if authorities insist.

PERFORMANCE ENHANCEMENT

Training methods have been revolutionized within the last decade by innovations such as stretching exercises, biological feedback, weight machines that can pinpoint particular muscle development, diet, and, of course, many new kinds of drugs and medication.

But this body (there go those unintended puns again) of knowledge is just beginning to accumulate. As we learn more and more exactly how to make a particular athlete more efficient at his or her particular activity, we also have to learn what sort of long-range side effects go with that training program. And unfortunately, the emphasis on world-class athletes who break records results in a failure to address the more important question of how ordinary people in ordinary athletic activities can do better and emerge healthier.

Participation sports are not the concern of our study, but mass-entertainment sports have a responsibility to take the lead in research in this area. Weekend tennis players can't organize to research tennis elbow and the possibility of eventual arthritis; large commercial sports organizations can. Television, which lives off sports, could contribute. And the government should.

GENERAL HEALTH

This is the real issue. With so much sports activity going on, inciting imitation, the sports field should be used as a laboratory for the increase of general knowledge — especially about childhood development. Just as space-program technology has produced unforeseen fallout in earthside products (from minicomputers to Tang), entertainment sports should provide the raw material for extensive studies about the behavior of the human body under certain kinds of stress.

The way such programs should be organized doesn't concern us, but the need for them should be articulated much more strongly than it has been by the sports establishment.

31. Clarify Legislation

"You don't have to be Jewish to like Levy's rye bread," read a famous advertisement depicting a smiling, elderly Oriental. And you don't have to be in the sports business to find your affairs in a bewildering tangle because of ambiguous, contradictory, illogical, and inconsistent laws and government regulations.

But American commercial sports enterprises face some special difficulties. Their relation to the antitrust laws cries out for clarification, and the unwillingness or inability of the last fourteen United States Congresses to come to grips with the subject in a comprehensive way has put an unfair burden on this industry.

The unfairness hasn't always operated in the same direction, and not everyone has complained about the status quo, as one group after another has found a way to turn some aspect of the ambiguity to its advantage. But in the interests of good government, good sense, and good business, not to mention setting a good example in so highly visible and influential an activity, Congress should weed out the legal jungle in four areas. It should establish uniformity of legal status for all sports, and make clearer definitions, once and for all, of what proprietary rights a club has, what antitrust provisions are not in the public interest when applied to sports, and which individual rights (of players and owners) may be curtailed to maintain the system as a whole.

Let's label these general topics Baseball's Exemption, Copyright Considerations, the Per Se Problem, and the Draft.

BASEBALL'S EXEMPTION

A simple one-sentence bill, stating that Congress does not intend baseball to have an antitrust status different from that of other sports, would undo the affront to logic and the palpable injustice that has existed for more than twenty years. A Supreme Court ruling in 1922, based on reasoning long since rejected in many relevant cases (that personal services are not "trade and commerce") and on premises indisputably false (that the business of staging baseball games is "not interstate"), made baseball exempt from antitrust laws. This exemption was reaffirmed in 1952 in a one-paragraph decision that explicitly disavowed any reexamination "of the underlying issues."

In the course of the six sentences that constitute the entire 1952 ruling (by a 7–2 vote), there are three errors of fact and one whopping omission (as pointed out by Lionel S. Sobel in his *Professional Sports and the Law,* published in 1977). Within the next ten years, the same Court, composed of substantially the same judges, ruled that other comparable activities, from theater operation to boxing to football, were subject to those laws. Each time, the Court referred apologetically or defensively to baseball's special position, and each time insisted that it was up to Congress to act to eliminate the contradiction. And in 1972, the Supreme Court said the same thing again.

Obviously Congress could — and probably should — pass a comprehensive bill spelling out how the antitrust laws apply to a business whose activity must be monopolistic in order to survive: The illusion that a world or national championship is being decided cannot be maintained unless all credible competitors come under some centralized ruling body. But passing such a bill has proved difficult, because many conflicting interests become involved. Each has lobbyists and plausible arguments in its support, and every proposal has the potential for arousing the ire of some particular group of voters, most of whom feel instinctively that they don't want the system they enjoy tampered with. (If they weren't devoted to it, they wouldn't be fans to begin with; and an awful lot of voters are fans.)

But that's no reason to leave baseball alone. Its exemption has two bad effects. First, it makes baseball's self-government too complacent and unresponsive to public pressure, because it prevents the possibility that another league will start up and force innovations. (New leagues in professional football, basketball, and hockey relied on antitrust suits to force mergers.) And second, it holds out the hope to other sports that the eventual resolution will be exemption for everybody.

Prompt action to strip baseball of its special status would improve the chances of producing a comprehensive law, because it would add baseball's considerable lobbying power to whatever united front the major team sports would then present. And a comprehensive law is needed to take care of the other three legal problems.

COPYRIGHT CONSIDERATIONS

Copyright may be the wrong term to use, but it is suggestive to me of the underlying issue. Antitrust law rests, more than most laws, on matters of definition. Murder is murder, theft is theft, and speeding is speeding, and the ordinary person has little trouble defining the act that constitutes a crime. The law then deals with establishing whether the crime happened or not, the degrees of responsibility, and proper punishment; but the nature of the alleged act is not mysterious.

In questions of monopoly, things aren't that simple. Exactly when restraint of trade takes effect in such a way as to go against what society has decided to outlaw is not always self-evident. Defining and describing the crime is part of what has to be decided. As a result, precedent and relationship to other cases play a large role in determining whether there is something to act upon, apart from the did-he-or-didn't-he questions we normally associate with trials.

Sports businesses have always claimed to be different from ordinary business, often pushing this claim to ridiculous and obviously self-serving lengths. They talk of their special need to be rivals and partners simultaneously, since they must act as partners to carry out the conditions that make rivalry possible, and they maintain that ordinary legal concepts of free competition can't be applied to them.

Clearly, there is truth in the basic position. That teams and leagues try to use this authentic peculiarity as a tool to obtain privileges and advantages that go far beyond it doesn't alter the fact that the circumstances are true, and unique to sports. An automobile manufacturer doesn't *need* an equally solvent competitor to build his own cars; but a contest needs a comparable opponent to create the contest.

It seems to me that the trouble lies in defining the product accurately enough. The product is *not* "The Dallas Cowboys," getting together with another product called "The Philadelphia Eagles." The product is a National Football League game. What is being "produced" is the entire *show* of a game that counts in league standings and has other publicly accepted trappings. The product is not merely the actions of the component parts.

If each league were organized as a single legal entity, with all players under contract to it instead of to the separate clubs, and all receipts completely shared, no antitrust question about its internal activities would arise. It would still be open to charges of monopoly with respect to rival leagues and to cornering the market in top talent, but not with respect to such matters as selling television rights, locating franchises, moving players from team to team, and setting ticket prices.

But such an arrangement would run smack into another peculiarity. For historical as well as psychological reasons, the public would be suspicious of such centralized control; and that whole set of illusions on which sports interest depends would become compromised. Spectators must be able to *believe* that one team has a motive to surpass another, not only in the action of that day's game but as an organization competing for the best players and coaches. A "syndicated" league, the dream of major-league originators and attempted unsuccessfully by others, carries the flavor of results "arranged" to seem exciting, as wrestling does.

Appropriately written laws can solve this dilemma. They can recognize the relevant legal right to "the NFL game" as an entity, without forcing formal amalgamation of all the clubs. That's why I call this issue a "copyright" question. The author of a book, or the producer of a play, is given complete control over the disposal of the product of his imagination and effort. No one can disseminate his product, or tamper with its content, without his permission. He sells that permission in various ways, according to his good or bad judgment, but his legal right to own and assign it is protected for many years, just like a patent on an invention. Well, the NFL game is the product of the NFL's collective effort and imagination in exactly the same sense. It deserves the same protection.

This approach would help untangle one troublesome question that arose in the 1970s. With FCC permission, cable-television stations have been allowed to pick up games already on the air and redirect them to places and times the clubs feel are harmful to their interests, with no compensation to, or permission from, the clubs. That's like saying that once my book is published, anyone else can *republish and sell* it, without asking or satisfying the original publisher. That's what copyright laws prevent.

But the copyright approach, as a concept, helps make other relationships clearer, too. Combined television negotiations, on a league level, would not need exemption from antitrust laws (whereas, say, a package deal attempted by the NFL and major-league baseball would). And it would simplify the handling of the two remaining topics.

THE PER SE PROBLEM

Antitrust violations are treated in two ways. Some activities— such as agreements to fix prices — are considered so innately harmful and open to abuse that they are called *per se* violations (meaning they are "in and of themselves" forbidden). In these cases, it is only necessary to show that such a thing is being done; the activity cannot be justified on any grounds.

Other activities are subjected to a "rule of reason." A policy may be found to be illegal in one set of circumstances but not in another. The deciding factor in such cases is the *necessity* of the practice to the business involved (taking into account the larger social costs and benefits that go with it). In general, if it can be shown that an alleged "combination in restraint of trade" is essential to carry out an otherwise beneficent business interest, the practice will be permitted (if that's what a court decides).

The simplest example of this is scheduling. The various competitive businesses called teams must act together to make a league schedule, and in doing so they "restrain" the right of the Yankees to schedule twenty-seven lucrative dates with the Dodgers. But the rule of reason would nonetheless protect schedule-making from the charge of monopolistic abuse.

Sports authorities have always maintained that they will take their chances with any rule-of-reason defense, and be able to live with the consequences, win or lose. What terrifies them, and hangs over them as a perpetual threat, is the possible finding that something is a per se violation. The per se doctrine is generally applied to price fixing, group boycott, and territorial division of markets — activities built into sports as we know it. Some indication, by means of legislation, that in antitrust cases, sports businesses can have the rule of reason applied to *all* their operations, would ease the climate without threatening the safety of the republic or the legitimate rights of anyone.

THE DRAFT

Most vulnerable to per se interpretation is the draft of college players by professional teams. It's pretty hard to justify by rule of reason too, but that way, at least, one has a chance. No matter how you slice it, though, a draft system *is* price fixing, group boycott, and one kind of territorial division.

Here we come upon a recent development. The old "reserve-system" regulations, which had evolved as a means of controlling players who were already pros, were challenged under antitrust laws. But the real answer to the problem turned out to be effective labor unions. Reserve-system rules, strong or loose, are clearly "working conditions" that unions can bargain for, and the labor-relations laws afford a context in which to do that. So from now on, antitrust will not be a pressing issue in labor relations, since workers are allowed to accept or reject (by striking) almost anything they want, and both sides are allowed to bargain collectively. And one of the things all the player-union agreements have accepted is some form of draft.

But the draft limits players who are *not* pros yet, who do *not* belong to the union making the agreement, and who are clearly competing for the jobs of the union members who agreed to it. These are muddy waters indeed. It is true that *all* unions create entry-into-the-system rules that affect, in some way, incoming workers who have not yet voted on the regulations. But a draft, which is based on the principle "Work for me, or stay out of the profession," goes well beyond ordinary rules.

Yet it is hard to see how professional team sports could operate without something comparable to a draft. The essential feature of the drafting process is not the order-of-choice provision by which weaker teams pick first, nor is it the lower price an incoming star must accept when no other team can compete for his services. These are, from the club's point of view, highly desirable and enormously profitable by-products, but not the central issue. What the draft ensures is the *distribution* of playing talent: each team gets only one pick per round, so that no one team can load up on *all* the best players.

The draft is part and parcel of the competitive equality fostered by roster limits and related regulations. It makes it impractical for a team to sign up and not use talent some other team could — as was customary in baseball in the heyday of farm systems, in the 1930s.

The legality of the draft is so tricky that specific legislation permitting it, with appropriate safeguards for the people being drafted, should be enacted. If it is unjustifiable, it should be outlawed — again by specific legislation, since any attempt by an individual player to challenge it in court would mean sacrificing that player's career, even if, years later, the case is won.

Mass-entertainment spectator sports — the phenomenon we've called the sports establishment — is a big enough part of our society to get serious and prompt consideration from our lawmakers.

32. Reform the NCAA

THE NATIONAL COLLEGIATE Athletic Association was created some seventy-five years ago for the purpose of standardizing the playing rules of football for colleges across the country. It acquired the same function for other sports, and became a clearing-house for various administrative matters, but had little real power until after World War II.

Then two things happened. The simultaneous growth of college population (because of the GI bill and other new opportunities) and of intersectional competition in commercially viable circumstances created a desire for more-uniform eligibility and recruiting standards. And the arrival of television required a central set of rules to keep the strong from overwhelming the weak in the marketplace.

The NCAA seemed a natural repository for those responsibilities. It was already conducting national championships in sports like basketball, swimming, and track. It had a central office and lines of communication to its members, comprising all the major sports colleges and many of the minor ones. And it was free of regional loyalties. Recruiting and eligibility regulations were written and adopted by the membership, and a special committee was created to negotiate contracts for football telecasts.

But this development put the NCAA in the policing business, and it created enormous vested interests for the top NCAA bureaucracy. The adage that power corrupts could be illustrated in a detailed history of the NCAA, but two very general points are enough for our purposes.

The regulations concerning recruiting were made incredibly

complex (on purpose, in my opinion), so that every single possible infraction can be found to violate some letter of some law. But the NCAA can't investigate and judge every single infraction, only those that are brought to its attention, and then only to a limited degree. Thus it has the absolute power of selective certification, perfected by other amateur ruling bodies and still in use by the International Olympic Committee. In such a set-up, the more complicated the rules the better.

The NCAA's television operation amounts to controlling the flow of money — important money, in the college context. The original idea was to keep big attractions, such as Notre Dame, from televising every week and destroying the live attendance at smaller schools everywhere. If television appearances are to be rationed, the one who controls the rationing obviously wields enormous arbitrary power. (A television appearance means more than the money a school gets; the benefits of publicity and exposure are important for recruiting and fund raising.) So the NCAA, with a handful of secret investigators who ordinarily violate most of the accepted guidelines about self-incrimination, hearsay, weight of evidence, and relevance, can choose to discipline (by means of probation) one school and not another. And one aspect of probation punishment is that television appearances are forbidden.

Today, the control of television is not in itself a terrible problem. College athletic teams need some central negotiating body anyhow, the policy of "protectionism" has worked well, and no one has proposed an alternate system that sounds better. Anyhow, it is a business matter to be handled in a businesslike way by whoever does it.

But the policing of eligibility is another matter. Trying to monitor cheating or carelessness in hundreds of institutions involving thousands of people is an impossibility, for a handful of central-office investigators. Those they catch are necessarily a random minority. To be more effective, they would have to be a secret-police organization on the scale of the Gestapo. And even in theory, no set of regulations can be written that will apply fairly to the varied circumstances of several hundred American colleges.

There is, however, a simple and practical way to get the NCAA out of the policing business without weakening its other powers. Junk all the detailed restrictions concerning recruiting methods, high school grades, scholarship limits, and the rest, and zero in on the basic idea and basic problem. Call it graduation. The relevant standard for a college athlete should be his bona-fide status as a student working toward a degree. He is being presented to the public as that, not as an achiever of certain grades, or a person with a certain income, or one who spoke with his prospective coach only three times. A student. And the measure of a student's success, as a student, is graduation. He gets his degree.

My proposal, then, would work this way. First, determine the "normal" percentage of graduates at any particular college. Then require every athletic squad to meet (or exceed, if you want to be stricter) that figure.

Each year.

Any year in which the percentage isn't met, that school would go on probation (in that sport) the following year, and stay on probation until it gets back to the required percentage.

That's all. That's the whole rule. It would be self-policing. It would be effective. And it would be to the point. All the NCAA would have to do would be to process the graduation records submitted by the college presidents. It would collate and enforce, not judge.

Cheating would not miraculously end. The pressures that surround college football and basketball would not disappear. But I doubt that college presidents would fool around with the integrity of a degree the way they tolerate a snap course, an unearned credit, or an undeserved grade. Too much is at stake in the academic reputation of an institution, to faculty, alumni, and other students, for it to risk being caught with phony graduates. That's exactly why such a high proportion of top athletes never graduate. The schools are willing to support and exploit them in all sorts of ways, but they don't hand out illegitimate diplomas.

If the NCAA is cut back to a bookkeeping and television-negotiating agency, it can be reorganized along more sensible lines. Its unwieldy convention process won't have to deal with all those bewildering regulations, written in such tortuous wording. Its administrative hierarchy won't have to be defensive or overburdened. Accusations of favoritism, vengeance, and violation of civil rights will disappear.

It will also be in a better position, out of the line of investigatory fire, to settle a more pressing matter — the proper integration of women's and men's programs into a single administrative structure. On that topic, I have no background and no suggestions, but to carry it out will require some major restructuring of the NCAA sooner rather than later, apart from other issues.

33. Rethink Little League

IT IS FITTING that we end this exploration of the sports
business — a brutally competitive, often cynical, hard-
headed business whose realistic operations we have explored by
emphasizing their non-idealistic side — by discussing children.
The children who play miniature versions of mass-spectator
games are not earning a living, or even, for the most part, seeking
college scholarships. They are abstracting from a professional entertainment its purest qualities: play (as opposed to "work") and
exhilaration.

Play in some form is vital to child development, in every culture. Imitating adult activities is also a fundamental childhood
occupation in every culture. But for it to be truly play, the imitated adult action must be modified. When boys (of twelve or
younger) act out their father's occupations as hunters or warriors,
they don't use real lethal weapons. When little girls play with
dolls, they don't use living infants. When kids play store they
don't use real money, nor do they use real medicines to play doctor. Every once in a while, a child does try to play with the real
grown-up objects, and the result is tragedy.

Organized sports of the Little League pattern, modeled on
major professional sports, lose sight of this distinction. The promoters of Little League (and its equivalents) are generally well
meaning. There is an element of self-aggrandizement for some
adults, of course, and mindless rooting by some parents. By and
large, though, they believe they are doing children a favor. But
they're not.

Overorganized games have at least four harmful effects on
children:

1. They make competitive results too important too early. Winning and losing, in all their extensions, may indeed be inevitable in adult life, but childhood is only the training period. You wouldn't let someone begin learning a high-wire act without a net. Yet that's what we do when we add the burdens of publicity, recognition, blame, and false importance to the outcome of a child's game, just because those things are part of adult professional games.

2. They segregate children by athletic ability, socially as well as in the make-up of teams, at an age when such classification is undesirable and unfair. It's unfair because physical growth and coordination change rapidly, almost from month to month, and pigeonholing a child on the basis of whether he or she makes the team, which is reasonable among adults seeking a paying job, is not reasonable among fifth graders.

3. They rob the children involved of the opportunity to learn to do things themselves. The most important part of play is learning how to set up the game, choose up sides, argue with your peers, make compromises, figure out answers, submit to *self*-directed rulings so that the game can continue, and so forth. These important civilizing functions are bypassed by adult-run leagues.

4. They entice some children into physical actions that are bad for growing bodies. The most obvious example is a twelve-year-old trying to throw a curve ball. Most of the actions natural to big-league games are abnormal strains put on abnormally conditioned, full-grown bodies. By 1980, doctors were speaking out publicly against the lifelong injuries that can result from the too-early exercise of motions that will be relatively safe later.

Specifically, the Little League mentality, especially when applied to swimming and gymnastics, can lead to damaging results. Super-conditioning to a punishment level is a virtue for a grown professional athlete; an equivalent training program designed specifically for the special needs of a growing child might be justifiable; but blind imitation of adult exercises is irresponsible. Doctors, trainers, and many coaches know this. So do most professional athletes who went through the Little League ranks. Not all agree with what's just been said, but many do, and they should speak out much more forcefully than they have.

What should the adults who are devoted to Little League organizations be doing instead? They should supply as many kids as possible with equipment — balls, bats, gloves, shoes — especially the economically disadvantaged. (Forget uniforms.) They should supply facilities — fields, gyms, and playgrounds — and keep them in good repair. They should contribute transportation when necessary. They should offer instruction in technique, in the most rudimentary form, when asked. And once the kids begin to play games, the adults should keep hands off and even leave the premises. In short, they should function like librarians. They should be caretakers of the equipment, keep some sort of order, and help with problems. But they shouldn't do the reading for the children, or tell them which page to read when.

In my view, such changes in approach are needed for the general mental, physical, and social health of the next generation. But that is just one layman's opinion, and not necessarily relevant to sports, journalism, or society, our main concerns. What is relevant, however, is the long-range effect Little League has on the sports establishment. It turns off more young people than it turns on. It works *against* building the complex of illusions and childhood associations that go into fandom.

Creating a new generation of fans is not, of course, a major social goal, but it certainly ought to be the selfish goal of the sports establishment. And if great virtues of some other kind resulted from Little League pursuits, spreading an antifan attitude might well be worth it. But there are no compensating virtues, and the Little League system exists only because adults *are* fans. It is a mirror to the mass-entertainment sports system, and a cruelly distorting one. Jonathan Schwartz's passion for the Red Sox did not grow out of Little League experience.

34. Conclusion

HAVING DISCUSSED all these reforms, let's not forget one important fact: no medicine at all is preferable to the wrong medicine. So the first priority should be resisting proposals that sound plausible and even exciting but couldn't be carried out in the real world, or might make things worse if they were. A little knowledge is a dangerous thing, the saying goes. Solutions to sports problems are frequently offered by legislators, academics, writers, researchers, and fans, who have exhaustively explored the subject that interests them but have never grasped the whole picture and how the interrelated parts work.

"You can't get there from here," says the Down East farmer to the lost motorist in an old joke, and that is often a profound truth. All sorts of utopian formats for realigning leagues, altering regulations, enforcing observance, regrouping colleges, establishing championship tournaments and rating systems and satisfying television viewers look great on paper. Some of them really would work very well if we were starting from scratch. But to be feasible, any change must take into account the existing vested interests and the acceptability of a new system's features to all those already involved.

In short, change must take into account the things this book has tried to make clear: the realities, not the myths, of sports, journalism, and society.

—02